EVALUATING THE NATIONAL HEALTH SERVICE

STATE OF HEALTH SERIES

Edited by Chris Ham, Director of Health Services Management Centre, University of Birmingham

EVALUATING THE NATIONAL HEALTH SERVICE

Martin A. Powell

Open University Press
Buckingham · Philadelphia

Open University Press
Celtic Court
22 Ballmoor
Buckingham
MK18 1XW

and
1900 Frost Road, Suite 101
Bristol, PA 19007, USA

First Published 1997

A catalogue record of this book is available from the British Library

ISBN 0 335 19530 X (pb)   0 335 19531 8 (hb)

Library of Congress Cataloging-in-Publication Data

Powell, Martin A., 1961–
    Evaluating the National Health Service/Martin A. Powell.
        p.   cm. — (State of health series)
    Includes bibliographical references and index.
    ISBN 0-335-19531-8 (hbk)   ISBN 0-335-19530-X (pbk)
    1. National Health Service (Great Britain)
    I. Title.   II. Series.
RA412.5.G7P79   1997
362.1′0941 – dc21   96-39950
                                          CIP

Typeset by Type Study, Scarborough, North Yorkshire
Printed in Great Britain by St Edmundsbury Press,
Bury St Edmunds, Suffolk

To my mother and father

CONTENTS

LIST OF TABLES

SERIES EDITOR'S INTRODUCTION

Health services in many developed countries have come under critical scrutiny in recent years. In part this is because of increasing expenditure, much of it funded from public sources, and the pressure this has put on governments seeking to control public spending. Also important has been the perception that resources allocated to health services are not always deployed in an optimal fashion. Thus at a time when the scope for increasing expenditure is extremely limited, there is a need to search for ways of using existing budgets more efficiently. A further concern has been the desire to ensure access to health care of various groups on an equitable basis. In some countries this has been linked to a wish to enhance patient choice and to make service providers more responsive to patients as 'consumers'.

Underlying these specific concerns are a number of more fundamental developments which have a significant bearing on the performance of health services. Three are worth highlighting. First, there are demographic changes, including the ageing population and the decline in the proportion of the population of working age. These changes will both increase the demand for health care and at the same time limit the ability of health services to respond to this demand.

Second, advances in medical science will also give rise to new demands within the health services. These advances cover a range of possibilities, including innovations in surgery, drug therapy, screening and diagnosis. The pace of innovation is likely to quicken as the end of the century approaches, with significant implications for the funding and provision of services.

Third, public expectations of health services are rising as those who use services demand higher standards of care. In part, this is stimulated by developments within the health service, including the availability of new technology. More fundamentally, it stems from the emergence of a more educated and informed population, in which people are accustomed to being treated as consumers rather than patients.

Against this background, policymakers in a number of countries are reviewing the future of health services. Those countries which have traditionally relied on a market in health care are making greater use of regulation and planning. Equally, those countries which have traditionally relied on regulation and planning are moving towards a more competitive approach. In no country is there complete satisfaction with existing methods of financing and delivery, and everywhere there is a search for new policy instruments.

The aim of this series is to contribute to debate about the future of health services through an analysis of major issues in health policy. These issues have been chosen because they are both of current interest and of enduring importance. The series is intended to be accessible to students and informed lay readers as well as to specialists working in this field. The aim is to go beyond a textbook approach to health policy analysis and to encourage authors to move debate about their issue forward. In this sense, each book presents a summary of current research and thinking, and an exploration of future policy directions.

Professor Chris Ham
Director of Health Services Management Centre
University of Birmingham

ACKNOWLEDGEMENTS

I am grateful to colleagues in the School of Social and Historical Studies, University of Portsmouth, for providing that inevitable feature of book acknowledgements, a supportive environment. Comments on earlier drafts were provided by Professor Graham Moon and Dr John Mohan of the University of Portsmouth, and Dr Enid Fox. The latter made her usual valiant attempt to improve my grammar and writing style, while tolerating my mixed metaphors; it is usual to absolve all others of blame, but I am certain it would be a better book if I could read her writing. Jacinta Evans and Joan Malherbe at Open University Press provided a constructive, but tolerant, editorial touch. The series editor, Professor Chris Ham, provided useful guidance in the twenty-fifth hour of his day.

It is a pleasure to follow the convention of thanking friends (human and animal), although their prime function appears to provide alternative attractions to writing. Nevertheless, I am grateful for all their efforts. Finally, I should like to thank my parents for all their support, delivered in many ways over many years. After some 80,000 words, it is strange that the words to express adequately this remain so elusive. All I can do is to dedicate this book to them in the belief that a first (and last?) book should be dedicated to parents, irrespective of the age of its author.

1

INTRODUCTION

According to Aneurin Bevan, the Minister of Health in the 1945 Labour government that introduced the British National Health Service (NHS), it was 'the biggest single experiment in social service that the world has ever undertaken' (quoted in Timmins 1996: 101). It has been termed also a unique experiment in social engineering (Klein 1995a: vii). Experiments are usually accompanied by evaluation. Indeed, it has been written that 'The problem of evaluation is the first priority of the NHS' (Cochrane 1972: 25). Yet, after over 50 years of the NHS, we still lack clear ideas of how well this experiment is working. For some, it is the finest service in the world, but others consider that the experiment should be abandoned as a failure. To some extent, these different perceptions represent inevitable political debate. However, the terms of the debate are rarely specified. How should the NHS be evaluated? What are its successes and failures? Are these inevitable, and common to all health-care systems, or a unique product of the NHS? Will the changes of the Thatcher and Major Conservative governments make it better or worse?

This text attempts to examine these issues. Impatient readers who now turn to the Conclusion for answers will be disappointed. Some indications will be found, but no definitive answers, nor should we expect them. This is for three main reasons. First, judgement entails many concepts that lack precise definition, let alone accurate measurement. In statistical terms, there are problems of validity and reliability (Phillips *et al.* 1994: 47–51). Second, much research remains to be done on evaluating the NHS. In particular, very little evaluative work on the recent NHS reforms has yet emerged. This text, as a preliminary exercise, should be seen as an attempt to stimulate thinking about the questions rather than providing answers. Third, where politics is a basic ingredient of the debate, there can never be full agreement. There are different views on ends and means of the NHS. An outcome may be viewed as 'good' by one commentator but as 'bad' by another; what is important is that the criteria should be clearly stated.

THE BRITISH NHS

The NHS occupies a special place both in the British welfare state and among other health-care systems. It is the only social service in Britain that is comprehensive in scope in the sense of looking after the entire population and in being organized around an ethical imperative (Klein 1995a: vii). Unlike much of the rest of the welfare state, which aims only to provide minimum standards, the NHS is meant to deliver the best services to all British citizens. Neither is this care dependent on any insurance benefits based on contributions. The premature baby needing special care gets it before paying a penny in direct or indirect taxation; its parents need not have paid value added tax (VAT, or sales tax) on a single packet of nappies before their baby is in its incubator (Iliffe 1988: 47–8). Access to health care is a right of citizenship: just as everyone is equal in the eyes of the law, everyone is equal in the eyes of the NHS. In short, the NHS offers a free gift of resources based on need (Iliffe 1988: 47). Indeed, for many years, visitors were entitled to free care, in a British gesture of a civilized principle to the world (Bevan 1978: 104–6). Internationally, too, the NHS is unique. It is the only national health-care system, centrally financed and directed, operating in a Western democracy (Klein 1995a: vii). As Glennerster (1995: 53) states, the 1946 National Health Service Act created 'a health care system unique in the western world'.

The NHS also occupies a special place in the hearts of the British people and of its founder, the British Labour Party. It is central to the 'cradle to grave' concept of the welfare state and many people feel grateful for treatment ranging from the minor to the expensive and life-saving (for example, see Titmuss 1974; Griffith *et al.* 1987: 237; Owen 1988: 1–2). The credit that has been given to the NHS as the 1945 Labour government's greatest achievement (Campbell 1987: 165) might well be extended to the Labour Party in general. Both at its foundation and subsequently, the NHS has been judged to be the most socialist of the 1945 Labour government's welfare reforms. In the issue of 3 March 1950, *Tribune* called it 'the most socialist measure introduced by the last Parliament'. According to Michael Foot (1975: 293), Bevan's biographer and later to become the leader of the Labour Party, the NHS is the greatest socialist achievement of the 1945 Labour government.

It has been argued that the NHS contributes to the health of the British polity and society. For Titmuss (1970: 254–5) it expresses and reinforces a sense of individual altruism and collective responsibility. Consequently, it strengthens social cohesiveness and social solidarity, and was 'the most unsordid act of British social policy in the twentieth century'. As Klein (1989: 146) puts it, from this perspective the NHS represents an important social good, even if it has not cured a single patient. As Aneurin Bevan argues:

> No society can legitimately call itself civilized if a sick person is denied medical aid because of lack of means. . . . Society becomes more wholesome, more serene, and spiritually healthier, if it knows that its citizens have at the back of their consciousness the knowledge that not only they, but all their fellows, have access, when ill, to the best medical skill can provide.
>
> (Bevan 1978: 100)

Similar extolments of the NHS may be found throughout Bevan's writing and speeches (Bevan 1978: ch. 5; Foot 1975; Webster 1991a). How can anyone argue against such persuasive prose, let alone the original oratory? According to right-wing critics, this is precisely the problem: rational analysis of the NHS is almost impossible (Jewkes and Jewkes 1962; Whitney 1988). As Klein (1995a: 248) points out, the Bevan tradition sees health care as a secular church. It follows that anything less than complete faith amounts to heresy.

It has been said that public services in general are different from the rest of the economy, applying a number of distinctive criteria (Pollitt and Harrison 1992). Similarly, it has been claimed that health care in particular has its own distinctive criteria (Reisman 1993; Titmuss 1968: ch. 12). Equity is perhaps the key criterion that distinguishes the public from the private. Differences in the provision of market services result from differences in demand: a mixture of income and preferences. Differences in subscription to satellite television stations do not lead to calls for equality: a National Satellite TV Service. This is because it is in the realm of the market: differences are relatively unimportant and result from wants rather than needs. Even in a society of equitable income distribution – 'Egalitaria' – different consumer preferences would lead to differences in ownership of consumer goods (Klein 1988). However, in most countries it is felt that the market ought not to distribute health care. While it is acceptable that low incomes may mean that some people who desire satellite TV have to go without it, it is not acceptable that lack of income should lead to people going without health care. The market and consumer demand can be allowed to distribute satellite TV broadcasts, but not health care. In this sense, access to health care is a right while access to satellite TV is not: questions of equity and citizenship are relevant for health care but not for satellite TV.

In a crude sense, the difference between the state and the market hinges on the difference between need and market demand. This has implications for the issue of acceptability. To oversimplify a little, just as the welfare state is built on the notion that 'the gentlemen in Whitehall know better' (Timmins 1996: 101), the NHS is built on the notion that the doctor knows best. While individuals may be the best judges of their market preferences, the professional is the best judge of their needs. In short, the NHS is built on paternalism rather than consumerism. Responsiveness has been identified as a problem for the NHS. An enquiry into the NHS in the 1980s argued that 'Businessmen have a keen sense of how well they are looking after their customers. Whether the NHS is meeting the needs of the patient, and the community, and can prove that it is doing so, is open to question' (DHSS 1983: 10). According to Holland (1983: 27): 'Acceptability is a very important although often overlooked aspect of health care. If the health care offered is unacceptable then regardless of its effectiveness or efficiency it may fail to achieve the stated objective if the population refuses to utilize it.'

Issues of acceptability and responsiveness are bound up with professionalism and consumerism. As Pollitt and Harrison (1992: 13–14) write, a feature of the late 1980s and early 1990s has been the emergence of a strong rhetoric around the notion of improving the quality of public services. The most obvious example can be seen in the Citizen's Charter initiatives. The definition of quality and who defines it have been subject to great debate. Quality can refer to inputs, processes, outputs or outcomes. The term was arguably used more promiscuously during the early 1990s than 'efficiency' was in the 1980s. However, most of the literature stresses user or consumer judgements. Thus, concerns of quality shifted to a new agenda. Previously, the only judge of quality was the individual professional. This was a central feature of the 'medical model' (Morgan *et al.*

1985; Jones and Moon 1987: ch. 1; Baggott 1994a: ch. 2; Allsop 1995: ch. 7). More recently, quality became a collective professional responsibility. An individual clinician's work has increasingly been subject to the scrutiny of other professionals in the form of initiatives such as medical audit. Most recently, quality is seen in consumer terms. Traditionally, there was a clear power structure within health services (Ham 1981, 1992; Wilding 1982). The patient was seen as a passive client. The doctor had the monopoly of relevant knowledge and this asymmetric knowledge meant that the patient could not challenge what the doctor said. However, the consumer view may conflict with professional views. The professionals have been challenged by management and the public. However, the challenge is largely based on lay rather than clinical criteria. For example, Charter initiatives give the public entitlements based on waiting times rather than on what happens at the end of the wait. The 'consumer watchdogs' in the NHS, the community health councils, tend to judge hospitals on 'hotel' rather than clinical criteria. Put another way, the NHS is a store that is judged by the service rather than the quality of the goods. The product may be poor, but if it is well packaged in terms of a short waiting time, a pleasant and clean environment and the 'personal touch' of a good 'bedside manner', it will pass inspection. In one sense, this is similar to the retail model, but the 'grocer's NHS' falls short in that there are few money-back guarantees.

As Klein (1982: 386) points out, the NHS is a very complex organization. It is a policy arena distinguished by its complexity, heterogeneity, uncertainty and ambiguity. It is complex because the provision of health care requires the cooperation of a wide mix of skills, ranging from those of doctors and nurses to those of laboratory technicians and ward orderlies. Its heterogeneity derives from a variety of very different activities, ranging from the provision of curative services for the acutely ill to care for the mentally handicapped. It is marked by the large degree of uncertainty about the relationships between inputs and outputs, means and ends: while a shoe manufacturer may be reasonably certain that a given input of leather, labour and capital investment in machinery will yield boots as a final output, there can be no equivalent certainty that a given input of resources will produce a given quantity of health at the end of the day. Finally, and linked to the uncertainty, the health-care policy arena is remarkable for the ambiguity of the available information: a patient treated may be seen either as an indicator of success (if the objective of the organization is defined as being able to provide treatment) or as an indicator of failure (if the objective is defined as the prevention of ill-health). Moreover, the NHS, unlike the shoe factory, does not attempt to respond to consumer demand. Once the consumer has decided to contact the NHS (usually via the general practitioner or GP), most decisions concerning treatment are taken by professionals. The NHS is largely a supplier-dominated service, shaped not by consumer preferences but by producer norms. Lastly, the NHS defines and selects, to a large extent, its own clientele. The population of hospitals is not defined by statute (except in the case of a small minority of the mentally ill); it is not legislation that determines who visits the GP's surgery.

FRAMEWORK FOR EVALUATION

The most widely known framework for assessing quality in health services is Donabedian's (1980) model of structure–process–outcome. Structure refers to the physical and organizational setting, and available resources for providing health care. Process involves what is done to the patient in terms of advice, diagnosis, treatment and after-care. Outcome relates to the change in the health of the patient. A number of writers have provided general frameworks for evaluating health services that are related to the Donabedian scheme (Holland 1983; Long and Harrison 1985; St Leger *et al.* 1992; Long 1992; Roberts 1990). Each uses slightly different terms, but in general produces a framework of inputs, outputs (or activity) and outcomes. Inputs are what go into the health-care system. The most obvious input – the lowest common denominator – is expenditure. This can be divided into revenue and capital expenditure. Revenue expenditure includes staff and drugs, which have to be paid for continually and which cannot be used again and again: an hour of a doctor's time, a wound dressing or a spoonful of medicine cannot be re-used. On the other hand, capital expenditure relates to buildings and equipment such as beds and X-ray machinery, which can be used time and time again. What is bought with expenditure (such as staff and drugs) are generally termed intermediate inputs. Inputs are used to produce outputs such as operations and radiographs. These outputs should combine to produce an increase in patients' health outcome. This is generally taken to mean that the patient should leave hospital in a more healthy state than when he or she entered. However, there are cases in which an increased state of health is not possible. Here, the focus changes from cure to care, and outcome can be thought of in terms of a person's quality of life, with criteria such as comfort, pain relief and dignity, for the same state of health.

A focus on the above concepts and the relationships between them generates a general set of criteria of evaluation (Harrison *et al.* 1990; Long 1992; Phillips *et al.* 1994). Effectiveness, or efficacy, concerns the extent to which the inputs produced a positive outcome: for example, did the bundle of staff time and associated drugs produce a more healthy patient? In its crude sense, efficiency relates to the ratio between inputs and outputs. It is generally expressed in financial terms: for example, the cost per day of a stay in hospital. The hospital with the lowest cost per day is generally termed the most efficient. Expressed in these terms, whether the hospital stay cured the patient is not relevant. Thus, a technically efficient processs may yield no benefits. 'It is possible to kill people efficiently or spread litter efficiently' (Pollitt and Harrison 1992: 13). Clearly, such a notion does not – or at least should not – have a place in the NHS. A more useful sense of efficiency or cost-effectiveness, by contrast, relates to the cost per unit of desired outcome, such as the cost of a successful hip-joint operation or the cost per person with eyesight restored. Thus, efficiency is a ratio between inputs and outputs, while cost-effectiveness refers to the ratio of inputs to outcomes. A neat summary is given by Drucker (1968): efficiency is concerned with the question 'Are we doing things right?' while effectiveness refers to the question 'Are we doing the right things?' Equity is concerned with the degree of variation between individuals in terms of the inputs, outputs and outcomes.

EVALUATING THE NHS

There have been a number of attempts to evaluate the NHS (Klein 1982; Harrison *et al.* 1990). In the 1950s the Guillebaud Committee, set up to examine the cost of the NHS, defined performance in terms of a single criterion: value for money, or efficiency, but equated efficiency with economy. Like many of its successors, Guillebaud (1956) did not manage to get to grips with efficiency in the full sense, but concentrated mainly on economy (costs) – the input half of the efficiency ratio. When the Royal Commission on the NHS (1979) looked at the performance of the service, it found itself almost as flummoxed as the Guillebaud Committee had been

23 years before. The questions put by the Royal Commission were a good deal more sophisticated and wide-ranging than those of the Guillebaud Committee. But the answers were scarcely more convincing. Almost a decade later, the Social Services Committee of the House of Commons (1988: xi) stated that:

> The last major weakness of the National Health Service is that it is not possible to tell whether or not it works. There are no outcome measures to speak of other than that of crude numbers of patients treated. There is little monitoring on behalf of the public. As a result, the correct level of funding for the NHS cannot be determined and the public and politicians cannot decide whether or not they are getting value for the resources pumped into the National Health Service.

The debate on the NHS has been termed naive (Owen 1988: 3) and limited (Ranade 1994: 2). It rarely gets beyond statistical claims of 'underfunding' and accusations of breaking the principles of the service. Debates about what a modern health-care system can be expected to provide, how limited resources can be used to best effect and what needs to be done in a broader sense to improve the health of the population are edged to the margins or never addressed. The principles of the NHS are equated with a particular set of institutional arrangements which, like a sanctified ancient monument, cannot be touched but continue to crumble away under the onslaught of wind and weather (Ranade 1994: 2).

EVALUATING THE NEW NHS

The reforms introduced by the Conservative government in 1991, following the 1989 White Paper 'Working For Patients' (WFP), (DoH 1989) has been viewed as a watershed in the NHS, marking the end of the 'old' NHS and the beginning of the 'new' NHS. Certainly, there now appear to be new concerns expressed in a different vocabulary. However, whether this amounts to a new agenda is less clear, partly because there have always been different views about these issues.

The concern of equity was very much associated with the 'old' NHS. However, for many years, there was little empirical examination, as it was assumed that the problem of equity had been solved by making the service free and universal. With the discovery of inequity in the 1960s and 1970s, academic and policy concerns developed together. In particular, policies addressed geographical inequities in the NHS (Mays and Bevan 1987; Beech *et al.* 1990). The highwater mark of this concern is perhaps the Black report (Townsend and Davidson 1982).

Efficiency or economy has always been a concern for governments, and has been a recurring theme in the 1980s and 1990s (Harrison *et al.* 1990: 85–6), but examining the efficiency of the service is a relatively recent academic concern. Effectiveness, in contrast, has been an academic concern, but saw little practical expression in the NHS until recently. It was left to individual clinicians. Clinical freedom led to variations in medical practice and no questions were asked, although the discovery of variations predates the NHS (Glover 1938, in Ham 1988b). Consumerism or acceptability has only recently appeared on anyone's agenda.

Future directions regarding the importance of and criteria of evaluation in the NHS are unclear and may be contradictory in places (Long 1992). On the one hand, the increased visibility of evaluation and monitoring has been stressed. Walsh (1995: 219) claims that the market-based state is an evaluative state. St Leger *et al.* (1992: 6) argue that the reforms of the NHS do have one great merit, in forcing consideration of value-for-money issues: 'So the evaluation of health service effectiveness will be a growth area'. It has been pointed out that there have been initiatives in evaluation and monitoring since the 1980s (Harrison *et al.* 1990; Ham 1992) and it has been claimed that evaluation has moved squarely on to the national political agenda (Harrison *et al.* 1990: 151). However, on the other hand, the government did not commission any evaluation or trial of its recent reforms. In general, all potential evaluators of the NHS have stressed the difficulty of the task and have provided more questions than answers. Part of the problem is a lack of information, but another part of it is the lack of an appropriate framework for analysis. WFP makes no mention of how its reforms will either contribute to or, as many fear, detract from the guiding principles of the NHS. There is no framework to drive the reforms, no benchmark against which to measure their success or failure, and no apparent concern with outcome or impact (Harrison *et al.* 1989: 12). In other words, 'evaluation' may be of greater importance, but the 'who' and 'what' questions of evaluation remain unanswered. First, professional and consumer views may conflict. For example WFP strengthens professional (audit) and consumer perspectives, which may be in tension (Harrison *et al.* 1990). For example, on the issue of closure of hospitals, professionals stress the value of centralization in large hospitals, while consumers value localism and accessibility. Second, the criteria of evaluation may also be in conflict. Certain types of evaluation may have dominated the stage. For example, the Audit Commision has had a major impact in demonstrating that some places appear to squeeze more out of their available resources than other places (e.g. Audit Commission 1990, 1991, 1996). It has been claimed that evaluating health services has become a cost and efficiency exercise; it is time to add a human and moral dimension. The future is to look beyond efficiency to equity, effectiveness and acceptability (Long 1992: 70) and to separate rhetoric from reality.

Moreover, the link from policy evaluation to policy often remains distant. At a time when ministers are arguing that medicine should be 'evidence based', is it not reasonable to suggest that this should also apply to health policy? In short, it is clear that evaluation should inform policy, and 'the case for evidence based policymaking is difficult to refute' (Ham *et al.* 1995: 71).

PLAN OF THE BOOK

Chapters 2–4 provide the context for evaluation. Chapter 2 provides a brief history of health policy in Britain before the NHS. It examines the provision of health services just before the introduction of the NHS and attempts to evaluate these services. Thus, this chapter analyses the provision that the NHS inherited in 1948 and that can serve as a baseline for assessing subsequent developments.

Chapter 3 examines the formation of the NHS. It covers the debates surrounding the evolving plans for the service and assesses the resulting National Health Service Act of 1946 which led to the service coming into being two years later. It critically examines the principles of the service.

Chapter 4 briefly outlines the structures and policies of the NHS since 1948. Within a chronological framework, it focuses on three main topics: finance, management and policies.

The next three chapters evaluate the NHS from different perspectives. Chapter 5 is concerned with temporal evaluation. This examines the changing NHS over time, using the framework of inputs, outputs and outcomes. The main issue is whether the NHS today is better or worse than the system it replaced. There are two main problems with addressing this issue. First, there is that of how to measure the NHS over time. Second, there is the problem of determining to what extent the changes that are detected have been caused by the NHS or whether they would have occurred with a different health-care system.

Chapter 6 is concerned with intrinsic evaluation. It examines the extent to which the NHS has been true to its founding principles. How far has the service lived up to its aims of being free at the point of use, comprehensive and equitable? In other words, this chapter compares objectives and achievements, or the rhetoric and reality of the NHS.

Chapter 7 is concerned with extrinsic evaluation. The NHS, which is often taken as a model of a national, taxation-based system, is compared with other health-care systems. First, the structure and performance of the systems of industrialized Western countries are examined. Then, other health-care systems are presented in order to illustrate different models of provision. Germany's is presented as an example of a national insurance system. Sweden's is a comprehensive system based on elected local authorities. The USA's system is based on insurance with a state safety net. Finally, the NHS is located within the comparative context, and the possibility of learning lessons from other countries is reviewed.

The final chapter brings together the main points of the study, and offers some speculations on the future of the NHS.

2

HEALTH CARE BEFORE THE NHS

Conventional wisdom is largely critical of health-care provision before the NHS. For example, on the fortieth anniversary of the NHS, a *Guardian* editorial (1988) claimed that before the NHS there was:

> A two-tier system under which millions were left uncovered and unable to afford medical care. The gross disparities in the distribution of medical facilities would make our modern inequalities seem virtual perfection. . . . In short, what 100 years of private enterprise, competition and the voluntary ethic produced was an irrational, uncoordinated and uneconomic apology for a health care system.

This neat summary of the conventional wisdom, which is partly due to poor information and partly due to a hostile ideology, is at best only partially true.

This chapter examines the development of health and health care in Britain, culminating in the situation just before the introduction of the NHS. This historical account is necessary for two main reasons. First, the NHS's inheritance in 1948 was the zenith of the previous system, and so serves as a good reference point for assessing the performance of the NHS since that date (Chapter 5). Second, the objectives and nature of the NHS derived in part from the limitations and problems of the prewar system (Gray 1991:258). Thus, the system before the NHS influenced both the principles of the NHS and the measures that were taken to achieve them. The planning of the NHS could not start from a blank piece of paper: its shape in many ways was determined by incremental developments from the previous system.

THE DEVELOPMENT OF HEALTH POLICY

The term 'health policy' is a convenient one under which to examine a number of very different issues. However, it is one which would not have been recognized during much of the period under discussion, which was characterized by piecemeal developments rather than being shaped by an overall coherent policy. Indeed, it is still said today that Britain has a policy for health services, but no health policy. Health policy includes consideration of all factors that have a significant effect on health. In the extreme, all public policy is health policy because issues such as poverty, unemployment, housing and pollution all have effects on health. Nevertheless, 'health' is often equated with 'health care'. Although curative health services are the most visible symbols of health policy, their contribution to the nation's health has been questioned (see Chapter 5). Moreover, the earliest legislation on health policy was not concerned with personal health care, but with public health.

Public health

The most pressing health problems in industrial Britain were associated with the rapid population increase and urbanization of the nineteenth century, which threw up living and working conditions that are barely imaginable today in Britain (Herbert 1939: 25–30; Doyal 1979: 142–7; Fraser 1984: ch. 3). The health problem was clearly shown by the high mortality rates that occurred throughout much of the nineteenth century, and which increased further during outbreaks of infectious disease such as cholera. It has been said that the population was living on a dungheap and was being poisoned by its own excrement (Bruce 1968: 63). It was claimed at the time that 'the annual loss of life from filth and bad ventilation is greater than the loss from death or wounds in any wars in modern times' (quoted in Bruce 1968: 65). However, there were social and geographical variations in mortality. In the 1830s the mortality rate in the country districts was 18.2 per 1000, compared with 26.2 in the urban areas. The average age of death for the upper middle class was 38 years in Manchester and 35 years in Liverpool, compared with figures for the labouring class of 17 and 15, respectively (Doyal 1979: 50–1). Such figures clearly indicated the link between the environment and ill-health, as much illness was due to infectious disease that was associated with unhealthy living conditions.

The solution to these problems was seen to be public health reform, meaning environmental improvements (Fraser 1984; Baggott 1991). The stimulus for action is generally said to have been two main factors. The first was rational self-interest. Infectious disease could strike at the rich as well as the poor. Therefore, reducing the level of infectious disease suffered by the poor made life safer for the rich. Second, ill-health imposed financial costs on the wealthy in the form of rates raised for expenditure on the poor. This was because when the breadwinner was sick and unable to work, the whole family would be supported at public expense. Thus, disease was inextricably entangled with the Poor Law, as expenditure on relief of the poor could be reduced by taking preventive action with regard to the environment to keep the family breadwinner at work (Fraser 1984: 62). Out of this awareness grew Edwin Chadwick's famous *Report on the Sanitary Condition of the Labouring Population of Great Britain* of 1842, 'perhaps the greatest of the nineteenth century Blue-Books (Fraser 1984: 62). The problem was seen to be insanitary housing and deficient sewerage and water supply, and the solution was through civil engineering. Slowly this led towards the Public Health Act of 1848, 'a great landmark in social reform' (Fraser 1984: 70), which permitted local areas to pursue sanitary reform. Later legislation made action compulsory rather than permissive. Chadwick's earlier blueprint led to a patchwork structure which evolved into a public health system by the Public Health Act of 1875, which remained the essential basis of all public health activity until 1936 (Fraser 1984: 75–7).

What impact did these measures make on the health of the population? At first sight, the record is impressive. Death rates fell almost continuously from the 1870s to become about 12.0 per 1000 in the 1930s. A major part of the decline in death rates came from the reduction of deaths through infectious diseases, such as tuberculosis and typhoid. The infant mortality rate (IMR) continued to remain high throughout the nineteenth century, but subsequent improvements are indicated by a decline from 142 per 1000 in 1900 to 61 per 1000 in 1940 (Stevenson 1984: 203–4). However, Webster (1984) has challenged the optimistic view that these figures suggest. He points out that that falls in the IMR were slow when compared both with other countries and with earlier periods in Britain. Aggregate national figures hid geographical and social variations which may have become more marked during the economic depression of the interwar period (Laybourn, 1990: ch. 2; Jones 1994: ch. 4). Moreover, a decline in death rates does not tell the full story of the health of the population. According to Herbert (1939: 20) some 41 per cent of the men called up for military service during the last year of the First World War were classified in the lowest grade of physical fitness: 'C3'. By 1935 no fewer than 62 per cent of prospective recruits were below the relatively low standard of physique required by the army.

Primary care

Many working men belonged to friendly societies, 'the most important providers of social welfare during the nineteenth and early twentieth century' (Green 1993: 30), which, in return for contributions, provided the services of a doctor and sick pay (Green 1985, 1993). In his National Health Insurance (NHI) scheme of 1911 David Lloyd George, Chancellor in the Liberal government, effectively nationalized this arrangement for all workers earning less than £160 per year (Gilbert 1966; Carpenter 1984). The workers had to pay 4d per week, which was added to contributions from the employers and government to produce Lloyd George's '9d for 4d'. In return for contributions they were entitled to join the list or 'panel' of a general medical practitioner (or 'panel doctor') and receive free medical care and sick pay when they were unable to work owing to illness. This scheme did not provide for hospital treatment, except for tuberculosis, or treatment for dependent women and children. As a health scheme, the omission of women and children was a major problem, but the scheme was primarily to prevent poverty. It enabled the breadwinner to be treated and return to work as soon as possible, with sick pay to tide the family over in the meantime. From this point of view, medical care for other members of the family was not necessary (Fraser 1984: 167). As Carpenter (1984: 72) puts it, the NHI scheme was conceived primarily in terms of income maintenance. Insurance was seen by Lloyd George as a temporary expedient. He likened himself to an ambulance driver responding to an emergency (Fraser 1984: 167–8). By 1938 nearly half the population were entitled to consult 'panel doctors' under the NHI scheme. The rest, including children aged below 14 and most women, either paid the doctor directly or deferred medical care, except that which might be available through the local authorities' services described below.

The NHI scheme was inefficient and unequal. Administration was entrusted to 'approved societies' and contributors could choose between them. The societies ranged enormously in size and extraordinary duplication of effort was involved. For instance, in a factory in the south-west, 337 employees were members of 37 different societies, 16 of which had only one member at the firm; and in 1926 it was stated that 98 societies had one member each in Glasgow. The range involved may be seen from the fact that though 65 per cent of the societies insured 2 per cent of the population, 76 per cent of the population were insured by 2.5 per cent of the societies (Fraser 1984: 199–200). While some societies paid only minimum benefits, others paid for dental and optical treatment, hospital treatment and nursing homes. By 1936 it was estimated that some 13.1 million people were entitled to dental benefit, as compared with 11.3 for optical benefit and 1.9 for hospital care (PEP 1937: 206). In other words, equal contributions led to unequal benefits. Problems associated with the NHI scheme were well documented in both official and unofficial accounts (Gray 1991), culminating in a devastating critique of conditions inherited by the NHS. Collings (1950) claimed that the overall state of general practice was bad and deteriorating. Inner-city practice was described as at best very unsatisfactory and at worst a public danger. Rural practice was an anachronism and suburban practice was a casualty-clearing service (see also Tudor-Hart 1988; Digby and Bosanquet 1988).

A major concern of the early twentieth century was with the health of women and children (Herbert 1939: ch. 9; Ham 1992: 9–11; Leathard 1990: 12–13). One of the stimuli was the discovery of the poor state of health of army recruits for the Boer War. This led to the establishment of the Interdepartmental Committee on Physical Deterioration. The resulting 1904 report recommended improving child health through the provision of school meals and school medical inspection. Acts setting these up in 1906 and 1907, respectively, although limited in many ways, 'marked the beginning of the construction of the welfare state' (Gilbert 1966: 102). Concern over the high rates of maternal and infant deaths led to a series of provisions associated with maternal and child welfare. Midwives' registration and certification was introduced under the Midwives Act of 1902; the permissive Notification of Births Act of 1907 opened the way for systematic home visits, intended to promote good child care, and beginning within days of a baby's birth. Further legislation, most notably the Maternity and Child Welfare Act of 1918, empowered local authorities to extend their range of services for expectant and nursing mothers, and for children under school age. These could include sudsidized home midwives, maternity homes, and infant welfare clinics, as well as the home visits undertaken by the health visitors for whom, by the 1930s, professional qualifications had been established and were required for their work. The 1936 Midwives Act placed local authorities under a duty to provide the services of salaried midwives. The development of the various services for mothers and young children proceeded in parallel with that of the school medical service, which by the 1930s went well beyond its original function of medical inspection and advice. However, as the services for women were limited to maternity care and related matters, and as the emphasis both of the school and the infant welfare services was very much on preventive rather than curative care, local authorities' services by no means compensated for the lack of provision for the dependants of people covered by the NHI scheme.

Hospitals

As regards secondary care, there were two hospital systems. Richard Titmuss (1950: 66) points out that the dominant feature of the situation before the Second World War was:

> the existence of two distinct and contrasting hospital systems – voluntary and municipal. Both had grown up without a plan. Their origins and histories were dissimilar; they were differently organized and financed and in some respects they catered for different sections of the population.

The oldest and most prestigious hospitals were in the voluntary sector, which dated largely from the eighteenth century, the 'golden age of hospitals'. Voluntary hospitals were run by boards of governors and were originally financed by philanthropy through the 'donations of the living and the legacies of the dead' (Abel-Smith 1964: 405). Doctors attended in an honorary (unpaid) capacity. The voluntary sector was diverse, with variations in size, function and quality. At the apex of the sector were the teaching hospitals, where doctors were trained. These tended to be large, general hospitals with a high reputation, and were staffed by many of the leading doctors of the time. At the other extreme, some hospitals had a handful of beds. Some of these, mainly 'cottage hospitals' in rural areas, attempted to be 'mini' general hospitals, but others were 'special' hospitals, concentrating on a particular type of disease such as those affecting the ear, nose and throat, or a particular group of patients such as women and children.

The traditional function of the voluntary sector was to provide free services for the poor financed by the philanthropy of the rich. However, admission was generally restricted to the 'deserving poor'. Hospitals tended to exclude also 'incurable' or 'chronic' cases as well as those with infectious disease. Moreover, a patient with an influential patron stood the best chance of admission. The teaching hospitals favoured those who presented an 'interesting' case compatible with the requirements of medical education (Abel-Smith 1964). In the twentieth century the voluntary sector experienced increasing financial problems, in that the 'funding gap' between cost and revenue had become a pressing matter. The response to this problem was seen in the increasing use of contributory insurance schemes, means testing and pay beds: a combination of 'trade with charity' (Abel-Smith 1964: 338). In short, the voluntary hospitals continued to exist partly by abandoning their original objective of providing free care for the poor. In spite of these initiatives, it has been argued that by the 1940s the voluntary system as a whole was bankrupt and voluntary in name only (Webster 1984: 28). Indeed, some parts of the system had never subscribed to the original aim of free treatment for the poor: many cottage hospitals, staffed mainly by general practitioners and located mainly in the rural areas, and which appeared from the 1850s onwards, usually required payments from patients either directly or in the form of subscription schemes from the outset. Similarly, special (as opposed to general) hospitals had always tended to charge patients (Abel-Smith 1964: 102–3, 156–8).

Municipal hospitals were provided by the local authorities and financed largely through local taxes. The municipal hospital system was even more varied and complex than the voluntary system, as local authorities were given permissive powers to deal with different problems at different times. The largest segment of the publicly funded hospital services grew up almost accidently as an appendage to the workhouse system established under the Poor Law Amendment Act of 1834 (Webster 1988a: 5). Poor Law medical services were intended to cater for paupers who became sick. Sick paupers were treated in workhouses run by the local Poor Law guardians under the shadow of 'less eligibility', and this accounts, in part, for the contrast between the Poor Law medical service and the voluntary sector in terms both of standards and client group. 'Less eligibility' implied inferior standards to those prevailing in the voluntary hospitals, which was reinforced by the objective of economy. Patients tended to be the chronic as opposed to the acute sick, as well as those not deemed to be 'deserving', such as un-married expectant mothers and people with venereal disease. The common attribute of such a diverse body was that the voluntary hospitals were often unwilling to admit them. Standards were low, but by 1866 this sector was larger than the voluntary sector and was termed in an enquiry by the *Lancet* 'the real hospitals of the land' (quoted in Abel-Smith 1964: 64). This period saw pressure for work-house reform. The President of the Poor Law Board, Gathorne-Hardy, introduced the Metropolitan Poor Bill with the words,

> There is one thing ... which we must peremptorily insist on, namely, the treatment of the sick in workhouses being con-ducted on an entirely different system, because the evils complained of have arisen mainly from the workhouse manage-ment, which must, to a great degree, be of a deterrent charac-ter having been applied to the sick, who are not proper objects for such a system.
>
> (Quoted in Abel-Smith 1964: 77)

Abel-Smith (1964: 82) writes that:

> The Metropolitan Poor Act of 1867 was an important step in English social history. It was the first explicit acknowledge-ment that it was the duty of the state to provide hospitals for the poor. It therefore represented an important step towards the National Health Service Act which followed some eighty years later.

Standards did improve from the late nineteenth century, notably in London and some other large cities, where the sick were likely to be treated in separate infirmaries rather than in part of the general mixed workhouse. By the early twentieth century some infirmaries had the latest equipment such as X-ray machinery and sunlamps, and performed an increasing number of surgical opera-tions. Some even received medical students and accepted paying patients (Crowther 1983: 184–5). In short, the better infirmaries were becoming more like acute general hospitals, although claims that the infirmaries were equal to the latter should be regarded more as a hopeful aspiration than as a statement of fact. In some places that lacked access to voluntary hospitals, the majority report of the Royal Commission on Poor Laws stated in 1909 that the Poor Law infirmary had become *de facto*, if not *de jure*, a general hospi-tal for the community (quoted in Abel-Smith 1964: 206). However, advances were less marked in many rural areas, where patients were treated in conditions more like those of the nineteenth-century workhouse than of the more modern infirmaries found in some urban areas (Crowther 1983: 186–8). Abel-Smith (1964: 215) states that by the early twentieth century, 'though a number of good infirmaries had been built, the majority of the sick were still housed in unclassified institutions, some of which had been condemned forty years earlier'.

A historical account of provision for mental health is problematic for two main reasons. First, the area is characterized by anachronistic terminology and, second, many of the standard accounts devote little space to the subject. This is in spite of its historical importance since: 'The County Asylums Act of 1808 constituted a significant precedent because it was the first piece of legislation in which public funds were made available in all administrative areas for providing hospital accommodation' (Webster 1988a: 9). Wilson (1946: 72) writes that 'Mentally afflicted persons fall into two groups, each of which (broadly speaking) is the subject of distinct legislation and of different methods of care'. The first group comprises people with mental health problems ('lunatics'). The 1808 Act enabled local authorities to set up asylums. In practice, county asylums were not developed into a comprehensive system until after the Lunatic Asylums Act of 1845. The Lunacy Act of 1890 placed an obligation on local authorities to maintain institutions for the mentally ill. The Mental Treatment Act of 1930 introduced new terminology of 'persons of unsound mind' and 'mental health hospitals'. The legislative framework may have become less draconian after this date, but the old asylums continued to be large, isolated, overcrowded institutions providing a largely custodial as opposed to a therapeutic regime (Means and Smith 1994: 27–9).

The second group consists of people with learning difficulties ('mental defectives'). Attempts were made to isolate this group from the rest of society by removing them to an institution under the 1886 Idiots Act. This process was reinforced by the Mental Deficiency Act of 1913. Many in this group were housed in farm and industrial colonies, largely outside the realm of medicine (Means and Smith 1994: 29–31). The interwar period saw some developments in the treatment of, and the terminology associated with, mental health. However, the two groups continued to be separated from those suffering physical illness and probably encountered more problems of overcrowding and understaffing.

Patients with infectious disease were often treated in the only public facility available, namely the workhouse, where they might be placed in the next bed to someone without the infection. In the latter half of the nineteenth century sanitary authorities were empowered to provide isolation hospitals. As always, permissive legislation led to uneven results, with many small authorities constructing hospitals with a mere handful of beds, if they took up their new powers at all. It was not until the twentieth century that local authorities assumed responsibility for the treatment of tuberculosis. In this case, powers were entrusted to the 150 or so major local authorities (counties and country boroughs) instead of all 1400 authorities, which included a motley collection of non-county boroughs and urban and rural districts with populations that fell to below 1000 people.

In the interwar period, local authorities started to assume powers to provide institutional maternity care through powers that were consolidated and extended by the Maternity and Child Welfare Act of 1918. 'Welfare authorities' (the major local authorities and some of the larger urban areas that were not county boroughs) were enabled to augment provision made by the Poor Law guardians. This provision was often to be found in small municipal maternity homes.

By the twentieth century, then, the granting of health powers to different authorities at different times had resulted in a confused pattern of different administrations with a mismatch between powers, duties and capacities, that has been termed 'a multiplication of health authorities and the disintegration of functions' (Robson 1931: 296). The 1929 Local Government Act was intended to bring some order into this confusion, essentially by attempting to concentrate responsibilities on the major local authorities. This was to be achieved in two main ways. First, some powers exercised by the lesser local authorities were handed over to the major ones. Second, the boards of Poor Law guardians were dissolved and their functions were taken over by the major local authorities. It was intended that every service, whenever possible, should be transferred from the public assistance committees of the local authorities (which handled the former Poor Law functions) to the relevant functional committees (the public health committee in the case of medical services). Thus the counties and county boroughs were enabled to 'break up the poor law', to use the famous phrase of the Webbs (see Abel-Smith 1964: chs 14, 22–3). So, by the 1930s, agency and client group had changed: municipal provision was, in theory, available for the whole population. It was provided, in varied degrees of quality and quantity, by some 150 major local authorities: the county boroughs and county councils that served populations of over 4 million to around 20,000.

The quantity and quality of local authorities' provisions depended on factors such as the size of the local authority area, the financial capacity of the area, and the attitudes of councillors and officers (Wilson 1938; Powell 1995b). In some cases, these factors worked in the same direction: for example, the London County Council was large, rich, powerful and progressive, and it was proud of its municipal empire of beds, which outnumbered London's voluntary beds by a factor of more than five (Abel-Smith 1964:372). Outside London, the county boroughs tended to have better provision than the county councils. It might be thought that richer areas would have better provision than poorer ones, but the affluence factor often conflicted with the political factor. Many poorer areas had Labour councils, which spent more on health provision. Thus, the relative importance of the factors determining expenditure on municipal medicine before the NHS remains uncertain (Wilson 1938; Lee 1988; Powell 1995b) although it seems clear that financial capacity was a constraining and not a determining factor in the provision of local authority services.

By 1938 there were some 3100 hospitals for the physically ill in England and Wales, providing some 263,000 beds (Pinker 1966: 49, 57). The voluntary sector contained about a third of all beds, but a majority of acute beds and, with one exception, all the teaching hospitals. The municipal sector provided some 175,000 beds at 1900 hospitals, and was responsible for the vast majority of beds for the chronic sick and for infectious disease. Although both sectors were varied, containing large and small and general and special hospitals, the municipal sector was generally and correctly deemed to be the lower tier in terms of quality of provision. Estimates about provision for mental health are less clear (Herbert 1939: 158; Leathard 1990: 9; Webster 1988a: 9). As Gray (1991: 249–50) states, reliable information on the numbers, cost, or staffing in this area is very hard to obtain. However it is probable that the size of the mental health sector approximated municipal provision for the physically ill (see PEP 1937: 275–9; Means and Smith 1994: 28, 31).

CRITICISMS OF HEALTH-CARE PROVISION BEFORE THE NHS

The general tenor of comment about health provision before the NHS is one of criticism. This is true both of contemporary commentators such as Wilson (1938) and Leff (1950) and of subsequent accounts such as Eckstein (1958), Walters (1980), Whitehead (1988) and Gray (1991). Isolated voices of praise come from Jewkes and Jewkes (1962) and Green (1985, 1993). Most of the criticisms of health-care provision before the NHS may be examined under a number of convenient themes. Wherever possible, the criticisms will be evaluated using primary data. These are from a semi-official survey of England and Wales undertaken during the Second World War, but the data refer to 1938. The country was divided into ten survey regions and a team of leading medical and lay surveyors collected information on virtually every hospital in their region. The surveys were published in ten volumes (NPHT/MoH 1945–6) and summarized in the *Domesday Book of the Hospital Services* (NPHT 1946).

Barriers to access

In some accounts, and in the popular wisdom, lack of money is often seen as the main barrier to access. PEP (1944: 5) commented that 'To-day a person in need of medical care meets with financial barriers at almost every point'. To the extent that most people had to pay something towards health care (Whitehead 1988: 9–12), this is accurate. However, the term 'barrier' suggests that people were prevented from using health care because of lack of money. It is clear that some people were prevented from consulting for some conditions, but the generality of these circumstances remains unclear. Health care was not wholly divorced from ability to pay for it, although great progress had been made towards eliminating the financial barrier (MoH 1944: 6). About half the population had access to a panel doctor, and some had additional benefits such as dental and optical treatment. However, many women and children lacked such coverage. Their options were either voluntary insurance, direct payment or foregoing or at least deferring medical treatment. In primary care, then, it was women and children who bore the main burden of neglect in terms of treatment, although, at least in theory, they had access to a number of municipal preventive services (Wilson 1938, 1946).

In the case of secondary care, national estimates of subscribers vary from about 5 to 10 million (Cherry 1992: 479). However, Cherry claims on the basis of a study of East Anglia that hospital contributory schemes were almost as extensive as NHI and that the national estimates given above may be too low. The most optimistic national estimates suggest that some 10 million people subscribed to hospital insurance and that, with dependants, some 22 million may have been covered (PEP 1944: 5). In theory, for voluntary hospitals, the rest contributed what they – or more likely the hospital – considered they could afford on a means-tested basis. Municipal hospitals were required to recover charges on a means-tested basis. However, it has been estimated that only about 10 per cent of costs were covered in such ways, and some local authorities were effectively offering free hospital treatment to their citizens (Webster 1988a: 6).

In some ways, it was not the poorest groups who suffered the greatest problems of financial access. Some contemporary commentators argued that the rich and poor got treated by the same doctors, but the middle classes were neglected. Indeed, an article entitled 'The advantages of poverty' argued that the poor got better treatment than the rich, who were often treated in their own homes or in nursing homes (Walters 1980: 35–40). Eckstein (1958: 9) has argued that 'the social distribution of the British medical services . . . was biased very much in favour of the lower classes . . . Mayfair, in certain respects, did not come off as well as Limehouse'. He continues that the 'lower classes' enjoyed not only financial but also geographic advantages in access to hospital and specialist services as the vast majority of the larger hospitals were located in metropolitan areas where the population was preponderantly poor (p. 38). In addition to abnormal metropolitan concentration *per se*, the better hospitals tended to be located in the poor parts of the cities (p. 39). The urban poor, therefore, enjoyed almost every conceivable advantage over the rest of the population in access to good hospitals and specialists (p. 40).

Money, then, was a barrier to some, but not to all, and it was not simply the case that the poor suffered the greatest problems of access. Moreover, the financial barrier was not the only nor, in some cases, the most important one. Others existed, and to some extent remain today.

Distance was a barrier in some cases. Travel difficulties for rural dwellers were formidable. Sometimes, people travelled many hours for an outpatient appointment lasting a few minutes. In South Wales, the rate of outpatient attendances for populations in the three largest towns was some five to six times higher than for those in the surrounding areas (Trevor Jones *et al.* 1945: 36). Sometimes, for municipal hospitals, 'an arbitrary line drawn on a map [administrative boundary] often determines whether a patient shall have access to a well-staffed, relatively modern hospital . . . or be sent some distance away to an unsatisfactory institution' (Parsons *et al.* 1945: 7).

Psychological barriers such as stigma existed. Municipal hospitals, despite the change of name, were still often known as the workhouse, and were repellent to many for reasons of reputation, standards, and other clients. For example, the South Wales surveyors said of maternity provision in the least progressive institutions: 'facilities and equipment . . . are of the barest and . . . there is little pressure on the beds because they are rarely used except for unmarried mothers and for confinements of women of the mentally deficient type . . . ordinary patients will not willingly enter such institutions' (Trevor Jones *et al*. 1945: 20).

The fact that money was not the only barrier is suggested by the fact that despite the NHS effectively removing it, use of facilities is still unequal (see Chapter 6).

Adequacy

Health-care provision was seen to be inadequate on both quantitative and qualitative criteria. According to the national survey of hospitals by teams of surveyors during the Second World War, Britain needed a further 98,000 beds. This meant that the existing stock of 225,000 beds needed to be increased by some 40 per cent. Moreover, the general inadequacy of hospital accommodation was much greater than this would suggest, as the existing number of beds included 'bed overcrowding' (estimated by one team of surveyors as 20 per cent) and unsuitable premises (NPHT 1946). On the other hand, estimates of bed requirements from the 1950s onwards were much lower (Jewkes and Jewkes 1962: 10; Godber 1983: 6–7). With the benefit of hindsight, the wartime reports may have adopted over-ambitious standards, but the surveyors could not be expected to foresee that advancing medical technology would mean lower lengths of stay in acute hospitals and that much provision for tuberculosis and infectious disease would shortly cease to be necessary. There were hospital waiting lists, but often in terms of days or months, shorter than today. Little is known about the vast amount of undetected illness not making its way on to waiting lists. To some extent, this 'numbers game on hospital beds' (Godber 1983: 6) is a pointless exercise. However, the critics were on firmer ground with respect to the qualitative dimension of hospital accommodation and the quantity and quality of the staff.

It is suspected that one of the most serious problems of the interwar system was the quality of the care that was delivered (PEP 1944; Gray 1991), although this is perhaps the most difficult aspect to examine. Many hospitals were deficient in structural terms. Every team of surveyors found inadequate buildings (NPHT/MoH 1945–6; NPHT 1946). In his Annual Report for 1946 the Chief Medical Officer commented that 'A fact which is strikingly brought out of the reports is that many hospital buildings are out of date and fall far short of modern requirements in planning and in the facilities which they provide for efficient and convenient working' (quoted in Leff 1950: 226). In South Wales the surveyors considered that several of the buildings used for the treatment of the sick were obsolete and should be abandoned as hospitals as soon as possible. They classified up to a half of all hospital accommodation as unsatisfactory (Powell 1992c). Sir George Godber, one of the hospital surveyors and later to become Chief Medical Officer at the Ministry of Health, recalls that one institution was 'almost as it had been in Poor Law days; there was even a treadmill – unused of course,' and one local authority claimed to have a smallpox hospital that proved to be a field in which they could pitch a tent (Godber 1983: 10, 12).

The *Domesday Book of the Hospital Services* (NHPT 1946: 9) stated that, serious as the bed shortage was, there was an even more serious shortage of medical staff, most obviously of consultants: one survey team considered that consultant staff could at least be doubled. This shortage resulted in a considerable amount of surgery being undertaken by general practitioners. All the surveying teams commented on the problem of the 'general practitioner surgeon' (NPHT 1946: 12; Leff 1950: 228–9). Bradford-Hill (1951) estimated that 'general practitioner surgeons' did a total of 2.5 million operations in 1938, which represented an average of three operations per general practitioner per week. In his maiden speech to the House of Lords in 1943, the President of the Royal College of Physicians, Lord Moran, said, 'You may be surprised to hear that there are some great areas of England, towns with a population of 100,000 where the major surgery and everything else is done by general practitioners. All this must end; it is one of the greatest evils of our time in the medical world' (quoted in Honigsbaum 1989: 111). Tudor-Hart (1988: 3) gives an example from as late as 1952 of a general practitioner surgeon who operated on a woman with acute intestinal obstruction: 'Never having met this unusual condition before, he waded into the macaroni without planning his return'. He telephoned a London consultant and waited four hours for the latter to arrive, which led to the eventual happy ending of the patient surviving.

The limited evidence available suggests that clinical standards in hospitals were low. For example, Gray (1991: 256) cites a survey of 1935 that reports that permanent incapacity resulted in only 1 per cent of cases treated at a fracture clinic compared with 37 per cent of cases treated elsewhere. The disability periods for an ankle fracture were 11 weeks and 38 weeks, respectively.

The incentives of the NHI system led to cost minimization, restricted quality of service and high throughput (Digby and Bosanquet 1988; Gray 1991). 'The working tradition from which present general practice stems was a local sick shop where the doctor, unconvincingly disguised as a scientific gentleman, remained a shopkeeper, but a shopkeeper paid increasingly by the state rather than customers' (Tudor-Hart 1988: 42). Essentially, the panel doctor was an overworked businessman operating from an under-funded sick shop where consultations were rushed and examinations were rudimentary. As late as 1952, Tudor-Hart (1988: 7) recalls working in a practice in inner London which had some equipment which was 'redundant but . . . kept on standby in case the nineteenth century returned'. His workload included seeing some 20 or 30 patients each morning and evening, with some 15 housecalls between surgery sessions.

Inefficiency

Eckstein (1958: 62–71) points to the lack of coordination within and between the voluntary and municipal hospital systems before the NHS. Indeed, as PEP (1944: 41) put it, Britain had hospitals but no hospital system. There were, at best, two badly coordinated hospital patterns, each consisting of a large number of equally poorly coordinated parts (Eckstein 1958: 71). Rational planning was difficult, if not impossible, as there was much unfriendly competition, if not overt hostility, jealousy and rivalry between the 'systems' (Eckstein 1958; Walters 1980; Whitehead 1988). The problem was that hospitals had grown up without a national or even an area plan (MoH 1944: 7). Eckstein (1958: 62–3) concludes: 'irrational organization, particularly in the hospital system, was, in many ways, the most serious fault of the pre-Health Service medical system'. Sir Ernest Morris of the London Hospital in 1934 asked the questions: 'but are we to compete? And is not that idea of competition the very mistake we are all making?' (quoted in Rivett 1986: 184). In 1943, Niven McNicholl, a civil servant in the Ministry of Health, wrote that 'commercial competition among doctors is at the root of most of the evils of private medical practice today' (quoted in Honigsbaum 1989: 49). This lack of coordination had a number of consequences.

First, it led to wasteful duplication and the over-development of facilities on one hand and the existence of many small hospitals on the other (NPHT 1946; Whitehead 1988). Hospitals competed to acquire the latest items of equipment, whether they needed them or not. There were examples of cottage hospitals having the latest X-ray equipment which remained unused for most of the time. When it was used, the matron acted as radiographer. Local authorities tended to erect their own small hospitals rather than combining to build a larger unit: for example, two 50-bed hospitals may have existed a few miles apart across a local authority boundary when joint action might have led to the more satisfactory solution of one shared 100-bed hospital. Britain was littered with small hospitals. For example, in 1938 the average size of hospitals was 84 beds, but this fell to 68 beds for voluntary general hospitals and 15 beds for voluntary maternity hospitals (Pinker 1966: ch. 9). Each hospital strove for an impossible self-sufficiency. Each adopted the course of action most likely to enhance the individual hospital rather than that most likely to produce the best facilities for the patient (NPHT 1946). Pinker (1966: 59) concluded that the consequences were 'somewhat depressing by economic and possibly also medical criteria. It is very likely that the prevalence of small institutions for the physically ill was a burden on running costs which limited the equipment and amenities available to patients and staff.'

Second, there was a division of labour between the systems. The voluntary hospitals received a preponderance of spectacular cases, and the public hospitals a clear majority of routine ones. Indeed, the municipal hospitals, owing to their obligation to treat patients, 'were often nothing more than dumping grounds for the expensive chaff of the voluntary system' (Eckstein 1958: 67). In view of this, the public came to associate spectacular cures and sensational surgery with the one system and long-stay, incurable and terminal cases with the other (Eckstein 1958: 66–7), in spite of the fact that some voluntary hospitals were very bad and some municipal hospitals were very good. In other words, the factors influencing where a patient was treated sometimes depended more on the hospital's history and legal status rather than what was best for the patient.

There was also the problem of the division of labour within systems. As hospitals attempted to be self-contained, there existed a:

bad distribution of cases to beds. . . . Often a complicated case is occupying a bed in a hospital with neither the staff nor the equipment to treat it, whilst a simple case is occupying a bed in a hospital with a high standard in staff and equipment, thus utilising facilities which might be used for other and more diffi-cult cases.

(NPHT 1946: 8)

Some hospitals had long waiting lists, while others had empty beds. Sometimes this was a result of the prestige of the hospital, but sometimes it was the outcome of contributory schemes. Patients might be restricted to the hospital covered by their scheme, even if other hospitals had shorter waits or better facilities for treating that particular disease. A further consequence was that contributors with less need might be treated ahead of non-contributors with more need (NPHT 1946: 14). In short:

The anomalies of large waiting lists in one hospital and suitable beds empty at another, and of two hospitals in the same area running duplicated specialist centres which could be better con-centrated in one more highly equipped and staffed centre for the area, are the result of a situation in which hospital services are many people's business but nobody's full responsibility.

(MoH 1944: 56)

This judgement applied not only to hospitals, but to health services as a whole. As Robson (1931: 296–7) explains:

The members of a single working-class family may be tended within a short space of time by half a dozen separate health agencies. If the father is in work and falls ill he will be treated by the panel doctor and draws benefit under the National Health Insurance scheme. If he is accidently injured while at work he will be examined by the local certifying surgeon appointed by the Home Office in connection with the Factory Acts and Workmen's Compensation Acts. If he becomes unemployed and receives relief from the Public Assistance Committee he may be treated medically by the Poor Law medical officer. If he contracts an infectious disease he will be cared for in an isolation hospital maintained by the local auth-ority. If he suffers from war wounds or disease attributed to service with the military forces, he will be treated by the Local Pensions Committee. If his wife is confined she will be visited by the District Nurse and advised by the medical officer

connected with the maternity and child welfare clinic run by
the district or borough council. If certain diseases supervene
before the child is born the county council will become
responsible through their medical officer for her medical treatment. If there is another child in the family, a boy aged ten, let
us say, the health of that child will be cared for by the School
Medical Officer of the local education authority. When the lad
leaves school and wants a job in a factory, it is the certifying
surgeon – who has never seen him and knows nothing of his
medical history – who is alone empowered by statute to decide
whether he is sufficiently fit to take such employment. If he
develops tubercular trouble it is the County Medical Officer
who is responsible for his treatment and care.

An equally long passage describes how responsibility for the health
of an individual is shifted from one local body to another at different stages of the individual's life.

Inequality

It is generally claimed that inequality was one of the most serious
problems of health care before the NHS. Much of the discussion
has concerned geographical inequality (Powell 1992a). At first
sight, there appears to be plenty of evidence of this (Eckstein 1958;
Stevens 1966; Walters 1980; Hollingsworth 1988), and it appears to
speak with one voice. However, on closer examination, it is found
that this is the case because it *is* only one voice, or rather two. In
other words, most subsequent accounts are based on two sources
that are recycled, sometimes referenced to the primary sources,
sometimes to secondary sources and sometimes unreferenced, until
the apparent unaminity becomes convincing. These two planks of
evidence are PEP (1944) on GPs and Titmuss (1950) on specialists.
However, far from providing a firm foundation, these planks show
signs of analytical woodworm. Their great oaks of criticism have
risen from tiny acorns of selective quotation of unreferenced and
possibly problematic data (Powell 1992a, 1995c).

The evidence that exists is rarely subjected to critical analysis.
Many accounts of the maldistribution of doctors rely on scraps of
evidence. There tends to be much reliance on assertion and anec-
dote. As a result, many hypotheses masquerade as explanation.
Indeed, it has been argued that, 'apart ... from a few scrappy
comments, heavily loaded with political overtones, of the apparent

surplus of doctors in such places as Kensington or Bournemouth, the critics have not gone to much trouble to examine the facts' (Jewkes and Jewkes 1962: 13). Thus, despite apparently voluminous evidence on the distribution of health-care provision before the NHS, the basis for many of the claims can be traced to the two problematic sources referenced above. It is claimed that hospital beds and doctors were unequally distributed, but the distribution of doctors is considered to be a more serious problem, since:

> Considerations of structure, condition and equipment were overshadowed by the crucial problem; the number and quality of the medical and nursing staff. For a good doctor can in an emergency overcome material deficiencies, while a bad doctor will still be a bad doctor however excellent the hospital and its equipment.
>
> (Titmuss 1950: 70)

The main claims are of inequality on north–south and urban–rural axes. They will now be examined on the basis of primary data.

Degree of inequality

It is claimed that the uneven distribution of doctors across the country was of the order of sevenfold (PEP 1944), but the degree of inequality depends on the class of the local authority and the scale utilized. Among major local authorities the range was approximately fourfold for county councils and sixfold for county boroughs. However, for the London Metropolitan Boroughs the maximum and minimum areas are Saint Marylebone (which includes Harley Street), with 8.54 doctors per 1000 population, and Shoreditch, with 0.35: a variation of approximately 24-fold. For all areas above a threshold of 5000 population, the variation rises to about 65-fold (Powell 1995c). The variation is approximately sevenfold for all hospital beds and 14-fold for acute hospital beds. In other words, the conventional wisdom tends, if anything, to underestimate the degree of geographical inequality.

Urban–rural differentials

It has been claimed that in many respects rural areas were poorly served compared with urban areas (Pater 1981: 20; Webster 1988a: 13). In terms of hospital beds, this is perfectly true, but unexceptionable. As today, hospitals tended to be located in urban rather than rural areas. The urban county boroughs had 8.00 beds per 1000 population, compared with 4.73 for the rural county councils. For acute beds, the corresponding figures were 4.56 and 1.88 (Powell 1992b). However, as today, many rural dwellers travelled to the town both for inpatient and outpatient treatment. This was particularly so for towns surrounded by large rural hinterlands, such as Norwich, Chester and Lincoln, where the town's residents accounted for less than half the patients in the town's hospital. More Lancashire residents were treated in the voluntary hospitals of the Lancashire county boroughs than in the county council area itself. Movement across boundaries for municipal hospitals was much more limited, but still not uncommon (calculated from NHPT/MoH 1945–6: appendices; see also Eckstein 1958: 40, 58, 70).

Moreover, not all county boroughs had high levels of provision, nor was it necessarily low for county councils. In three of the nine English survey regions, county boroughs as opposed to county councils had the fewest beds per capita (Powell 1992b).

The gradation along the urban–rural axis was less clear for doctors. The county boroughs and county councils exhibit remarkable similarity in their aggregate provision. However, this similarity disguises regional differences. In the London region (with nearly a third of the population of England and Wales) the county council areas had more doctors per capita than the county boroughs. In the north-west, the West Midlands and the eastern regions, the two types of area had a similar level of provision. However, in the remaining regions the county boroughs reasserted their traditional advantage over the county councils, with the greatest differences being found in South Wales and the Berkshire, Buckinghamshire and Oxfordshire region. At the national and regional levels, then, the rural areas did not necessarily have fewer doctors per capita than the urban areas (Powell 1995c).

However, it was clear that large urban areas tended to have more specialists. It was reported by the teams of wartime hospital surveyors, and noted by the *Domesday Book* summary of the surveys (NPHT 1946: 9), that specialists were confined to the larger and/or richer urban areas. Indeed, an official report of 1948 claimed that about 37 per cent of specialists practised in London (Powell 1995c). The question now becomes one of proximity to such areas rather than one of the number of specialists located in administrative areas. As the north-west surveyors noted, if a place was near Manchester or Liverpool it could get all the service that it needed from these towns without difficulty (Carling and McIntosh 1945: 14).

The north–south divide

It is sometimes claimed that the south of the country was better
served than the north (Pater 1981:19). While the NPHT/MoH
surveys show that the south did tend to have more beds than the
north, the north-west region was relatively well provided for, with
6.7 beds per 1000 population, 3.7 acute beds per 1000 and 71
medical staff per 1,000,000, making it second only to the London
region for these categories. Conversely, the Berkshire, Buckinghamshire and Oxfordshire region had the lowest provision of total
beds (5.4 per 1000) and the Eastern region was worst off in terms
of acute beds (2.2 per 1000) and medical staff (42 per 1,000,000).
Moreover, each region had a wide variation of provision, and at the
local authority level some northern areas compared favourably
with many southern areas. For example, some northern local
authorities such as Liverpool and Halifax had more beds per capita
than the authorities with most provision in both the eastern and the
Berkshire, Buckinghamshire and Oxfordshire region (Powell
1992b).

The regional maldistribution of doctors outside London is not as
large as might be expected. There is some suggestion of a
'north/south divide' (with the eastern region being part of the
'north'), but the difference is not particularly large. However, it is
the Midlands rather than the north which is most obviously 'under-
doctored', with six towns in the bottom ten nationally. The concept
of a simple north/south divide is further undermined by variations
within regions and within counties being large in comparison with
variations between regions. For example, the county of Lancashire,
with the towns of Ince-in-Makerfield (bottom place nationally) and
Lytham (twelfth place nationally), has almost the full national range
of doctors per capita in a ranking of over 600 towns (Powell 1995c).

Thus, it has been shown that while existing accounts give a
broadly accurate picture of the geographical distribution of doctors
before the NHS, they omit a number of qualifications and caveats,
and lack detail. Generally, the south and urban areas did have more
provision than the north and rural areas, respectively, but, on closer
examination, it may be seen that some northern areas compare well
with their southern counterparts and some rural areas are well
provided for compared with urban areas. In other words, there was
no clear north/south or urban/rural divide. Moreover, the degree of
inequality may have been reducing over time. One crude comparison shows that the London bed–population ratio was about three

times that of the provinces in 1861, but only 17 per cent more by 1938 (calculated from Pinker 1966: 84).

Geographical inequity

Some writers have claimed that not only was the pre-NHS distribution of medical facilities unequal, but that it was also inequitable. In other words, it is asserted that high-need areas tended to have low service provision: this situation may be termed 'territorial injustice' or the 'inverse care law' (Tudor-Hart 1971), as opposed to the situation where high-need areas have high levels of provision, which has been termed 'territorial justice' (Davies 1968). Assertions of inequity are commonplace. After mentioning the sevenfold variation in GPs per capita (above), the PEP study claimed, without evidence, that, 'the disparity in distribution is even more serious than it appears from these figures, because under-doctored districts are usually also poor districts with high rates of sickness and mortality and in special need of a good medical service' (PEP 1944: 7). Aneurin Bevan (1946a: col. 44), with no apparent supporting evidence, claimed that the best hospital facilities were available where they were least needed. Similar assertions include the famous and often quoted phrase of Abel-Smith (1964: 405): 'the pattern of [voluntary] provision depended on the donations of the living and the legacies of the dead, rather than on any ascertained need for hospital services'. This implies that a system based on philanthropy led to greater resources in the richer areas. Finally, Webster (1988a: 14) has asserted, 'health standards precisely mirrored diversities within the health services'. In other words, the correlation between health status and health care was perfectly positive. These assertions of a negative correlation between need and provision all conform to what Tudor-Hart (1971) termed the 'inverse care law': 'the availability of good medical care varies inversely with the need of the population served' (see Powell 1990).

The only study that attempts to examine the degree of 'territorial justice' for hospital care before the NHS is that of Powell (1992d). This analyses the situation in 1938, the last full year of the pre-NHS system before it gave way to the Emergency Medical Service of wartime. For the county boroughs, it is found that while voluntary beds and staff tended to be negatively correlated with need, municipal beds and staff tended to be positively correlated with need. When both sectors are aggregated to make the total number of beds, the opposing directions of the correlations cancel each other out and the correlations between need and all beds are statistically insignificant. Thus, for hospital beds, the countervailing force of municipal provision eliminates the degree of inequity associated with voluntary provision. However, when staff are aggregated, the strength of the correlations for voluntary staff outweigh those for municipal staff, leaving a situation of more staff in the less needy areas. This preliminary analysis, then, finds that while voluntary provision tended to favour the less needy areas ('the inverse care law') municipal provision tended to favour the needy areas ('territorial justice') and, indeed, managed to compensate for the inequitable nature of voluntary provision of beds, but not of staff.

Doctors as a whole were significantly more inequitably distributed than beds or full-time medical staff: doctors were more strongly associated with areas of high rateable value and low infant mortality rates. The geographical distribution of doctors was clearly related to the geography of affluence. For the county boroughs the resorts and spas – the so-called 'watering holes' – or the 'bath chair towns' had the most doctors while the poorer areas had the least. For the county councils, the affluent Home Counties such as Surrey, and coastal areas such as Devon, had the most doctors (Powell 1995c).

Crisis

It has been claimed that the voluntary system was on the edge of bankruptcy and that the municipal system was virtually static. The voluntary hospitals were certainly short of money (Walters 1980: 47–54), but this applies to most hospitals at most times. By the end of the interwar period some hospitals had an accounting deficit. However, voluntary hospitals as a whole had a surplus. Revenue had increased between the wars, but there was a trend away from the classic philanthropic model towards one based on provident funding (Braithwaite 1938; Finlayson 1994). Moreover, financial problems were caused more by the expenditure side of the coin. Voluntarism saw increases in bed numbers during the interwar period and attempted to keep pace with changing medical advances by introducing new technologies and equipment (Prochaska 1992: 127–9). London's voluntary hospitals had an aggregate deficit in 1938 of £146,608, but this was on a turnover of nearly £5,000,000 and it was only the third aggregate deficit since 1921. The overall deficit of 1938 was no greater than it had been 40 years earlier, despite the vast increase in provision. Many institutions were in real financial difficulty, including several of the teaching hospitals, but hospital finances in the 1930s suggested not 'bankruptcy' but 'stability' (Prochaska 1992: 129). While it is important not to underestimate the financial difficulties, it is equally important not to draw premature conclusions of bankruptcy and crisis (Prochaska 1992).

Similarly, many are critical of the limited progress of the municipal system (see Powell 1997). However, it has recently been claimed that this view is too pessimistic. By the end of the interwar period, most suitable hospitals had been taken out of the 'Poor Law' (or public assistance) and turned into 'public health hospitals'. The 1930s saw, in times of economic difficulty, increasing revenue expenditure, capital expenditure on extensions and repairs that were some three times the capital budget of the early NHS, and a number of new hospitals, compared with none during the first decade of the NHS. Activity in terms of operations and outpatient attendances also grew strongly. In short, municipal provision was 'an expanding service' (Powell 1997).

CONCLUSION

It has been shown that the British health-care system before the NHS, while far from perfect or even having reached adequacy, was not as bad as the pessimists have claimed. As Prochaska (1992: 242) writes, it is often described, far too facilely, as defective and chaotic. His verdict on voluntarism is that:

> Historians have contributed their share to the misunderstanding of 1930s hospital provision. Typically they conjure up an ideal form of hospital administration and distribution against which the inter-war medical provision looks chaotic. Treating the rise of state provision as inexorable, they fail to give the voluntary sector its due.
>
> (Prochaska 1992: 130)

This assessment applies also to the municipal sector (Powell 1997). In other words, it is unfair to judge provision on post-hoc collectivist criteria. For example, the criticism of inequality is meaningful only to a 'system' of provision such as the NHS rather than a collection of individual providers such as existed in the 1930s. Each board of governors was responsible for its own voluntary hospitals. Each local authority was responsible for health care in its area. Moreover, there were few coordinating mechanisms. Indeed, according to some, diversity in local authority provision should be celebrated as an outcome of local democracy rather than criticized as a deviation from national uniformity (Robson 1953). In other words, the main contemporary criterion remained the adequacy of the individual voluntary hospital or local authority. On these terms, and bearing in mind the state of medical knowledge and the national economy at the time, institutions ranged from good to scandalous. Moreover, in a dynamic context, there were some signs of improvement (Powell 1997). Rapid medical advance means that hospitals quickly become anachronisms. In some ways more progress was made during the interwar years than in the early years of the NHS (see Chapter 5).

Nevertheless, contemporary and historical opinion is correct to suggest that health-care provision before the NHS suffered from severe problems. To what extent the NHS has solved them, or whether the NHS was the best way to address them, is less clear.

3

THE SETTLEMENT OF 1948

The NHS is said by some to have been constructed by political consensus and by others to have been built single handedly by the Minister of Health in the 1945 Labour government, Aneurin Bevan, as his monument to socialism. It is also claimed that the NHS was either the only or the best design available. An examination of the formation of the NHS shows that the eventual shape of the service was not the only possible design. Indeed, it emerged fairly late in the day, and ran contrary to many earlier trends and plans. For many years after its inception, despite criticism of secondary features and matters of detail, the fundamental structure of the NHS was seldom questioned. However, in recent years there have been increasing calls to examine alternatives. Some on the political right favour a basis of social insurance while some on the left favour services based on local government. Both options were considered, but were rejected in the settlement of 1948. Indeed, in some ways, the recent reforms of the NHS have more affinity with the proposals of the wartime coalition government than with the NHS as implemented by the Labour government of 1945 (Powell 1994b,c). Similarly, the Labour Party's current proposals draw more from the wartime Conservative Minister of Health, Henry Willink, than from their own Aneurin Bevan (Powell 1995d). Clearly, it is appropriate to reappraise the rejected plans of the 1940s. Likewise it is appropriate to reappraise the principles of the NHS. These have been generally assumed to be clear, but closer inspection shows them to be opaque and ambiguous.

This chapter examines the political architecture of the service and the details of the settlement of 1948. It aims to explain why some options were chosen and others rejected. An assessment of the 1946 Act is made and then the principles of the service, which form the basis of the evaluation in Chapter 6, are outlined.

THE FORMATION OF THE NHS

A comprehensive health service was discussed within the Ministry of Health in 1936, but it was not until 1938 that the issue appears to have been taken more seriously. A range of possibilities were considered. Some in the Ministry favoured extending NHI to cover hospital services, and this was also the favoured option of the British Medical Association (BMA), the doctors' 'trade union'. The nationalization of the hospitals – their eventual form within the NHS – was briefly considered and quickly rejected on the grounds that this would dry up the flow of voluntary subscriptions and so increase the burden on the ratepayer and taxpayer, would be opposed by the medical profession and would radically change existing Ministry of Health policy. It soon became clear that the Ministry's favoured option was a service administered by the major local authorities, in keeping with the established policy for all the services that were within the Ministry's remit.

The Second World War stimulated the development of a comprehensive hospital service, as the Ministry realized that it would be impossible to return to the prewar state of affairs. This was for two main reasons. First, the voluntary hospital sector was considered at best to be in severe financial difficulties and at worst to be in terminal decline. Second, as war became likely the Ministry of Health attempted to organize health-care resources to meet the needs of military and civilian casualties. This led to the formation of the wartime Emergency Medical Service. The Ministry took a good deal of indirect control over health care, and the scheme translated 'a collection of individual hospitals into something of a related hospital system' (MoH 1944: 57). Webster (1988a: 22–3) argues that the scheme, created as a temporary expedient, marked a secular shift towards a nationally planned and rationalized hospital service which on points both of structure and detail left a permanent mark on the postwar hospital system.

In 1941 the Minister of Health, the National Liberal Ernest Brown, made an announcement in the House of Commons that committed the government to a coordinated system of voluntary and municipal hospitals, based on larger areas than the current local government units, but he made it clear that the service would not be free. It appears that the Beveridge report (1942), the blueprint for the postwar welfare state, provided the pressure to introduce two vital changes: first, reform was extended to the health services as a whole rather than merely to hospital rationalization;

and second, the service would be free at the point of use. This second change took a longer time to evolve. As Honigsbaum (1979: 196) notes, the government's expressed commitment to a comprehensive health service stressed that the service would be available to all as opposed to being free to all. Thus, the commitment to a universal health service preceded the commitment to one that was free. In 1943 a plan emerged in the name of the Minister of Health, still Ernest Brown. The 'Brown plan' had some radical features, including a salaried GP service, but opposition from the medical profession in the subsequent negotiations forced the Minister to shelve it. The Ministry was in retreat when the Conservative, Henry Willink, replaced Brown as Minister of Health in late 1943. The subsequent White Paper, 'A National Health Service', published in February 1944, was largely an erosion of proposals that originated from Brown's tenure at the Ministry. Earwicker (1982: 270–2) charts the dilution of Brown's plan, as pragmatism triumphed over rationality. The White Paper, then, represents both a party political compromise between the partners in the coalition government, and a practical compromise in the sense of an attempt to respond to the objections of a powerful interest group.

Its main features can be briefly described. The health service was to be free and comprehensive. Hospital planning was to be in the hands of 'joint boards', which were to be committees representing the constituent local authorities in the larger administrative areas that a hospital service was considered to require. A joint board would secure services from municipal and voluntary hospitals in its own area, with contracts covering arrangements with the latter. Where necessary, it would be able to contract for additional services from hospitals of both types outside its area. Payment for services would come from a mixture of funds from both local and central government. GPs in 'health centres' run by the local authorities were to be salaried, and subject to greater local authority control than were those who continued in 'individual practice'. The latter were to be in contract with the Central Medical Board, which would have local committees, and the doctors would be free to undertake private practice. New GPs would not be allowed to set up in areas that were judged already to have an adequate number of doctors. The government would discuss with the doctors the future of the sale of practices. In addition to running health centres, local authorities would run clinics and their traditional range of domiciliary and environmental health services.

Following the publication of the White Paper, Willink continued to hold confidential negotiations with the medical profession over some 18 months, with little reporting to the coalition government's Reconstruction Committee. Many in the Labour movement feared the worst, and in 1945 the Party conference condemned the suspected retreat from the White Paper. The *New Statesman* claimed that this was a 'disastrous climb down by a weak Minister, yielding to pressure by the vested interests. For a second time in its history the BMA is doing its best to wreck a scheme which would result in a vast improvement in the people's health' (quoted in Earwicker 1982: 293). It is now clear that Willink had made a number of important concessions to the medical profession, which appeared to concede little in return. Thus, although Willink claimed his concessions were points of minor detail, the resulting 'Willink plan' was clearly a regression from the White Paper in a number of important details. The medical profession gained a large degree of representation both on central and local bodies; the Central Medical Board's powers to control the geographical distribution of GPs were reduced; health centres were to be introduced only experimentally; and there were to be no direct financial relationships between local authorities and voluntary hospitals – the distribution of money at local level was to be via a 'clearing house'. Perhaps the most important concession was the designation of the larger areas only as planning bodies. So, 'the cardinal principle of combining planning and execution in the same local hands' was lost (Pater 1981: 104). Godber (1988: 38) has claimed that one vested interest after another eroded the broader concepts, and the outcome was a plan which appeared to amount to little more than an extension of the NHI system with hospital services provided by existing owners under contract .

After the general election of 1945, the new Labour government announced that it did not deem itself bound by the outcomes of Willink's negotiations and proposed to go 'back to the White Paper'. However, the Minister of Health, Aneurin Bevan, produced a scheme which differed from the White Paper in important respects. The most important change was that the hospitals were to be nationalized and run by non-elected *ad hoc* bodies. In one bold stroke, then, Bevan overturned the long tradition of municipal administration, to which both the Ministry of Health and the Labour Party had subscribed, in favour of a policy which had generally been regarded as not practical politics only a few years earlier. This decision was fought against in the Labour cabinet, notably by

Herbert Morrison, a former leader of the London County Council, and usually seen as a friend of municipalism.

The NHS would be administered by a tripartite system. Hospitals would be run by some 400 hospital management committees (HMCs) grouped into 13 regional hospital boards (RHBs), with Wales acting as a region. However, the teaching hospitals were to retain much of their independence by remaining outside the main RHB–HMC structure and being administered by boards of governors. Family practitioner services would be run by executive councils, which differed from the insurance committees that ran NHI only in that the former were to be more numerically dominated by the professions. GPs would be paid a basic salary, but would continue to receive the bulk of their income from capitation (that is, according to the number of patients on their list). Local authorities were stripped of their hospital functions, and were left with a range of domiciliary, non-institutional and environmental health services. The tripartite system perpetuated the largely separate development of the health services before the NHS.

Bevan tended to reverse many of the concessions given by Willink to GPs. However, Bevan, like Brown and Willink, was forced by the medical profession to concede on some points: pay-beds in NHS hospitals, generous merit awards for consultants and a large degree of medical representation on NHS bodies. At the eleventh hour, in order to break the apparent deadlock with the doctors, Bevan announced that his basic salaries would be only temporary and for new entrants, and that salaries for GPs would be introduced only by means of a new Act of Parliament.

AN ASSESSMENT OF THE 1946 ACT

The 1946 Act sometimes appears to mean all things to all people. It has been claimed that it represents a political consensus or settlement between the parties. On the other hand, it has been asserted that it was the finest achievement of the 1945 Labour government and represents both a triumph of socialism and superiority to any other proposal for a health service at the time.

Consensus

The NHS has often been seen as the result of political consensus. Addison (1975: 14), in *The Road to 1945* states that:

all three parties went to the polls in 1945 committed to the principles of social and economic reconstruction which their leaders had endorsed as members of the Coalition. A massive new middle ground had arisen in politics. . . . When Labour swept to victory in 1945, the new consensus fell, like a bunch of ripe plums, into the lap of Mr. Attlee [the Labour Prime Minister].

Recent historical research has tended to question this notion: it has been claimed that much greater attention has to be focused on the road *from* 1945, on events that followed – rather than preceded – the ending of the wartime coalition (Jefferys 1987, 1991; Brooke 1992). Similarly, in the field of medical reform, the notion of consensus as portrayed by an agreement on ends, but disagreement on means, or 'conflict within consensus' (Fox 1986: 106–14; Klein 1995a: 6), has been criticized by Webster (1990): general agreement was virtually limited to points upon which universal assent would be impossible to withhold. It is unrealistic to portray the health debate as proceeding on two isolated planes, one related to ends, the other concerning means, as questions of ends and means became inextricably interwoven. It is clear that the White Paper meant different things to the different parties. The Parliamentary debate on the White Paper shows that for many Conservatives it represented the limit to which they were prepared to go, while for Labour Members of Parliament (MPs) it represented a minimum on which to build for the future: a compromise measure, representing, at best, a half-way house to a socialist health service. In general, reassurances from Willink and the Parliamentary Secretary, Florence Horsburgh, were almost exclusively aimed at the fears of their own party. Moreover, as shown below, Conservatives in general tended to prefer the revised Willink plan to the White Paper of 1944.

It is generally agreed that there would have been some type of health service under a Conservative government in 1945, but that it would have fallen short of the proposals in the 1944 White Paper (Jefferys 1987: 144; Campbell 1987: 165–6). A secret Conservative committee on the Beveridge report had favoured an expanded NHI scheme, with protection for voluntary hospitals and private practice (Addison 1975: 221; Jefferys 1991: 131). However, any Conservative health service that subscribed to the concepts of free access and universal provision would almost certainly have been an advance over prewar thinking (Webster 1988b: 34) and the coalition government's commitment of 1941. Conservative MPs always took care to stress their commitment to a free and comprehensive service, even in their amendments to Bevan's Bill on its second and third readings, although, as Foot (1975: 156) notes, Parliamentary practice is that an opposition tables an amendment on the third reading only when it is opposed to the principle of a Bill. However, Conservatives tended to distance themselves from the 1944 White Paper *per se*, arguing that it was more 'green' than 'white', in the sense of being a consultative document. In general, Conservatives expressed approval of Willink's revised scheme, with greater freedom for doctors, more private practice, and thriving voluntary hospitals set to be a permanent fixture. Indeed, these themes were stressed in their 1945 manifesto and in election addresses (Jeffereys 1987, 1991). Lord Woolton admitted that the health service would be very different under a Conservative government from what it would be under a socialist government (Jeffereys 1991: 196).

Labour's NHS?

As Brooke (1992: 133) notes, the protracted birth of the NHS has inevitably raised the question of parentage. Until recently, the Labour Party has rarely received much credit. Some have suggested that the NHS was an orphan child of prewar and wartime consensus, left on Labour's porch in 1945. Harry Eckstein (1958: 102, 108fn) claims that:

> of all the people and organizations articulating concern with medical reform before the war, the socialists were the last, and in some ways, the most half-hearted in the field. . . . The Labour Party was certainly not in the vanguard of the agitation. It joined the team, at best, in the middle of the game.

A number of authors have filed a paternity suit on behalf of Labour (Marwick 1967; Earwicker 1982; Morgan 1984; Brooke 1992; and particularly Webster 1988c, 1990). They have shown that both before and during the war Labour did have a radical health policy, for a free and universal service staffed by salaried doctors and based on the local authorities, which was largely developed by the Socialist Medical Association (SMA). In other words, a convincing case has been made that the NHS was not founded on consensus and there was a 'Labour effect'. However, it can be shown that the Labour government's NHS was very different from that indicated by earlier Party policy. Moreover, the extent to which socialism is reflected in the Act of 1946 is a matter of debate.

Much research highlights the differences between Party policy and the Act. During the war, the Labour Party (1943) issued a policy document entitled *National Service for Health*. This was heavily influenced by the SMA. In addition to the traditional concerns for a free and universal service, the NHS was to be based on reformed local government, with a full-time salaried service, health centres and no private practice.

One of the most long-standing policies was for a service based on local government. 'Above all else', stated Somerville Hastings (1941: 20), President of the SMA, 'the hospitals must be under local democratic control'. The Labour Secretary of State for Scotland in the coalition government, Tom Johnston, attacked *ad hoc* health authorities as a 'system of continental dictatorships', inconsistent with the principles of representative government (Webster 1988a: 49). However, Labour ministers in the coalition turned away from a local government service, as the necessary local government reform was postponed. They rejected the idea that the hospital service could be placed on the existing local authorities in 1943 (Brooke 1992). Nevertheless, the 1945 Labour Party conference stated that no scheme that did not give local authority control was acceptable. In other words, although a local government service was still official Party policy, its rejection was already decided, as far as hospitals were concerned.

However, the other elements remained as 'real' as opposed to 'nominal' Party policy. A memo from Woolton to Eden in 1944 (quoted in Brooke 1992: 207) stated that the Labour Party found it very difficult to swallow the idea of doctors in health centres who would not be salaried servants of the state. This idea was much more palatable two years later. Bevan (1946a, col. 55) said that he was not in favour of a full-time salaried service. All GPs would receive a basic salary, although they would continue to be paid on a largely capitation basis. He claimed that one of the main reasons for this change in Party policy was that the medical profession was not ripe for it.

For the SMA, health centres were inextricably linked with a salaried service. Their supporters desired, and opponents feared, that they would be the Trojan Horse to bring in a salaried service. In the Reconstruction Committee Labour fought for the increased prominence of health centres in the NHS and, again, were critical of indications that they were losing ground as policy developed.

However, the definition of a health centre was always unclear. For some, it meant little more than 'group practice' or a communal consulting room. For some Communists associated with the SMA, it meant a revolutionary change in health care (Honigsbaum 1979: ch. 25): health centres would bring socialism to the surgery in the forms of breaking down professional barriers and emphasizing prevention, or 'positive health'. Bevan (1946b: col. 509) stressed the importance of prevention: 'If we can get a stream of healthy people attending the health centre, it becomes a health centre; but if we merely have morbid cases going to a health centre it becomes a morbid centre'. Labour MP Dr Taylor (1946: col. 509) argued that the health centre proposal was really the key to the GP service as constituted in the Bill: 'The thing will stand or fall by the success of the health centres'. In this sense, the health centre symbolized the difference between the socialist and non-socialist conception of the NHS (Webster 1990: 139) and was the criterion on which the NHS would be judged. Although health centres gained a good deal of prominence in Labour's 1946 scheme, it has been claimed that Bevan led Labour supporters of health centres to believe that he would develop them at a faster rate than he intended or that building shortages would permit (Honigsbaum 1989: 95). Labour's commitment to, and proclaimed importance of, health centres was clear. The failure to develop them represented the most obvious case of non-compliance with a central provision of NHS legislation (Webster 1988b: 382). Eckstein (1958: 252) has termed this 'perhaps the greatest failure of the Service.'

Labour's policy in the 1930s and its practice in the Reconstruction Committee tolerated no combination of public service and private practice. This fitted in with the idea of a salaried service and the experience of the 'panel' of the NHI scheme, where some doctors were said to neglect their panel work to concentrate on their private patients. Bevan (1946a: cols. 56–7) allowed private practice and pay-beds within the NHS, while acknowledging that both would be repugnant to some of his colleagues. His justification was that if he did not allow them, the best doctors would not serve in the NHS and there would be a growth of private nursing homes. In other words, it was a necessary evil to achieve true universalism. It appears that Bevan was convinced on this matter by Lord Moran, President of the Royal College of Physicians, but both at the time and subsequently it has been argued that Bevan's fears would not have materialized, as so few doctors would have been able to rely totally on private patients. In other words, if faced with the decision of choosing between the devil of the health service and the deep blue sea of private practice, few would have taken the plunge. The *Lancet* regarded the decision to allow private practice as remarkable: 'We should perhaps be thankful that Mr Bevan, in storming the Bastille of the hospitals, shows no inclination to proclaim the complete revolution in medical organisation which logic or his personal convictions might dictate' (quoted in Player and Barbour-Might 1988: 18). According to *The Guardian*, private fees were 'the reef on which this splendid venture may flounder' (quoted in Pater 1981: 123).

Many Labour supporters were critical of Bevan's concessions (Earwicker 1982: 370–7; Webster 1988a, 1988c; Brooke 1992: 337). But the extent of the concessions suggests that these criticisms tended not to be particularly spirited. Honigsbaum (1979: 292) writes that Bevan's concessions eroded the SMA's expectations so far that it had little to cheer about other than the principle of universal coverage. Earwicker (1982: 314) claims that:

> At a stroke, Bevan intended to deprive the municipalities of the central place they had occupied in successive Labour plans since 1919. Appointed as opposed to elected bodies contravened the letter and spirit of every Labour party policy document on health.

Similarly, Brooke (1992: 337–8) writes :

> The NHS showed most departure from the plans of the war years. During the war, the distinctiveness of Labour policy had been clearest in this field of social policy, with its emphasis on a salaried service working through health centres [run by local authorities]. Bevan stood Labour policy on its head, nationalizing the hospitals yet allowing the doctors to avoid a salaried service.

If SMA and Labour Party health policy is regarded as 'socialist' (in other words, what the Labour Party says as opposed to Herbert Morrison's famous definition of 'what a Labour Government does'), earlier coalition plans were to a large extent 'socialist'. Campbell (1987: 166) considers the Ministry's thinking leading to the 'Brown plan' to be surprisingly radical. Earwicker (1982: 270) claims that it was 'a programme of which any Labour Minister would have been proud'. Webster (1988c: 194) writes that Labour ministers on the coalition government Reconstruction Committee were no doubt gratified to find that the proposals presented by Brown coincided closely with their own thought.

Labour criticized Willink's retreat from the Brown plan on issues from which the Labour government was later to retreat. Many criticisms of Brown's and Willink's concessions can be aimed with equal, if not greater, force at Bevan: for example, the Labour reaction to the infinite regress of 1943–4 with respect to salaries and private practice (Brooke 1992: 203–9). We may detect an inverse radicalism law, in the sense that the further away people were from the negotiations, the more radical they were: Labour's Thomas Johnston, Secretary of State for Scotland, warned against antagonizing the doctors and favoured a gradual approach. On the other hand, Clement Attlee, Stephen Taylor and Evan Durbin, rarely regarded as radicals, argued against any compromise. In short, if 'a salaried health service based in health centres had long been an objective central to socialist health policy' (Brooke 1992: 208), then Bevan's scheme was scarcely more socialist on this point than that of Willink and less socialist than that of Brown. Indeed, in some cases, Bevan's concessions went beyond those of Willink (Honigsbaum 1979: 289; Campbell 1987: 168).

It is clear that the Labour government and Bevan made a difference to the shape of the health service. However, the change in direction was not closely related to Labour Party policy. It was probably more socialist than the White Paper of 1944 and almost certainly more socialist than the Willink plan and the likely shape of a Conservative health service. However, in some ways, the most socialist plan was introduced in 1943 by a National Liberal. It is far from clear that the NHS represented a triumph for socialism (Powell 1994a). Webster (1988b: 34) writes that:

> in many important respects, the structure of the NHS repre-
> sented a final capitulation by the Government in the war of
> attrition waged by the effective and influential medical and
> voluntary groups since the original plan for a simple and
> unified system of health service administration was unveiled in
> 1943.

Elsewhere he claims that vested interests caused the policies for socialized medicine evolved by the Labour Party over three decades to be abandoned to such an extent that 'the NHS was reduced to an empty shell' (Webster 1988c: 199). As Brooke (1992: 337) puts it, the NHS 'was neither the child of the SMA nor of the Churchill Coalition'.

Why, then, did Labour's NHS fall so short of a socialist health service: less socialist than Party policy of the 1930s and 1940s, and in some ways less socialist than the plan introduced in the name of a National Liberal in a coalition government? Why did the Labour Parliamentary dog, including 12 members of the SMA, fail to bark? Why were many similar concessions labelled by Labour as a climb-down by Brown and Willink but as statesmanlike negotiation by Bevan? As Honigsbaum (1979: 297) writes, nothing was more strik-ing than the way SMA leaders succumbed to the compromises Bevan made. Why did SMA leaders who had been so dogmatic become so pliable when a socialist sat in the minister's chair?

There are a number of reasons why the NHS did not closely reflect the SMA's thinking that became Party policy (compare Lowe 1993: 166–75). Bevan was remote from the SMA, and his relations with the group were not particularly close. Criticisms may have been muted in public for reasons of Party loyalty. As Earwicker (1982: 302) points out, it was no simple process to trans-late Labour's ideas into legislation. There was no ready-made blue-print, in spite of Party policy, as Party policy was generally marked by ambiguity and indecision. The Party's recent policy document (Labour Party 1943) had stressed reformed local government, and as the health service could not wait for local government reform, the local government solution was not feasible. In any case, Labour was moving away from municipalism, local democracy and diversity towards centralization and uniformity (Robson 1953). According to Honigsbaum (1989), the faith in Bevan and his per-sonality – in the words of Labour MP Fred Messer, 'the way in which he applied anaesthetic to the supporters on his own side, making them believe in things they had opposed almost all their lives' (Messer himself was anaesthetized) – was only a partial explanation. The most important explanation may be the intensity of Labour MPs' faith in the '100 per cent principle'. On this reading, Labour was prepared to settle for the most important item on its socialist shopping list and to let the others go. On the other hand, they may have mistakenly believed that a universal service would lead inevitably to their other demands. As Campbell (1987: 169) puts it, Bevan's socialism was in terms of a universal or '100 per cent' service:

> His decision was not a betrayal of socialism but a choice between conflicting goals of socialism. A doctrinaire attempt to impose the SMA's service . . . might have been the 'correct' solution on paper, but it would have meant a two-tier system in practice. Bevan secured an alternative socialist objective

much more in tune with the instincts of the Labour Party and the mood of the times, a universal NHS.

Klein (1989: 17–19) paints a similar picture: '1946 reflects as much a defeat for some of Bevan's colleagues as an assertion of socialist at the expense of Conservative ideology'. He portrays the cabinet battle between Bevan and Morrison as partly reflecting different values: responsiveness versus efficiency, differentiation versus uniformity and self-government versus national equity.

Superiority

While Labour's NHS may not have represented full-blooded socialism, was it superior to the alternative plans of the time? It is generally claimed that the Labour health plan 'went much further than both the 1944 White Paper and the revised plan favoured by Willink' (Earwicker 1982: 320; Godber 1988: 38; Digby 1989: 60; Berridge 1990: 239; Jefferys 1991: 212). Marwick (1967: 402) writes that the 1946 Act was in advance of the political 'consensus' and previous vague Labour utterances on the subject. Earwicker (1982: 294) points out that it was the revised White Paper that indicated the gulf between the coalition partners in health reform. Morgan (1984: 154) writes that Willink's ideas, especially in their final, watered-down version, fell short of Bevan's proposals in vital respects, notably on hospitals and health centres. However, the criteria of evaluation are rarely specified. It appears to be assumed that a superior service is one that is more free and universal, more democratic and more unified. It is probable that Bevan's proposals were more advanced in the areas of free and universal provision, but it is arguable that some elements in earlier plans were more advanced with respect to democracy, while the situation as regards integration is less clear.

Free and universal service

There is little doubt that the NHS had a stronger commitment to being free at the point of use and universal than any likely Conservative plan. Conservative regard for private practice would, at best, have led to a merely nominal universal service in which all would be eligible, but in practice there would have been a two-tier service, with money buying a better service, as in education or housing. The Conservatives adopted the idea of a free service late in the day and their commitment to it remained unclear.

Democracy

If democracy can be simply equated with the franchise, then the NHS was less democratic than envisaged in plans based on local government. However, in the absence of local government reform, a localist health service would not have been based on the existing local authorities but on joint boards, indirect authorities at arm's length from the voters. Nevertheless, it can be argued that indirect local control may be more democratic than remote control from Westminster.

The Conservatives saw their chance to become the defenders of localism: to support the man in the town hall as opposed to Labour's gentleman in Whitehall. Localism is concerned with decisions being made by local people through the local ballot box. It tolerates local diversity rather than imposes national uniformity. At the price of mixing metaphors, while the Labour dog failed to bark, the Conservatives pinched his clothes while he was bathing. Conservative speakers argued that health care, like the education service, could be entrusted to local government and claimed that the loss of health services would sign the death warrant for local government. Localist writers such as D. N. Chester (1951: 328–42), J. M. Mackintosh (1953: 165–70, 180–91) and W. A. Robson (1953) criticized the Labour Party and Bevan for their treatment of local government.

However, in the Parliamentary standing committee examining the NHS Bill, the Conservative objections appeared to be not so much on the grounds of appointment as opposed to election, but on central as opposed to local control. They attacked the concentration of power in Whitehall as opposed to the periphery: the centre of gravity should move to the periphery, the autonomy and independence of the RHBs and HMCs from the Minister should be increased and policy should be 'bottom up' as opposed to 'top down' (*Hansard* 1946). The parameters of the debate, then, appeared to change. The democratic deficit was seen not so much in the principle of election versus selection, but in the locus of control, in the centre as opposed to the periphery. The question of power was more 'where' than 'who'.

These issues have a clear relationship to inequality. As more autonomy is given to peripheral bodies, whether elected or not, it is likely that there will be greater variation between these bodies. While the centralism of the NHS aims to achieve national uniformity, the classical localist model celebrates diversity as an expression of local democracy (Robson 1953). Thus, while it is likely that a Conservative NHS would have been more unequal between different areas, this may have resulted from the principle of localism displacing that of equality.

Integration

A further argument in favour of a local government service was in terms of integration. After the demise of the Brown plan, neither the 1944 White Paper nor the NHS Act planned to secure a fully unified service. Conservative MP Sir Harold Webbe (1946: col. 367). considered that the system of local government that followed the Local Government Act of 1929 allowed public health to be planned as a whole, enabling a complete interlocking of the preventive and curative medical services. On this view, the NHS would reopen the gap between preventive and curative public health, and take the health services back to a position which would be worse than before the 1930s. The NHS would be administered in a tripartite system, leaving responsibility for preventive and curative treatment in different hands. This would result in a lack of unification both within the NHS and between it and the services of local authorities. Not only would responsibility be divided with respect to, say, tuberculosis and maternity within the NHS, but also between the NHS and local authority services such as housing (Leff 1950: 240–1; Mackintosh 1953: 154; Guillebaud 1956: see especially the note of reservation by former Permanent Secretary at the Ministry of Health, Sir John Maude). So, hospitals might discharge patients too quickly, because responsibility for them would pass to another budget. Patients could be discharged to unsuitable housing, with negative consequences for their recovery. Thus:

> All the fundamental criticisms of the NHS can be traced back to the decision not to base services on local authorities. The various medical services were fragmented instead of unified; the gulf between the GPs and the hospitals widened instead of closed; there was no provision for preventive medicine; there was inadequate financial discipline and no democratic control at local level. In retrospect the case for the local authorities can be made to look formidable, the decision to dispossess them a fateful mistake by a Minister ideologically disposed to centralisation and seduced by the claims of professional expertise.
> (Campbell 1987: 177)

Conclusion

The 1944 White Paper and similar locally based schemes were not inferior to Bevan's NHS on all criteria, notably that of local democracy and more arguably that of unification. The tripartite system largely perpetuated separate administrations. It is possible that the NHS achieved greater integration within the hospital sector at the cost of less integration *between* the hospitals and local health services, local authorities' social services and the family practitioner services.

However, in spite of any 'paper' advantages, the claim that the local government solution was not a practical possibility in 1945 is supported both by contemporary observers (Pater 1981: 169, 184; Godber 1988: 38) and subsequent writers (Stevens 1966: 73; Campbell 1987: 177; Berridge 1990: 241). In other words, the NHS may have been the best of the feasible options in 1945, illustrating that it, as well as politics, represents the 'art of the possible'.

THE PRINCIPLES OF THE NHS

> For many years countless advocates of the British health service have taken it for granted that the 'NHS principles' are clear, sound and completely understood. So great and so sustained has this complacency been that the principles have become an unquestioned, unexamined article of faith. They have become part of a deep-seated myth which holds that the NHS is theoretically perfect and based on fundamental moral axioms. But the evidence – once properly examined – does not support the myth: not only are 'the principles' philosophically complex, and open to several different interpretations, but the NHS has never been deliberately organised in accord with them.
>
> (Seedhouse 1994: vii)

According to Klein (1989: 203) there was a political consensus in the 1980s that all parties supported the principles of the NHS, but 'it is a consensus which may be more apparent than real since it contains disagreement about what the ' principles' of the NHS actually entail. It is as though rival religious sects were to lay claim to the body of the same saint in the name of their competing faiths.'

Outlining the principles of the NHS is more difficult than might be first thought. The Royal Commission on the NHS (1979: 9) traced the principles and objectives of the service, very broadly, to the 1946 NHS Act. However, it noted 'the absence of detailed and publicly declared principles and objectives for the NHS'. It is generally held that the founding principles of the service were equality of access, comprehensiveness, equity and services that were free at the point of use (IHSM 1988: 17; Social Services Committee 1988: 9). However, these objectives are seen as vague, implicit and determined largely by a series of *post hoc* rationalizations (Cooper and Culyer 1971; Maynard and Ludbrook 1982; Mays and Bevan 1987). The NHS's main strategy was the removal of the price barrier (Cooper and Culyer 1971: 3; Mays and Bevan 1987: 6).

> When the Labour Party founded the new service on the basis of equal access for equal need, it might be more correct to interpret this as the principle that determined the form of the NHS (tax financed, universal coverage and no charges to patients) rather than as an objective that it was thought necessary to pursue actively.
>
> (Maynard and Ludbrook 1982: 109)

There is some imprecision and ambiguity about the principles of the NHS, then, but together they seem to add up to the proposition that medical need should be the sole determinant of treatment, and that no other factor ought to distort the prioritization associated with need. As Iliffe (1988: 47) puts it, the NHS gives a gift of resources based on need. Aneurin Bevan saw this as the 'collective principle': 'resources of medical skill and the apparatus of healing shall be placed at the disposal of the patient, without charge, when he or she needs them; that medical treatment and care should be a communal responsibility, that they should be made available to rich and poor alike in accordance with medical need and by no other criteria' (Bevan 1978: 99–100). Elsewhere, Bevan termed this the 'therapeutical' principle and added the 'redistributive' principle: the service ought to be funded by progressive taxation rather than by direct charges to patients or payments from insurance funds. According to Bevan, this principle – the redistribution of the national income by means of financing the NHS through income tax – became overlooked (Webster 1991a: 202–17). Bevan gave two main reasons for his choice of finance. The first dovetails with the universal principle. Insurance is for a group within the community. If all the community is covered, it is not insurance: it is a tax. Moreover, 'you cannot give different types of treatment in respect of a different order of contributions. We cannot perform a second-class

operation on a patient if he is not quite paid up.' The second reason
stemmed from recent experience of the NHI scheme, where it was
generally claimed that the more affluent members got a better deal
in terms of additional benefits. A regressive method of funding was
rejected in favour of a progressive method: 'what more pleasure can
a millionaire have than to know that his taxes will help the sick? . . .
The redistributive aspect of the scheme was one which attracted
me almost as much as the therapeutical' (quoted in Webster 1991a:
208–9). However, it is unlikely in practice that many people see
the NHS as an engine of vertical equity. It may more properly be
seen as contributing to horizontal equity: redistributing from the
healthy to the sick and from people of working age to the young
and the old.

   'The principles' of the NHS are often discussed in the form of a
shoping list. However, it can be argued that the NHS is based on
two main principles: equity in distribution and equity in finance.
This boils down to the Communist notion of 'from each according
to their ability; to each acording to their need'. In other words, the
service should be financed largely by national progessive taxation,
and delivered to all on the basis of need. By this interpretation, an
equitable distribution of health care is the objective, and criteria
such as a free and comprehensive service are not ends in themselves, but means to achieve an end. They can be viewed as necessary, but not sufficient, conditions to achieve equity. Nevertheless,
before concluding, this chapter examines the means of a free and
comprehensive service and the end of an equitable service.

Free at the point of use

The free health service abolished any direct financial barrier
between the patient and the service. According to some, this is the
most important feature of the service (Thunhurst 1982: 30). Bevan
(1978: 100–1) stressed the freedom from fear of cost. 'It was *fear*
that Labour, and Bevan, set out to vanquish – the fear of having to
choose between being pauperised by doctors' bills and doing without medical attention' (Player and Barbour-Might 1988: 4). Treatment would be sought quickly as people would no longer wait to
see if their condition was serious enough to merit the associated
expenditure. There was also the benefit of removing medicine from
the marketplace. In 1911 George Bernard Shaw noted that: 'any
sane nation, having observed that you could provide for the supply
of bread by giving bakers a pecuniary interest in baking for you,

should go on to give a surgeon a pecuniary interest in cutting off your leg, is enough to make one despair of political humanity' (Shaw 1946: 9).

Bevan (1978: 109) claimed that 'A free health service is a triumphant example of the superiority of collective action and public initiative applied to a segment of society where commercial principles are seen at their worst'. The NHS substituted cooperation and rational planning for competition and the market (Powell 1994b).

A comprehensive service

The NHS was to be comprehensive in two senses. First, it was to cover everybody, as a right of citizenship. What was important, given the recent past, was that there were to be no means testing, insurance or any other eligibility checks. 'The link between contribution and benefit, fundamental to twentieth century British social policy, was abandoned. Coverage was to be universal and to be dependent upon nothing other than being alive and on British soil' (Cooper and Culyer 1971: 3). Marwick (1967: 387) claims that a 'comprehensive, classless (or "universalist") service' had been a central characteristic of Labour thinking on the subject since 1911. As Somerville Hastings put it at the 1932 Labour Party conference, 'I want a service that a millionaire may take advantage of, and I want it to be so efficient that he will be glad to do so' (quoted in Marwick 1967: 395). The '100 per cent principle' was important and Bevan strenuously resisted the BMA's claims that the service should be for 85 per cent or 90 per cent of the population.

> The really objectionable feature is the creation of a two-standard health service, one below and one above the salt. It is merely the old British Poor Law system over again. . . . The essence of a satisfactory health service is that the rich and the poor are treated alike, that poverty is not a disability, and wealth is not advantaged.
>
> (Bevan 1978: 101)

It was important not only that everyone was entitled to use the service, but that the vast majority did use it. The service was not intended to be open to all but used only by the poor, like the Poor Law. The coverage of the middle-income groups and above should be real as opposed to nominal. In other words, the NHS had to be a *de facto* as well as a *de jure* universal service. In his speeches,

Bevan laid great stress on the percentages of both professionals and the public who had signed up for the service. In September 1948 he claimed that practically 100 per cent of the population had joined GPs' lists. This meant that 'the health service would be a classless service and every section of the community would be in full enjoyment of its benefits' (quoted in Webster 1991a: 129). In a similar vein, Bevan hoped to attract all sections of the community into council housing by insisting on high quantitative and qualitative standards (Foot 1975: 75–8). It is clear, then, that the original idea of a universal NHS meant more than merely 'open to all'.

The second sense of comprehensiveness was that of covering all services. It has recently been pointed out that the dictionary definition of 'comprehensive' refers to 'comprising of much; of large content or scope' rather than being all-inclusive. On this definition, then, the NHS Act never promised provision for every conceivable need (Howell 1992: 1). This fits in with the economic point of view: that demand for health care will always outstrip supply. However, it seems that regardless of such semantics, the service *was* intended to be all-inclusive. There were to be no gaps or restrictions in terms of time periods, unlike health services in other countries (Whitehead 1988: 36). The NHS was meant to cover all illnesses and all parts of the same illness, unlike in the USA, where, for example, a given period of hospitalization exhausts entitlement to benefit. It is in contrast to private insurance, which sets thresholds beyond which certain conditions and costs are not covered, and which tends to desert contributors in their old age, at the very time when their need for care may rise. In the theoretical sense, the NHS is willing to sign a blank cheque for all citizens, guaranteeing care from the cradle to the grave. Titmuss (1974) gave the example of 'Bill', on whom he estimated that the NHS had spent some £250,000 at 1972 prices. It is the combination of the free and universal objectives that were the hallmark of the NHS. It stood virtually alone in giving free health care as a right of citizenship.

An equitable service

Although it has been claimed that the principle of equity is probably the bedrock of the NHS (IHSM 1993: 36), there was little *explicit* emphasis on 'equality' or 'equity' in Parliamentary debates and legislation on the NHS beyond the idea of equality of entitlement or eligibility, but this is merely another way of stating the universality objective. 'The health service had successfully dismantled the price barrier but had failed to deal with the others . . . there was nothing inherent in the 1946 Act which could have systematically brought equality about' (Cooper 1975: 64). The equity principle is difficult to conceptualize and even more difficult to achieve in practice. Full equality would presumably result if all with equal needs, endowed with equal propensities to consult and faced with equal access to health care, consulted with GPs of equal quality for equal lengths and equal contents of consultation. They would, if necessary, be referred, after an equal wait, to consultants of equal quality who treated them equally and achieved equal outcomes.

Unfortunately, the aims of the NHS regarding equity have never been made explicit by its founders or policy-makers. Seedhouse (1994 : 61–2) writes that equality in health care has been an ambiguous principle:

> contrary to the fashionable belief that equality at least is an unequivocal NHS principle . . . the NHS does not have a coherent egalitarian philosophy, and so possesses no practical egalitarian impulse to guide planning. In fact the aspiration to 'equality in the health service' could hardly be more vague.

As Le Grand (1982: 45, my emphasis) states, 'equality *of some kind* is . . . a major aim of policy makers concerned with the National Health Service'. However, 'there is no universally agreed interpretation of equity for the allocation of health care resources' (Le Grand *et al.* 1990: 115; see also Klein 1988; Whitehead 1992; Birch and Abelson 1993). Similarly, government policy statements on equity in the NHS 'are notoriously ambiguous and inconsistent' (O'Donnell and Propper 1991: 2). Often, brief policy statements refer to different criteria of equity such as equality of access and utilization, and it is unclear which is the more important. Sometimes, equity goals conflict: for example, some pronouncements claim to want to maximize both the overall quantity of health in a society and minimize the health gap between different groups. This is usually regarded as being impossible (Donaldson and Gerard 1993; Carr-Hill 1994; Mooney 1994).

There are a number of possible equity objectives of the welfare state (Le Grand 1982; Mooney 1986, 1994). However, it has recently been argued that they can best be described in terms of equality of entitlement, equality of status, universalism and social citizenship rather than the more demanding distributional, quantitative forms of equality as envisaged by Le Grand and Mooney. In other words, the 'equality' of the 'strategy of equality' (Le Grand 1982) is best considered in terms of eligibility rather than access, and status rather than distribution. The most important equality delivered by the NHS was treating rich and poor alike under one system rather than in separate systems (Powell 1995a). Equality was viewed in terms of universalism (George and Wilding 1984: 66), security and free access (Glennerster 1995). Thus, postwar social policy is symbolized by 'equality in non-differentiation rather than in distribution' (O'Higgins 1987: 13). On this view, the main test of the welfare state would be seen not in terms of distributive justice, but rather in terms of real as opposed to nominal coverage (did all the population actually use the service?) and the avoidance of stigma.

Moreover, it seems more reasonable to examine the NHS's commitment to equality on the basis of specific policy instruments and mechanisms to achieve this objective rather than on *post hoc* interpretations of vague statements from official documents. In other words, the NHS should be judged more by its actions than by its words. There are clearly mechanisms for securing equality of entitlement, namely the free and universal nature of the NHS, but those to achieve more demanding forms of equality are few and came into operation some 25 years after the foundation of the service. Abel-Smith (1984: 179) argues that if socialists believed 40 years ago that all that was needed to equalize health care between social classes was to remove the money barriers to access to health care, they were seriously mistaken. It seems that they did and they were! There do not appear to be any policy instruments that seek to secure equality for social class (or gender, race or client group). Indeed, decisions regarding the who, when and how of treatment are left in professional hands.

The only mechanism of achieving equality in the NHS, beyond equality of entitlement, is via the indirect route of geography. Apart from the micro-level allocations associated with need as assessed by individual clinicians, 'need' did not enter the stage of macro-level allocation until the 1970s, when the report of the Resource Allocation Working Party (DHSS 1976) attempted to distribute finance according to the relative needs of areas. As Culyer (1976: 113) points out, 'The idea of equal available care for equal need could never have been implemented in the first twenty or so years of the NHS's existence for the simple reason that "need" had never been given operational (or even meaningful!) content, nor was there much attempt to do so'. An equitable distribution at the inter-area level does not necessarily lead to an equitable distribution at the intra-area level, as accessibility may vary between different places within the area and different population groups. Thus, in terms of policy objectives, the NHS may preach equal access for equal need, but at best it practises equal input for equal need for hospital and community health care and equal input regardless of need for GP services. Moreover, this is at the area level only: there have been few comparable attempts to secure any version of equality with respect to social class, race or gender. In other words, if the NHS's attitude towards equality is judged by policy instruments and monitoring devices instead of *post hoc* interpretations of documents, then there is little support for the primacy of equality beyond a crude 'equality of entitlement'.

Thus, far from being a central concern of NHS policy as Le Grand (1982) argues, apart from limited and belated efforts to achieve some degree of geographical equity, equality appears to have had a low priority in NHS policy (compare Hindess 1987: 92–4). Certainly, for the NHS, it is difficult not to agree with Hindess (1987: 98) that far from showing that the 'strategy of equality' has been tried and failed, the record shows that it has played at most a limited role in the development of the British social services. So, while equality of use for equal need remains a convenient rallying cry, there has never been any explicit policy statement or, more importantly, any policy instruments that accept this aim. Achieving this objective is simply not fully in the hands of doctors, let alone government policy.

The decision to consult reflects consumer demand: doctors cannot drag in from the streets patients who look as if they may be working class. Similarly, part of the length and content of the consultation reflects the patient's input: an alarm clock giving equal five-minute slots would be unacceptable to all. Neither can the quality of doctors be made equal by edict: some doctors are simply better than others. Some problems are more qualitative than quantitative in nature. For example, general practice in inner London has been said to suffer problems of quality at the same time as being officially 'over-doctored' (DHSS 1981; Powell 1987). Moreover, professionals will decide to treat people in different ways. Decisions regarding the who, when and how of treatment are largely left in professional hands as a result of 'clinical freedom'. As was argued in a DHSS memorandum of 1970, quoted by the Royal Commission on the NHS (1979), 'it is important to note that the existence of clinical freedom substantially reduces the ability of the central authority to determine objectives and priorities and to control individual facets of expenditure'. It has been said that NHS managers can be compared with factory managers who have little control over their production managers. Klein (1988: 17) argues that the NHS cannot offer equal treatment for equal need, only equal access (or, more accurately, equal entitlement) to doctors who will then apply different criteria of 'need' and different kinds of treatment: these are termed 'differences' rather than 'inequalities'. In short, as long as doctors are human rather than androids, *full* equality will be impossible.

Thus, not only are many of the NHS's ascribed objectives unclear, but some are effectively beyond its control. The NHS can achieve equal entitlement in the shape of universality, and in geographically based forms of equal input and equal provision. However, it cannot achieve equal use, treatment or outcomes. (See DoH (1996b) for a recent discussion of the role of the NHS in addressing variations in health.)

This is not to minimize the validity of equality as a principal reference point for assessing, analysing and developing social policy. Rather, it is to argue that the specific aims of 'equality' must be more securely rooted, conceptually and historically, and more intellectually justified rather than being plucked from the thin air of the 'boo–hurray' school of social philosophy. Equality is more complicated and multidimensional than the current debate would imply (Rae 1981; O'Higgins 1987; Donaldson and Gerard 1993; Seedhouse 1994; Mooney 1994). It is a many-threaded tapestry that needs to be unpicked (Klein 1988: 4).

CONCLUSION

The settlement of 1948 did not emerge in some determinist fashion as the inevitable outcome of the Second World War and the Labour government of 1945. While these may explain in a very general sense the emergence of some form of health service, the detailed arrangements of the NHS defy simple explanation. It has been shown that the NHS did not represent a political consensus. On the contrary, it illustrated deep political divisions. The Labour government of 1945 had a decisive impact on the shape of the NHS, but that shape did not closely reflect Labour Party policy. Neither is it the case that the NHS was clearly socialist as compared with either conceptual criteria or earlier plans for the service. The NHS was a monument carved by the art of the possible. While it has been termed the best in the world, it may be more accurate to describe it as the best of the feasible options at the time.

The guiding principles of the service are generally said to be equality, comprehensiveness and free access at the point of use, although the reading here is that the first is the objective, to be achieved partly through the other two. It is simple to specify the criterion of a free service. It is relatively simple to indicate the nature of a comprehensive service, although there are increasing doubts about the ability of any system to deliver a fully comprehensive and free service. However, the equality principle is difficult to operationalize and there are severe doubts about achieving it in practice.

Chapter 6 examines the extent to which the 'principles' have been achieved, but it is first necessary to give a brief discussion of the working of the service.

THE NHS 1948–96

After 1948 the NHS quickly established itself as part of the political landscape. As Klein (1995a: 29) writes, the early years saw the transformation of what started out as a controversial experiment in social engineering into a national institution anchored in consensus. As an institution, the NHS ranked next to the monarchy as an unchallenged landmark in the British political landscape. Within a decade its fiercest opponents were taking it to their hearts: the medical profession had become its defender. All thoughts of the Conservatives voting against the NHS were banished as Iain Macleod, a former Conservative Minister of Health, claimed in 1958 that the NHS was largely out of party politics (quoted in Klein 1995a: 29).

This chapter will examine developments in the NHS from its inception until 1996, but with emphasis on the periods since 1979 and particularly after 1989. Three main themes – finance, management, and policies – will be examined in a chronological framework of periods largely arranged in decades.

THE 1950s

Although no new facilities or services were created by the NHS (Watkin 1978: 1), launching Britain's largest employer required much more than breaking a bottle of champagne against its side: organizational structures had to be created and staff had to be employed. It is hardly surprising that the formative years were ones of consolidation, of ensuring that the service worked. While the enormity of the administrative task was only too obvious, it appears that the size of the financial commitment was not. 'Nothing is more striking in the voluminous files of the discussions that led to the creation of the NHS ... than the lack of consideration given to the financial implications of setting up the NHS: even the Treasury dog did not bark' (Klein 1995a: 32). Within a few years, however, it was being claimed that the NHS was out of financial control. 'The National Health Service had barely begun before it was overtaken by the crisis over expenditure' (Webster 1988a: 13).

There are a number of reasons for this perceived crisis. First, it appears to have been assumed that cost could be estimated by extrapolating prewar expenditure trends. However, it soon became clear that a service with restricted access was a poor predictor of a universal one. The free health service was faced with a backlog of years of unmet need: people who had lacked access to health care now came forward to claim their birthrights, ranging from teeth, spectacles and wigs to deferred major operations. Second, the NHS was a victim of its own success. Producers and consumers had signed up for the service more quickly than expected. Third, pay awards for NHS staff had increased the wages bill to a higher than expected level. Finally, there were also unavoidable commitments consequent upon taking over a system verging on a state of dereliction. Buildings were decaying, staffing arrangements were untenable and medicine had failed to adapt quickly enough. In short, the system was weighed down with anachronisms. 'Adaption of this ramshackle and largely bankrupt edifice into a rational, modern and humane hospital structure to serve the whole population was inconceivable without revolutionary reorganisation and a secular increase in capital and revenue expenditure' (Webster 1988a: 261).

A close watch was kept on NHS expenditure in the Labour cabinet. Allsop (1995: 78) has claimed that in the early years 'the primary concern of policy-makers was to contain the size of the budget'. As expenditure outran estimates, there were calls to restrict it. In the 1950s the language was of economy. People were exhorted to swallow less medicine. The emphasis was on the patient making do with less: the austerity years of war necessarily continued into peace. Britain could not yet afford a three-course meal of health care, but had to manage on wartime Woolton pies. Ham (1981: 56) terms the formative period the 'years of make-do and mend'.

A Bill allowing prescription charges was passed in 1949, partly in order to raise revenue (to transfer public to private expenditure), but partly to prevent abuse. These prescription charges were never implemented, but in 1950 charges were levied on spectacles and dentures, leading to Bevan's resignation from the Labour government in protest against compromising the principle of a free health service (Webster 1988a: ch. 5; Campbell 1987: ch. 16).

The incoming Conservative government of 1951 was as concerned as its predecessor about NHS expenditure. The Treasury urged many economy measures on the NHS, resulting in a 'continuous programme of cheese-paring economies' (Webster 1994: 70). Although major changes were resisted, charges continued to expand throughout the 1950s. Moreover, revenue increasingly came from the flat-rate NHS contributions rather than income tax. The Conservatives appointed the Guillebaud Committee in 1953 to examine the service. It was hoped that this would supply the ammunition for an assault on NHS expenditure, but in its 1956 report the Committee pointed out the need for more, rather than less, NHS expenditure.

Administrative difficulties added to financial ones. As Morrison had pointed out, Bevan's NHS had to reconcile national accountability and local autonomy. The Minister of Health was to be accountable to Parliament for every penny of expenditure, yet local control was stressed. In a 1950 report this fundamental incompatibility between central control and local autonomy was pointed out (Klein 1995a: 43–5). Most commentators suggest that in this formative period, the centre had little effective control over the periphery. The Ministry could issue advice, guidelines and circulars, but these could be ignored, and in many cases were. It has been suggested that the hallmark of Ministry of Health policy-making in the 1950s was 'policy-making by exhortation' (Klein 1995a: 46).

The report of the Guillebaud Committee (1956) may be taken as an early evaluation of the NHS. It pointed out that there was no evidence of profligacy in the service: the cost of the NHS in terms of a percentage of gross domestic product (GDP) had fallen from 3.75 per cent in 1949–50 to 3.24 per cent in 1953–4. Capital expenditure had fallen to approximately a third of the prewar level in real terms. The report recommended that dental and optical charges, but not prescription charges, should be reduced as soon as possible. The management structure of the NHS was given a verdict of procrastination mixed with qualified approval: the only form of major reorganization that called for serious discussion was the transfer of health functions to the local authorities. However, it was concluded that a convincing case for transfer had not been made, and it was generally too soon to contemplate a major reorganization in a service only eight years old. However, Sir John Maude, the former

Permanent Secreatry at the Ministry of Health in the early 1940s, resurrected the idea that the NHS might be handed over to local government. In a note of reservation, he claimed that while the transfer of hospitals to local government would not be appropriate at that time, it might be desirable after a reorganization of local government.

Although it is generally claimed that equity is one of the fundamental principles of the NHS, there are few policy instruments that aim to achieve it, other than the free and universal nature of the service. Moreover, policy-makers have tended to be more concerned with the size of the NHS budget rather than its distribution. In 1948 the NHS achieved an unequal pattern of provision, and incremental resource allocation perpetuated this. This may be seen in two main ways. First, the better-provided geographical areas such as London continued to be favoured (Webster 1988a: 292–8). Planning was largely by decibels rather than any more rational indicator of need. Hospitals were allocated what they got the previous year plus a small amount for growth. It was a case of 'To him that hath more shall be given', rather than the meek inheriting the earth. Second, acute hospitals in general and prestigious 'high-tech' specialties in particular continued to be favoured over long-stay institutions. For example, in 1955, 73 per cent of consultants in neurology received merit awards, compared with 16 per cent in psychiatry (Webster 1988a: 315). Treatment for elderly people remained poor (Webster 1991b), while conditions in some mental hospitals were little short of a public scandal (Webster 1988a: 326–41). In the Leeds RHB studied by Ham (1981) the greatest cause for concern was over mental illness. Hospitals were grossly overcrowded. A report described one hospital as comprising old gaol-like buildings, with the accommodation best described as pre-Dickensian (Ham 1981: 119).

THE 1960s

This period saw the highest ever rates of real growth in NHS spending: 3.5 per cent for the Conservative government of 1959–64 and 3.2 per cent for the Labour government of 1964–70 (Appleby 1992: 43). However, the creeping transfer of finance towards flat-rate 'poll tax' NHS contributions and patients' charges rather than income tax continued, with the lowest proportion for income tax reached in 1962, when it was 70 per cent. The Labour Party came to power in 1964 with no notably new ideas, seeking only to restore the NHS to the glory it had been in 1948. The new government abolished prescription charges in 1965. However, the return to the 1940s was short-lived nostalgia. Economic difficulties of 1967–8 led to the devaluation of the pound and calls for economy from the Treasury. The Hospital Plan, a measure dating from the declining years of the Conservative administration, was maintained, but was partially financed by reintroduced – and higher – prescription charges (Glennerster 1995: 122).

The Hospital Plan of 1962 was the first real attempt to direct resources away from the inherited pattern. Introduced by Conservative Minister of Health Enoch Powell, it has been termed 'a marriage between professional aspirations and the new faith in planning: between what might be called medical expertise and administrative technology' (Klein 1995a: 67). It set down a series of planning norms, such as 3.3 acute beds per 1000 population, and aimed to achieve this through a series of district general hospitals of between 600 to 800 beds serving populations of 100,000 to 150,000. To some extent, the emphasis on the standard product made hospitals like hamburger restaurants. It should be noted that the emphasis was on equality rather than equity. In other words, the same number of beds were to be provided per capita regardless of any difference in the pattern of population need: 1000 healthy people 'needed' the same number of beds as 1000 ill people. As Klein (1995a: 70–1) notes, this attempt to achieve national uniformity via norms was subverted by two principles. The first may be termed the principle of infinite diversity: no two populations or communities are the same, no two consultants practise the same kind of medicine, and thus national norms inevitably have to be adapted to unique, local circumstances. The second may be called the principle of infinite indeterminacy: the future cannot be predicted, and we cannot know how changes in population structure, in the childbearing proclivities of families or in medical technology will affect the need for services.

Apart from building up a network of district general hospitals, the other main impact of the Hospital Plan was in the area of mental illness. The drug revolution and new treatments of the 1950s culminated in the Mental Health Act of 1959 and a governmental commitment to close the large psychiatric hospitals. Following this Act, a 'landmark in the development of mental health services' (Ham 1981: 124), which aimed to move from compulsory to voluntary treatment, from the asylums to the wards of general hospitals and from institutional to community care, the Hospital Plan proposed reducing the number of mental illness beds from 3.3 per 1000 population to 1.8. According to Enoch Powell, this aim of reducing the number of mental illness beds by half in 15 years implied 'nothing less than the elimination of by far the greater part of this country's mental hospitals as they stand today' (Ham 1981: 124). 'With the Hospital Plan, the era of community care had begun and has remained official government policy since 1962' (Murphy 1991: 59). However, while hospital provision was gradually run down, insufficient provision in the community took its place. As Baggott (1994a: 220) puts it, despite the growing support for community care during the 1960s it remained largely a paper policy. Murphy (1991: ch. 4) terms the period 1962 to 1990 'The Disaster Years' (see also Jones 1993; Allsop 1995: ch. 5).

THE 1970s

Real expenditure on the NHS increased at the rate of 3.1 per cent under the Conservative government of 1970–4 (Appleby 1992: 43). The period of economic growth was to come to an abrupt halt with the oil crisis of 1973–4. The external environment became hostile to public expenditure. The national economic growth that had made it relatively easy to finance annual increases in public expenditure halted. The NHS was now in an era of limited growth. 'To a remarkable degree, the NHS remained sheltered, if not insulated, from the harsh new economic and political environment in which it was operating' (Klein 1995a: 98). Despite the ritual of economic cuts, NHS expenditure grew, albeit at the reduced real rate of 2.3 per cent under the Labour governments of 1974–9 (Appleby 1992: 43). In comparison with other social services, the NHS was privileged. However, in comparison with past growth rates, it was pinched. Staff were accustomed to growth, and it was expected that money would always be available for the introduction of new treatments and an ever-expanding service. Expectations now conflicted with reality to produce discontent. Limited growth was enabled by the successive years' decisions to protect the revenue budget at the expense of capital expenditure: buildings and repairs could be put off until next year, while paying the staff could not. Capital spending fell throughout the period as successive Secretaries of State continued to trade reductions in the NHS's investment programme in return for safeguarding the current budget against cuts. In contrast, total spending on education and housing fell (Klein 1995a: 98).

Debates about the NHS's structure were dominant in policy discussions throughout the late 1960s and early 1970s. By the end of the 1960s it was generally felt that the tripartite structure was becoming unwieldy: this legacy of the pre-NHS times had perhaps served its purpose. Few people would have devised such a structure from scratch, and its disadvantages had always been evident to some degree. The problem was that prescriptions radically differed: it was agreed that the NHS should be unified, but there was no agreement on the shape of the unified structure (Watkin 1978: ch. 9; Allsop 1995: ch. 3).

In 1967 the Labour Minister of Health Kenneth Robinson announced an examination of the administrative structure of the NHS, which would proceed in parallel with the enquiries already set up into local government and local authorities' welfare services. Thus, the opportunity to reform the NHS simultaneously with local government had arisen. In 1968, Robinson issued a Green Paper entitled 'The Administrative Structure of Medical and Related Services in England and Wales' ('the First Green Paper'). Its central theme was unification under a single tier of some 40 or 50 area boards to cover all health services. The composition of these bodies was a 'very green' part of the Green Paper, but did not preclude the possibility that the area boards might be committees of the local authorities, which it was expected would result from the recommendations of the Royal Commission then sitting. This idea was sufficient to revive in the medical profession the old fear of local authority control, the option they had strenuously resisted in the 1940s, and they made their objections to this clear. The Crossman diaries, written by Richard Crossman, Secretary of State for Social Services in the Labour government between 1968 and 1970, reveal the rapid retreat from the First Green Paper. By January 1969 Crossman wrote, 'I ruled out the Green Paper in one stroke' (Crossman 1977: 329). Similarly, it seems that even before his cabinet colleagues had seen the recommendations on local government of the Royal Commission (the 'Maud report'), Crossman had ruled out 'the tentative suggestions Maud was going to make for bringing health under local government control' (p. 499).

In the Second Green Paper, of 1970, 'The Future Structure of the NHS', it was claimed that the government accepted the force of the Maud Commission's arguments about bringing health under local government, but in one paragraph this option was found to be unacceptable owing to the opposition of the profession and the insufficient financial resources of local government. On this issue, the Green Paper was white. The new plan was for some 14 regional health councils, which would have an advisory role and not be part of the chain of command, some 90 area health authorities (AHAs), which were to be coterminous with local government boundaries, and some 200 district committees (DCs). The composition of the AHAs was to be one-third professional, one-third from local authorities and one-third, plus the chair, appointed by the Secretary of State. The members of the DCs were to be the chair and half appointed and drawn from the AHA and the remaining half from people living and working in the district. In this way Crossman sought to reform the system from one in which many hospital authorities were controlled by 'self perpetuating oligarchies' that were aloof and remote from public opinion (Crossman 1972: 24).

Crossman did not have the opportunity to turn his scheme into legislation. The incoming Conservative government of 1970 had their own ideas on NHS reorganization. A consultative document issued by Sir Keith Joseph, the new Secretary of State, in 1971 made some changes to the original proposals. The regional tier was strengthened and placed more clearly within the central–local chain of command. The Secretary of State was to select the regional authority, and the region was to select the AHA, except that places were to be reserved for local authorities and medical schools. Regional members should include at least two doctors and a nurse, after consultation with the professions. However, the main criterion of selection was to be managerial ability rather than representing any interest group. The system was to be based on the principle of 'maximum delegation downwards, matched by accountability upwards' (quoted in Watkin 1978: 145). Below the area tier, Crossman's DCs were jettisoned and their representational role assigned to community health councils (CHC's), watchdogs to represent the community.

The 1974 reorganization did make some steps towards integration. The teaching hospitals lost their independent status under boards of governors and were brought into the AHA structure. Community nursing services were transferred from local government to the NHS and were effectively nationalized some 26 years after the hospitals, but local government retained its environmental health role. However, the administration of the family practitioner services remained separate, with the executive councils becoming family practitioner committees (FPCs). Thus, the essential tripartite administration of the NHS survived. The resulting structure was 'the most Byzantine ever imposed on a UK public service' (Glennerster 1995: 131).

In their turn, the Conservatives left office before the scheme could be implemented. When the Labour government took office in March 1974 , it was too late to alter the reorganization set for 1 April. As the Labour Secretary of State, Barbara Castle, put it in her diary, 'it was too late to unscramble Sir Keith's eggs' and some 'interim proposals to make the structure more democratic' were worked out (Castle 1980: 142, fn.). These included increasing the number of local government representatives on AHAs back to Crossman's figure of one-third, reserving on them two places for health workers other than doctors and nurses and strengthening the role of CHCs. These measures were set out in a document entitled, 'somewhat hyperbolically' according to Navarro (1978: 61), 'Democracy in the NHS'.

In spite of the hostile economic climate and the rapidly evolving organizational structure of the NHS, the 1970s may be seen as the decade in which the NHS recognized and partially responded to inequalities. In 1971 the 'Crossman formula' was introduced (devised by Crossman, but implemented by Joseph) to distribute money to different geographical areas (Mays and Bevan 1987: 10–14). This tentatively groped its way from the equality of the bed norm to the equity of responding to different circumstances through a formula incorporating indices of population, beds and cases. However, this had little time to operate as a more radical geographical policy was formed. The Labour government of 1974–9 set up the Resource Allocation Working Party (RAWP) to examine ways of distributing health-care resources according to need (Mays and Bevan 1987; Beech *et al.* 1990). The result was a method of measuring need by the proxy index of mortality. In other words, needy areas were those with a high standardized death rate. The result of the RAWP was to distribute expenditure away from 'over-resourced' London and the south towards the 'under-resourced' Midlands and the north.

It had long been recognized that there were client group inequalities in the NHS. It was generally agreed that long-stay patients got the worst deal. They are sometimes referred to as 'Cinderella groups', and include the mentally ill, the mentally handicapped and the elderly. In the 1970s services for the mentally ill, 'the slum of the NHS' (Klein 1995a: 72), moved on to the NHS agenda. Every Minister of Health had proclaimed the need to give priority to improving these services. In 1950 Bevan had warned his cabinet colleagues about the likelihood of scandals breaking about poor conditions in mental hospitals. As late as 1965, beds in one hospital were spaced so close together as not to allow lockers between them (Ham 1981: 122). To some extent, scandals were the motor which drove policy in the 1970s: action was due more to crisis management than any strategy, and was reactive rather than pro-active (see Watkin 1978; Ham 1981: ch. 5; Martin 1984). In 1967 an exposé of conditions affecting the elderly in hospitals, entitled *Sans Everything* (Robb 1967), was published. This was closely followed by a newspaper report revealing scandalous conditions at a hospital for the mentally handicapped at Ely. Crossman seized the rare opportunity of long-stay hospitals being in the media to press the RHBs to divert funds into the sector, and set up the Hospital Advisory Service, in effect an inspectorate reporting directly to the Secretary of State.

In spite of exhortation by the centre, there were few mechanisms and little extra money to achieve improvements for the Cinderella groups. As Digby (1989: 75) comments, 'even when Cinderella was eventually chosen to go to the NHS Ball, it proved difficult to allocate extra resources to allow her to do so in style'. The 1970s saw Green Papers on 'Better Services' for the mentally ill and mentally handicapped. However, in the absence of any earmarked funds, better services for one group could be achieved only by making services worse for other groups. Similarly, a document entitled 'Priorities' dissolved into exhortation (Klein 1995a: 116). Long-stay services remained a low priority in the medical pecking order. There was sometimes a gap between national policy and local action, a 'failure' in the implementation process. In the NHS the existence of powerful professional interests at the operational level is likely to be the main obstacle to the implementation of agreed policies (Ham 1981: 139, 197). In other words, the medical veto at local levels ensured that resources for acutely ill Peter would not be transferred to mentally ill Paul.

The final inequality to be recognized was that of social classes. In 1977 the Labour government set up a committee to examine inequalities in health between social classes. This committee had the misfortune to a report to a Conservative government in 1980. The hostile reception of the Black report (Townsend and Davidson 1982), and its attempted burial and rapid rejection, ensured that it received more publicity than it would have received if it had been sympathetically accepted. However, no policy initiatives resulted from this and there was little official recognition of inequalities concerned with race and gender.

The Report of the Royal Commission on the NHS in 1979 updated the Guillebaud report as a detached, impartial view of the service. This report has been termed not only 'the high-water mark of a particular style of policy making' (Mohan 1995: 1), but also 'a remarkable document, probably one of the most comprehensive reviews of a Health Service undertaken anywhere in the world' (Edwards 1993: 37). It gave an overwhelming, but not uncritical endorsement of the NHS. With regard to three key points, it was in general agreement with the Guillebaud report. First, although quantification was difficult, it considered that more money should be spent on the NHS. Second, charges should be gradually abolished. Third, the possibility of transferring the NHS to local government was examined. It concluded that the objections outweighed the advantages, and that 'we could not recommend it at the present', although the possibility might be explored again in the event of regional government. The report recommended that one administrative tier should be abolished, that AHAs and FPCs should be integrated and that the 'consensus management' of 1974 was largely sound.

THE 1980s AND 1990s

Restructuring the old NHS

While the Labour government of 1974–9 had been forced reluctantly to embrace the limiting of public expenditure, this was at the centre of the Conservative programme of 1979. The necessary evil became a desirable good. However, in spite of the government's stated objectives on public expenditure and the accusations of critics, expenditure on the NHS did not fall. It rose in 'real terms' (allowing for inflation). Nevertheless, the 1980s were marked by a continual debate about the level of NHS funding. Critics continued to claim that the NHS was underfunded. The problem with the debate is that it is very difficult to put a precise figure on what the NHS should spend (see Chapter 5).

As it proved politically impossible to reduce NHS expenditure, the focus changed to maximizing the output from that expenditure. In other words, as economy proved as problematic for the Conservatives in the 1980s as it had been for the Labour government that introduced the NHS, the concept of efficiency came to the top of the agenda. As Klein (1995a: 132) points out, this concern was not new to the NHS, but in the 1980s it increasingly dominated government policy: what had been a minor theme became the major one. One objective of increased efficiency was seen as largely attainable by injecting the NHS with the enterprise culture, consisting of the new managerialism plus a greater market orientation. This led to a number of diverse changes.

While the tripartite structure, with all its obvious faults, lasted some 26 years, the new structure of 1974 was to last only eight years. Klein (1995a: 113) writes that, 'Hardly had the new NHS structure been inaugurated, than the critics of Sir Keith Joseph's architecture appeared to have been justified. The new structure, it was widely agreed, was indeed too complex. Designed to please everyone, the structure satisfied no one.'

The Royal Commission had recommended abolishing one administrative tier and the tier that was shed was the AHA. It was argued that they were too small to be planning bodies and too large to be operational units. The 1979 consultation document issued by the new Conservative government, 'Patients First', stressed the local dimension. In contrast to arrangements under the reorganization of 1974, decisions were to be taken at local level, rather than being passed down the chain of command. The Conservative Secretary of State for Social Services Patrick Jenkin saw the NHS 'not as a single national organisation, but . . . as a series of local services run by local management' (quoted in Klein 1995a: 126). In the resulting reorganization of 1982, the structure was simplified. Essentially some 200 operating units based on district general hospitals became 'district health authorities' (DHAs) in their own right. Coterminosity was the main casualty of 1982: the largely common boundaries of AHAs with local authorities were lost and FPCs linked with the main hospital and community services since 1974, once again became free-floating bodies. The minor casualty was the reduction in the numbers of the local authority appointees on the new DHAs.

However, the rhetoric of delegation gave way to centralism almost as the ink was drying on the document. Klein (1995a: 144–5) points to the two-pronged attack of central administrative innovation in the shape of annual 'accountability meetings' throughout the hierarchy and the technical innovation of performance indicators (PIs), which are discussed later in this section.

In addition to structural changes, the NHS of the early 1980s saw an efficiency drive composed of a number of measures. These have sometimes been discussed as 'creeping privatisation' (Baggott 1994b), but as the term is problematic (Klein 1995a), 'market orientation' is here suggested as preferable.

The first two Conservative governments did not fundamentally alter the shape of the NHS, but attempted to increase its market orientation. In 1983 the government required DHAs to put their 'hotel services' – catering, cleaning and laundry – out to tender. The 'in-house' workers were forced to compete with outside private contractors. The lowest tender would normally secure the contract and any savings were to go towards patient care. It is generally argued that most tenders have remained in-house and that savings have been modest. Moreover, there has been a concern that any savings have been at the expense of quality, and financial savings to the DHA may be offset by increased social security income to the workers on lower wages (Pearson 1992: 231–5; Baggot 1994a; Mohan 1995: 180–2). Another example of the assumption that competition brings benefits may be found in optical services, where an internal market in spectacles was introduced in stages, resulting in a pilot commodification of health care (Taylor 1990; Pearson 1992: 238–9). In 1986 the NHS stopped supplying spectacles ('NHS frames'). People who would have been formerly entitled to them were given vouchers that they could use in the market. Thus, providers of ancilliary services were forced to compete for hospital contracts and opticians were forced to compete for customers. In hindsight, the seeds of the 'internal market' of the 1990s may be found in these policies.

From 1982 there were some special exercises under the auspices of Lord Rayner, the Prime Minister's 'Efficiency Advisor', known as 'Rayner scrutinies' and concerned with matters that included NHS residential accommodation and non-emergency ambulance services (Baggott 1994b).

In 1984 DHAs were obliged to find 'efficiency savings'. The term implies that cost would be reduced without cutting services to patients. However, it proved difficult to separate 'efficiency' from 'economy'. In other words, there is the possibility that some 'efficiency savings' were made at the expense of the quantity or quality of services for patients (Baggott 1994a,b).

Market orientation in health care also increased outside the NHS. The 1980s saw a large increase in commercial medicine, in terms of private hospitals, beds and health insurance (Griffith *et al.* 1987; Higgins 1988). It has been claimed that some of these increases are not due to the hidden hand of the market, but to the visible hand of government in the shape of planning decisions, changes to consultants' contracts and tax concessions. Moreover, the boundaries between state and private medicine have been blurred (Mohan 1995: ch. 7).

In 1983 Roy Griffiths, managing director of the supermarket chain Sainsbury's, was asked to examine management in the NHS. The contrast with the style of Royal Commissions was marked, and it was the Griffiths style that was to become the norm for the Conservative government. The Royal Commission on the NHS lasted three years, consisted of the 'great and the good', took evidence and published a detailed report. The Griffiths investigation involved four people, lasted six months, and while it consulted it did not take formal evidence. In short, it typified Prime Minister Thatcher's contempt of 'the establishment' and her preference for 'one of us'.

While it is said that the Russian Revolution took 10 days to shake the world, it took a mere 25 pages to transform the management style of the NHS. The recommendations of the 'Griffiths report' (DHSS 1983) were termed 'the most important single change to the NHS since 1948' (Timmins 1996: 409). Griffiths claimed that the NHS compared poorly with private industry. The main problem was seen as 'consensus management'. In an often quoted phrase, it was claimed that 'if Florence Nightingale were carrying her lamp through the corridors of the NHS today she would almost certainly be searching for the people in charge'. At all levels of the NHS, 'general managers', the counterparts of industry's managing directors, were to be appointed. It was hoped that many of these would come from industry, thus bringing a much-needed blood transfusion to the NHS. Griffiths stated that people in business 'have a keen sense of how well they are looking after their customers. Whether the NHS is meeting the needs of the patient and the community, and can prove it is doing so is open to question' (DHSS 1983: 10). In many respects the NHS was to be run like a supermarket: a virtue for Griffiths, but a vice and an object of derision for critics. General managers needed information on how well they were doing, and this was to be found in the newly introduced package of PIs. PIs enabled managers to compare their performance with other hospitals or districts, but were generally limited to conceptions of efficiency, such as patient's length of stay in hospital. They have been criticized on a number of counts (Allen *et al.* 1987; Roberts 1990: ch. 8; Carter *et al.* 1992: ch. 4; Klein 1995a: 144–6). First, PIs do not measure performance. They tend to be concerned with inputs and throughputs rather than outputs or outcomes. Second, they do not compare like with like. Third, the data used to calculate PIs are inaccurate.

The problems of this era of PIs and imposed targets may be shown by two examples. Many PIs examined hospital activity in terms of 'deaths and discharges'. In other words, for PIs, there was no difference between the two outcomes, a point of view unlikely to be shared by patients. Indeed, a hospital manager wanting to be judged solely on the basis of such PIs would be well advised to administer a lethal injection to patients on entry to hospital, which would have a dramatic effect on throughput. This hypothetical example is clearly ridiculous, but the following example is real. Klein (1995a: 144) points out that the Trent Region set a target of 2250 extra maternity patients, provoking somewhat ribald questions about who was to be responsible for increasing the birth rate.

The government attempted to introduce more competition into primary care in the 1987 White Paper 'Promoting Better Health'. Patients were to be enabled to change their GPs more easily: the idea was that they would 'vote with their feet' to register with popular GPs. At the same time, the proportion of GPs' income coming from capitation fees was increased. Reward was also tailored to performance by GPs getting more money for being active: for visits and immunizations. There was some degree of 'commodification' in that charges were to be levied for dental and optical checks (Baggott 1994b). This introduced 'a completely new principle' into NHS charges, namely charges for preventive measures (Johnson 1990: 86–7).

Creating the new NHS

'The most striking feature of policy towards the NHS, at least until 1988, was its continuity' (Le Grand *et al.* 1990: 93). As Holliday (1992: 23) explains, 'Thatcherism spent most of the 1980s trying to make the old NHS work better than had hitherto been the case. The means to this end . . . was managerial reform.' Holliday (1992: 59) sees a clear difference between the two reform programmes of the 1980s. The first is the shift to general management, which sought to increase efficiency through the creation of a clear managerial hierarchy. The second initaitive, that of the internal market, also seeks to increase efficiency, as well as having regard to other aims such as consumer choice, but it does so by means of competitive pressures.

Where the Griffiths reforms had sought to turn the NHS into an efficient but still unified business, the internal market reforms seek to split the NHS into efficient and competitive units. Efficiency thus remains a central objective, but it will now be generated not by an efficient monolith, but by the most efficient units in an internal market.

(Holliday 1992: 59)

This, it is claimed, is the essential difference between the 'old' and the 'new' NHS. In particular the new NHS can be traced to the 1990 National Health Service and Community Care Act. This drew on the proposals of two White Papers of 1989: WFP and 'Caring for People'.

While the Griffiths report provided the foundations of the new NHS, the superstructure came to be built in the 1990s. In 1988, amidst a crisis of expenditure, closed beds, postponed operations and legal action – all enjoying almost daily media headlines – a review of the NHS was announced (Timmins 1988). Its style followed Griffiths: a small, sealed membership, not formally consulting, and working quickly. Right-wing think-tanks competed to provide the most radical blueprint for the NHS. The review discussed, and eventually rejected, insurance schemes and funding by earmarked taxes: an exercise set up to deal with finance became largely confined to dealing with issues of service delivery. The Griffiths idea of the NHS being more like a business was followed to its logical conclusion. Businesses are said to be efficient because they compete in the marketplace and so the review examined ways of introducing competition into the NHS. A number of possibilities were considered. The main theme of the resulting 1989 White Paper WFP was to separate the NHS into purchasers and providers. Previously DHAs managed the provision of health care. Now, they would become purchasers of health care on behalf of their residents. Hospitals and community services became service providers. They could either become 'directly managed units', at arm's length from the purchasers, or they could decide to 'opt out' of DHA control and become 'NHS trusts'. An analogy might be that a DHA in the old NHS was like an insurance agent, aiming to maximize referral to its district general hospital. In contrast, DHAs in the new NHS would act like insurance brokers, attempting to survey the available options in order to get the best value for money from potential providers. This process essentially forced the NHS to put its clinical services out to competitive tender. Just as laundry contracts ensured that hospitals got the best deal for clean linen, the internal market would ensure that DHAs would get the best deal for clinical services. The 'wild card' of the package was the emergence of GP budget holders (GPBH) (Glennerster *et al.* 1994a, b). Practices with more than 11,000 patients (subsequently reduced to 9000 and later to 7000) could elect to hold their own budgets. They would then purchase a limited range of services, effectively becoming 'mini-purchasers'.

The regulatory route to achieving efficiency was to be continued in the form of audit. Consultants were to be involved in medical audit, examining their performance in comparison with others, leading to the identification and diffusion of 'good practice'. The Audit Commission was to have its remit extended from local government into the NHS. To some extent, this was the 'macro-level' complement of the 'micro-level' medical audit, albeit with a focus on efficiency rather than effectiveness. In a series of reports, the Commission examined issues such as day surgery, nursing resources and how many person-hours it took to change a light bulb.

Working for Patients (DoH 1989) argued that there was a lack of clarity about the role of health authorities, which were neither truly representative nor management bodies. This is a perfectly valid point. Health authorities have always suffered from the tensions of upward accountability to Parliament and downward accountability to the local community (Klein 1995a). This lack of clarity was to be resolved by clearly making NHS bodies (including trusts) management rather than representative bodies, and abolishing local authority representation. The CHCs set up in 1974, were intended to provide the 'consumer input'. Health authorities have been viewed by many as an example of the 'new magistracy': a result of patronage by ministers leading to a 'one-party state' of bodies with strong government leanings and connections (Mohan 1995: 201–4; Cooper *et al.* 1995: 31–9). The *Guardian* columnist Ian Aitken has described 'the unseemly scramble to pack hospital trusts, health authorities and hundreds of other quangos with the wives, aunties, cousins, party chairmen and (more than likely) the mistresses of Tory ministers and MPs' (quoted in Cooper *et al.* 1995: 33). However, highlighting that these bodies are not representative of the community misses the point, as the criterion of evaluation has changed: bodies are no longer intended to be judged on their degree of 'representation', but rather on a different type of accountability – in terms of service delivery. Former Conservative Secretary of State for Health William Waldegrave has argued that:

there is no guarantee . . . that by periodically expressing his or her democratic decision at the ballot box the citizen . . . will necessarily obtain on a continuous basis efficient, properly accountable, responsive public services. . . . The key point in this argument is not whether those who run our public services are elected, but whether they are producer responsive or consumer responsive. Services are not necessarily made responsive to the public simply by giving citizens a democratic voice, and a distant one at that, in their make up. They *can* be made responsive by giving the public choices, or by instituting mechanisms which build in publicly approved standards and redress when they are not attained . . . far from presiding over a democratic deficit in the management of our public services, this Government has launched a public service reform programme that has helped create a democratic gain.

(Quoted in Walsh 1995: xv–xvi, 219)

As Cooper *et al.* (1995: 11) explain:

Current health policy has effectively by-passed the problem of public accountability in the NHS by presenting health as a non-political, managerial issue. Governance is regarded as a matter of managing the market; efficiency is offered as an adequate substitute for accountability.

To oversimplify, the old DHAs could deliver poor service so long as they were representative; the new ones could be filled of card-carrying members of the Conservative Party so long as they delivered good service. Nevertheless the government was concerned with the apparent problems of legitimacy. Health authorities should be more responsive to the needs, views and preferences of local people. To achieve this, they were encouraged to involve the public through consultation exercises as they prepared their plans and allocated their resources. In other words, they must listen to 'local voices' in order to become 'champions of the people'. This initiative has been criticized as being 'long on exhortation but short on compulsion' and as 'the unaccountable in pursuit of the uninformed' (see Cooper *et al.* 1995: 46–74).

Most commentators point out that the rhetoric of localism, devolution and the local community appears to be merely a convenient cloak disguising the lack of local accountability. Devolution may just be an exercise in attempting to shift the blame for unpopular decisions away from government to the local bodies, while at the same time increasing central control. In this 'government-at-arm's-length' approach, it appears to be the case that upward accountability is being conveniently forgotten: if a minister is asked about a problem in constituency *X*, she or he can reply, 'That is a matter for the health authority'. The spectre of Eastern Europe has been raised to illustrate the terms of the political debate. The government claimed that the White Paper reforms were moving away from the old NHS form of centralist planning associated with Eastern Europe; the opposition claimed precisely the opposite: the extent of government control over appointments to the NHS would produce a 'board of management that will exist to implement central policy – exactly the sort of machinery of the clapped-out, centralised state that is being dismantled all over Eastern Europe' (quoted in Mohan 1995: 67, 203). Timmins (1996: 511) states that the NHS now has a line management system Stalin himself might have envied.

The community-care proposals in the 1990 NHS and Community Care Act resulted from perceived policy failure and a set of enquiries into community care in the 1980s (Means and Smith 1994: ch. 3; Wistow *et al.* 1994: ch. 1; Allsop 1995: ch. 5; Mohan 1995: ch. 5). The early 1980s saw an irony that a government committed to community care contributed to a vast increase in residential care. The supplementary benefit regulations were amended, making it easier for public funds to pay for places in private and voluntary residential homes for the elderly. This encouraged a mushrooming of new homes in the private sector, with the number of places increasing from about 47,000 in 1982 to over 161,000 in 1991. Those in receipt of social security payments increased from about 12,000 in 1979 to 90,000 by 1986, with total expenditure rising from £10 million to £459 million per year (Means and Smith 1994: 49–50). Income-support payments in the 1990s accounted for over £1.5 billion per year, some 20 per cent of community-care expenditure (Mohan 1995: 118). Two reports (Social Services Committee 1985; Audit Commission 1986) saw community care as an area of policy failure. Progress towards community care was being frustrated for a number of reasons. First, there was the perverse financial incentive associated with residential care, meaning that people might get financial help for residential care, but not for care in their own homes. Second, the pace of running down hospitals was far outrunning the provision of community-based services. This was described by the Social Services Committee (1985) as the 'cart and the horse ' phenomenon. Third, responsibility for the provision and funding of community care was divided between several agencies and there was little effective coordination. The reaction of the government was to appoint Roy Griffiths to conduct a review of community-care policies. The resulting report (DHSS 1988: 4) continued the theme of policy failure, arguing that 'in few areas can the gap between political rhetoric and policy on the one hand, or between policy and reality in the field have been so great'. Community care was described as 'a poor relation; everybody's distant relative but nobody's baby' – a criticism similar to that applied to hospitals before the NHS. It was proposed that local authorities should be seen as enablers rather than direct providers. Care managers would purchase an appropriate package of care in consultation with clients. Much of this report was translated into the government White Paper 'Caring for People'. In turn, 'Caring for People' became part of the NHS and Community Care Act of 1990.

The new NHS in action

There have been a number of developments since the new NHS came on stream in 1991. The regions have being amalgamated and transformed into regional offices of the NHS Executive. They are outposts of Whitehall, accountable to the NHS chief executive rather than to the regions in which they are situated, and staffed by civil servants rather than employees of the NHS (Mohan 1995: 213–14). Many DHAs have merged, in some cases to units similar to the old AHAs that were abolished in 1982. In April 1996 DHAs and Family Health Service Authorities (FHSAs) combined to become single purchasing authorities.

As we saw in Chapter 2, over time 'public health' gradually gave way to curative health care, increasingly located in hospitals. Recent years have seen a limited retreat from hospitals in two main directions. First, within health care, primary care has developed to the extent that care should be offered in a primary-care rather than secondary-care setting. The aim is a 'primary care led NHS' (NHS Executive 1996). Second, in the 1970s there was a growing recognition that the burden of illness in modern societies required something more than a narrow medical response. Many diseases, it was thought, were linked to lifestyle, and prevention was seen as the key. 'During the last two decades, health policy in the UK has become more informed by the broader concept of health status as opposed to health services' (Health Care 2000 1995). Some responses involved the introduction of screening, for example for breast and cervical cancer. However, most were 'health education' campaigns to persuade the public to change their behaviour:

individuals should exercise, give up smoking, not over-eat or drink. Perhaps the clearest example of the 'new public health' of exhortation were the safe-sex campaigns associated with AIDS. Critics saw an emphasis on 'victim blaming' and an avoidance of wider structural issues such as unemployment, housing and pollution (Baggott 1994a: ch. 11).

The publication of 'The Health of the Nation' White Paper (DoH 1992) – following a Green Paper of the same title a year before – is said to have marked a significant shift in public policy (Klein 1995a: 210). In the rhetorical sense, this is certainly true. The document stressed a commitment to health rather than simply to health care, and paid dues to social and public health, or collective as opposed to individual, issues in improving health. This general commitment was translated into 25 specific targets. The NHS Executive (1995: 3) claimed that 'Health of the Nation remains the central plank of government policy for the NHS'. However, critics point out that the targets appeared to be largely extrapolations of existing trends, designed to make sure that the government would be able to congratulate itself on making good progress towards them. Government action on unemployment, housing and pollution was conspicuous by its absence. In short, there appears to be little strategy and few mechanisms to achieve the targets (Baggott 1994a; Klein 1995a).

The 1980s and 1990s saw increased consumerism and individualism associated with the 'Citizen's Charter' series of initiatives. However, consumers did not have choice as in 'real' markets. Instead, they were to have information and a series of 'entitlements' but not legally enforceable rights. The guarantees of the Patient's Charter 'add to the rhetoric not to the reality of rights to health care' (Brazier 1993: 63). Performance targets would be published and aggrieved citizens would have 'well-posted avenues for complaint'. Some entitlements clarified existing ones, such as the right to be registered with a GP, some, such as courtesy and rights to information, were vague, and others gave entitlements but no legal redress, resulting in little more than an apology. It is claimed that the information 'will help you and your family doctor make informed decisions about your health care' and that 'You can influence the level and quality of service by making your views known – to your GP or direct to your local health authority' (DoH 1994: 4–5), but the mechanism of this influence is not specified.

In one sense, PIs went populist in the 1990s (Klein 1995a: 213), but while patients were armed with information, they could do nothing directly with it. They could not take their custom elsewhere in the NHS or shop around as, at least nominally, parents are able to do for their children's schools. They were not entitled to 'money-back' guarantees as in supermarkets or redress as in the case of the Passenger's Charter for British Rail. In other words, the mimic market produced a mimic consumerism (Klein 1995a: 212). Arguably, the information either did nothing or promoted increased expectations that led to discontent if they were not met. Recent government policy has carried with it an implicit assumption that greater consumer involvement in health care is both desirable and beneficial (North 1993; Shackley and Ryan 1994). However, it has been claimed that the limited scope of consumerism does little to empower patients (North 1993). Moreover, the existence of even this limited sense of consumerism is debateable since patients lack choice, which is fundamental to being a consumer. Contrary to the initial rhetoric of the internal market, it is not a case of 'money following the patients' but 'patients following the money'. In other words, patients are referred to providers that purchasers (DHA or GPBH) have contracts with: patients do not choose but rather are told where to consume. Moreover, even if they were able to act as consumers, there is little evidence that patients have much desire to do so (Shackley and Ryan 1994).

As Klein (1995a: 212–13) explains, the rights and standards published in the Patient's Charter were not particularly exigent. Like the 'Health of the Nation' targets, they appear to have been chosen largely because they were achievable. But, again, like the 'Health of the Nation', the symbolic importance of the Charter outweighed its immediate impact. It introduced a new rhetoric and a new set of expectations in the NHS, marking precisely the kind of shift of power from providers to consumers envisaged in the Griffiths report. The point is well illustrated by the standard for individual outpatient appointments. The fact that it was even necessary to make this a standard demonstrated the extent to which the NHS had been dominated by providers for the previous 40 odd years: the persistence of the custom of booking a batch of patients for the same appointment (usually the start of the clinic session) reflected the assumption that not a second of the consultant's time must be wasted but that the patient's waiting time was of no account.

The extent to which hospitals met the new targets was published in a comparative performance guide (DoH 1994). This covers targets such as waiting times in outpatient and accident and emergency departments, and waiting times for surgery. Stars were given for performance, as they are for children in an infant school. There were large variations both between and within hospitals. For example, in the South and West Region, the percentage of out-patients seen within 30 minutes varied from 63 per cent (*) to 100 per cent (*****). However, some hospitals that did well on some criteria did badly on others. For example, the United Bristol Healthcare Trust admitted 28 per cent of patients within three months for ear, nose and throat surgery (*), but 95 per cent for oral surgery (*****). The Winchester and Eastleigh Healthcare Trust carried out 7 per cent of cataract extractions by day surgery (*), but 92 per cent of its laparoscopy with sterilization in the same manner (*****). The Royal United Hospitals Bath NHS Trust saw 78 per cent of outpatients within 30 minutes (*), but assessed 95 per cent of accident and emergency patients within five minutes (*****). The next issue of the performance guide (DoH 1995) updated this information and added arrows to show whether a provider's performance had significantly increased or decreased. Many hospitals had increased their performance, but some were getting worse, and some hospitals were getting better in some areas, but declining in others. However, critics claimed that most of the information referred to waiting times and not to quality. Indeed, many of the most famous teaching hospitals in Britain found themselves at the bottom of the league tables, while little-known rural hospitals found themselves at the top. Under the headline 'Fury at teaching hospitals slur', an *Evening Standard* editorial claimed that:

> Only an idiot would put the finest teaching hospital in the world at the bottom of any ranking. But the Department of Health has managed it. . . . [They] have long waiting lists . . . because people want to use them. If you want to stay in a hotel you might not be able to get into the Ritz tonight. But finding a bed in an Edgware Road flop-house is no problem. According to Mrs Bottomley, the flop-house gets more stars than the Ritz.
>
> (Revill 1995)

The figures for 1995–6 (DoH 1996a) showed in the main con-tinued improvement, although critics continued to argue that they tended to remain invalid (measuring the wrong things) and unreli-able (measuring things inaccurately). Launching the 1995–6 league tables, Health Secretary Stephen Dorrell acknowledged wide-spread criticism that they did not go far enough, and did not rule out publishing in future clinical information such as death rates during and in the month after surgery and rates of wound infection after surgery.

The full implementation of 'Caring for People' came in 1993. This was likely to have three main effects for providers: first, the search for low-cost home care; second, the right to assessment of and consultation with clients; and third, a move away from the statutory sector into the mixed economy of welfare, in that 85 per cent of the budget had to be spent outside the public sector (Baldock and Ungerson 1994: 6). There was widespread scepticism among local authorities about the organizational principles underlying the changes, particularly about the capacity and quality of provision in the private and voluntary sector. Resources for inspection were limited and scandals over 'warehousing the elderly' occurred. There was 'near universal uncertainty and anxiety about resources' (Wistow *et al.* 1994: 68). However, while we know something of the concerns of directors and chairs of local authorities' social services committees (Wistow *et al.* 1994: ch. 4) we know little about the views of clients (but see Baldock and Ungerson 1994). Early indications are that, for many, the negative outcomes outweigh the positive. The services often fail to measure up to raised expectations. There is a lack of real choice, poor continuity of care resulting from the mix of provision, and the distribution of power between users on the one hand and purchasers and providers on the other remains unequal (Henwood 1995). Resource pressures in many areas clearly show that the system is not needs led, but rather cash led, in that although people are entitled to an assessment of their needs, local authorities have no obligation to meet them. In the case of the elderly, inadequate care may lead to neglect or great pressure on their informal carers. However, in the case of the mentally ill, there are examples of harm to themselves and others: one person entered the lions' enclosure at London Zoo; another killed a stranger on the London Underground.

There may now be a 'new consensus' on the NHS. The Labour Party has stated that it would neither continue with the internal market nor try to return to an old-style NHS but would offer a 'third way' (Beckett 1995), so affirming the purchaser/provider – or planning/delivery – split. However, the 'third way' would replace the market and competition with planning and cooperation. Rolling programmes or 'comprehensive healthcare agreements' would supplant year-on-year competition for contracts. It is claimed that these agreements would be very different from existing contracts.

First, they would not be along the lines of individual contracts to buy, say, 100 cataract or 50 hip operations (Beckett 1995: 13). But many existing 'block' contracts are not in this form. Moreover, the criteria of choice of the proposed agreements is far from clear: proximity, quality, costings, audit and comparative information on effectiveness are all mentioned. The Labour Party's attack on 'competition' may be anachronistic, since 'quietly in the night, competition in British health care has slipped away'. Markets and health care have been decoupled and the competition vogue may have had its day (Ham 1996: 70). Ministers certainly now longer talk the language of the market. Moreover, the 'market' was never as red in tooth and claw as favoured by its advocates or feared by its critics. There may, indeed, be much common ground between the political parties along 'the middle way between planning and competition' (Ham 1996).

The Labour plan of 1995 proposes that the governing bodies of trusts would be reconstituted to sweep away the 'one-party state', replacing it with 'representatives of patients, health professionals and people with local interests'. This appears to be a return to the health authorities roundly criticized by Labour in the past. Changing Tory for Labour nominees does not address the democratic deficit. It is axiomatic that nominated 'representatives' are rarely representative of their communities. The Labour retreat away from the elected authorities of 1943, despite the claim of Bevan (1978: 114) that 'election is a better principle than selection', continues. Moreover, while the Labour Party (1995: 19) complains that 'The government refuses to acknowledge, let alone take responsibility for, the chaos in the NHS', its policy statement has little to say about Parliamentary accountability and central–local relations.

It remains to be seen whether the differences between Labour and Conservatives are more than terminological (Paton 1995; Klein 1995b). Are the proposed comprehensive healthcare agreements (CHAs) merely a new name for the existing internal market contracts: the NHS's version of replacing the name of the unpopular nuclear reactor site at Windscale with the new name of Sellafield? As Klein (1995b: 76) says of the commitment to ending the internal market, there is less to this than meets the eye. Much of the Labour Party's 1995 document's 'policy fudge' (Klein 1995b: 76) relates to the problem of choosing between different providers. The other ingredients for an internal market are present. Is competition absent only in a terminological sense?

CONCLUSION

This brief journey through nearly 50 years of the NHS has revealed a number of themes. Some continuities may be observed. First, the NHS has always been liable to be described as in financial crisis: to some, it is a crisis of overspending, while to others it is one of under-spending. Expenditure will be examined in Chapter 5, but it is clearly a misuse of language to suggest that an organization can be in crisis for its entire history.

Second, another hardy perennial is the conflict between central accountability and local autonomy. Klein (1995a: 144) writes that the 'cycle of experiments with delegation quickly followed by rever-sion to centralisation provides ... one of the themes running through the history of the NHS'.

Third, the consumerism of the 1980s and 1990s is the 'soft consumerism' of the supermarket model, which does little to em-power the consumer (North 1993) or challenge the producers. Pro-fessional power in many areas – control of the area of work, power to define need, power in policy-making, power in resource allo-cation and power over people (Wilding 1982: ch. 2) – remains strong.

However, most commentators recognize a significant disconti-nuity: few would disagree with the WFP's proclamation as making the most far-reaching change in the NHS's 40-year history (Butler 1992; Holliday 1992). Although the internal market has been in operation for only a short time and it is difficult to disentangle its effects from all the other changes affecting the NHS, a preliminary assessment will be found in Chapters 5 and 6.

5

TEMPORAL EVALUATION

Temporal evaluation involves examining changes in the NHS over time. There are two main problems. First, what are the key indicators with which to measure the performance of the NHS? Second, to what extent are changes over the period of the NHS caused by the NHS? The first question is concerned with the level of change over the time period of the NHS. In other words, it seeks to establish whether there is an association between the existence of the NHS and changes over time. The second question examines the more difficult issue of the extent to which these changes are *caused by* the NHS, or whether they are caused by other factors and would have occurred with a different type of health-care system.

In crude terms the NHS can be thought of as a factory producing health. Inputs are combined in various ways to produce health-care outputs. However, health care is not valued as an end in itself. Rather, it is the means to the end of health. In other words, the NHS should, as far as possible, restore an individual to health (the curative function), provide care if restoring health is not possible (the caring function) and protect the individual from ill-health (the preventive function). However, in practice, the curative function has tended to dominate the NHS and the caring and preventive functions have been relatively neglected. It is perhaps more accurate to see the NHS as a garage: the human body is taken to the garage to be repaired after being damaged. The garage does little in the way of routine servicing of healthy bodies. Neither does it attempt much preventive work. Finally, the garage tends to lose interest if repair is not possible.

It is convenient to examine the NHS in the framework of inputs, outputs (or activity) and outcomes. Many people agree that the ultimate aim of the NHS is the optimum health of the population. In other words, the NHS should be judged by the health status of Britain. This is problematic for two main reasons. First, measuring 'health' is difficult. Indeed, it is generally 'ill-health', examined in terms of sickness (morbidity) or death (mortality), rather than health that is measured. Second, even if a perfect indicator of health were agreed, there is a large debate about the contribution of health care towards health. It is generally considered that the external environment (e.g. housing, unemployment, nutrition, pollution) affects health much more than health care. In other words, health is determined by factors outside rather than inside the NHS: the service's control over the major factors shaping health is extremely limited.

This chapter examines inputs, outputs and outcomes over time, and then examines the relationships between these, largely in terms of efficiency and effectiveness. (An examination of the topic of equity is given in Chapter 6.)

THE HEALTH PRODUCTION FUNCTION

'If there is one statistic with which the health of the NHS is (at least popularly) judged, it is the level of funding it receives' (Appleby 1992: 59). However, to extend one of the above analogies, this is like judging a factory on the amount of steel it uses rather than the product that it makes with this input. Money is certainly an indicator of the relative importance of the NHS in the eyes of the government in comparison with other areas of public expenditure such as education or defence. But an illness is not cured, just as a problem is not solved, by throwing money at it. Money is an input which is used to buy intermediate inputs such as doctors, nurses and drugs. The same amount of money can be spent in very different ways to purchase different bundles of health-care goods and services.

The production of health is a very labour-intensive process: over 50 per cent of the NHS budget goes towards staff salaries. In addition, other parts of current or revenue expenditure are used to purchase consumables such as drugs. In contrast, capital expenditure is used to buy items that can be consumed many times, such as hospital buildings and hospital beds.

Increasing the budget of the NHS has little *direct* impact on patients, as it mainly goes towards staff wages. A doctor or nurse with a pay increase is not automatically a better doctor or nurse. The pay increase may increase benefits to patients in a number of indirect ways. First, better pay may attract better-quality staff to the service. Second, it may increase staff morale, which may, in turn, lead to 'spin-off' benefits for patients. In contrast, money spent on drugs or new technologies may have a more direct benefit.

Staff carry out very different activities, for example surgical operations or physiotherapy. Staff tend to be very heterogeneous, both within and between categories. In other words, not only are doctors different from nurses, but they are also different from each other: for example, a cardiologist is not a good substitute for a geriatrician. The concept of professionalism is at the heart of this issue. Clinical freedom for doctors has always been guaranteed in the NHS. Non-clinicians such as managers, or indeed other doctors, cannot tell doctors what and how much to do – or, at least, this has been so until very recently, and it is too early to assess current indications of doctors' dissatisfaction with what they perceive as managerial constraints on their clinical decision-making. Some doctors may treat patients by means of chemotherapy, while others will decide to operate. Some doctors may treat patients in a day surgery, while others will treat them as inpatients, with differing lengths of stay. Finally, the workload, such as number of operations, between different doctors varies significantly (Ham 1988a).

Even if every patient in similar circumstances received the same treatment, it is likely that outcomes would differ. Just as no two doctors are exactly the same, neither are patients. Some patients may follow the doctor's prescribed regime exactly, while others may not. Even if they do follow advice, their circumstances may differ: one may be a smoker while another is not; one may go home to a damp house in contrast to the other; one may have family or community support, while another may have none. Thus, exactly the same clinical input may have very different impacts outside the surgery or hospital.

The production of health is therefore very complex. The relationships between inputs, outputs and outcomes are generally defined in terms of the 'three Es' – economy, effectiveness and efficiency (Carter *et al.* 1992). These terms are sometimes used in a different fashion by different authors, and so it is necessary to produce the definitions to be used here.

Economy

Economy is concerned merely with inputs, or cost-minimization. It is achieved with the cheapest option. However, the cheapest service is to provide no service. Thus, Carter *et al.* (1992: 37) see economy as the purchase and provision of services at the lowest possible cost consistent with a specified quality. Economy and efficiency are often confused in conceptual and in empirical terms. The main problem is in detecting whether like is being compared with like. An example is given by the contracting out of hospital 'hotel services' such as cleaning. The government has claimed that this policy led to increased efficiency – producing the same service with less money – while critics claimed that it was a false economy, as a worse job was produced for less money (Radical Health Statistics Group 1987: 122–30).

Effectiveness

Effectiveness 'is a concept that is fraught with ambiguity and confusion' (Carter *et al.* 1992: 38). It refers here to whether the process achieves its goal: in other words, whether it works. If the ultimate goal of the NHS is to achieve a healthy population, then an effective system is one that produces this. Effectiveness refers to the evaluation of outcome against a clearly stated objective. Evaluation of effectiveness is frequently hindered by the fact that objectives are not stated in terms that can be measured. We shall see in Chapter 6 that the apparently simple task of judging whether the NHS has kept to its original principles is a difficult one. For the moment, let us assume that the most important objective of the NHS is to achieve a healthy population. In other words, it should seek to reduce levels of morbidity and mortality or, in contemporary terminology, result in 'health gain'. Effectiveness can be thought of on macro- and micro-levels. The macro- or global level examines the extent to which the NHS as a whole contributes towards a healthy population. The micro-level examines the effectiveness of individual therapies, which is the domain of medical audit (Packwood *et al.* 1994) and of the randomized control trial (Cochrane 1972). However, the focus here is on the macro-level.

Efficiency

Efficiency may be divided into two different concepts. The narrowest may be termed 'operational efficiency' (Donaldson and Gerard 1993: 69). This refers to transforming inputs into outputs. In popular terms, it refers to 'productivity': whether a given process can achieve the same level of output with lower inputs, such as labour.

As Donaldson and Gerard (1993: 69–70) explain, operational efficiency asks the question, 'Given that some activity is worth doing, what is the best way of providing it?' Note that it is assumed that the activity is effective. It follows that, by this definition, ineffective therapies cannot be efficient, however inexpensive they are. Operational efficiency involves the selection between alternative means of achieving the same ends, and may therefore be interpreted as the pursuit of maximum output for a given level of resources, or minimum cost for a given level of output. For example, the question of operational efficiency would arise if a choice had to be made between an effective drug therapy and a surgical operation to treat a given condition. Assessments of the costs and effectiveness of each option determines which is the most operationally efficient. If one option is both cheaper and more effective, then it is clearly to be preferred. However, if one option is more expensive and more effective, then the cost–effectiveness ratio for both options must be calculated. The lower ratio – which is associated with less cost per unit of effectiveness – indicates greater operational efficiency.

The second and wider concept of efficiency is allocative efficiency (Donaldson and Gerard 1993: 70). In its broadest sense this is concerned with the returns to society associated with different activities. It may be applied to public spending as a whole. Does society prefer its money to be spent on defence or public services? Within public services should money be spent on education or health? Within the health field, should resources be switched from cure to prevention, from secondary to primary care, from acute provision to mental illness, from cardiac to hip surgery?

Many writers believe that what happens outside the NHS makes more difference to health status than what happens inside. In other words, health depends more on wider issues such as behaviour and the material environment (Townsend and Davidson 1982). On this view, money spent on improving the environment might have more of an impact on health status than if it were spent inside the NHS. The impact of medicine has been challenged by the 'professional dominance' and 'political economy' critiques (Allsop 1995: 141–7). Cochrane (1972) argues that many medical interventions remained matters of faith rather than proven by science. He advocates 'randomized control trials' (RCTs), which would subject therapies to scientific rigour and only those that had proved their effectiveness should be used. The historical debate on the efficacy of medical care is associated with the work of McKeown (1976), who argues that the improvements in health as shown by the decline in mortality rates of the nineteenth and early twentieth century was due more to social and economic factors, notably improved nutrition, than to the efforts of the medical profession. As Klein (1989: 166–9) notes, 'the case for the prosecution' (minimizing the contribution of health care towards health) is based on mortality rates, and neglects the issue of morbidity, or illness. It examines only the role of medical care in adding years to life rather than life to years: the quantity rather than the quality of life. It implicitly assumes that all the effort of the NHS goes into prolonging life. In fact, it is likely that only a small proportion of the NHS budget is spent in this way. For every life-saving operation there are many which make the quality of life better, such as cataract removal, hernia repair or hip surgery. Moreover, if the sole aim of the NHS was to extend life, this would suggest that all money should be spent on 'cure' as opposed to 'care'. To evaluate the NHS solely in terms of mortality rates is clearly only a partial view. A recent attempt to measure the effects of medical care (Bunker *et al.* 1994) concluded that clinical preventive services such as screening and immunization added some 1.5 years to life expectancy in the current century, with clinical curative services accounting for a further 3.5 years. Quality-of-life benefits were more difficult to estimate, but 'millions of people have experienced relief of pain and improvement of function from the use of therapeutic drugs, surgery, medical management, and medical devices' (p. 242).

Moreover, the McKeown thesis has been criticized for giving credit to nutrition without allowing for other possible factors such as public health provision (Szreter 1988, 1994; Guha 1994). Similarly, Klein (1989: 171–7) has criticized the 'social engineering' solutions of the Black report, which saw the solution to health inequalities primarily in terms of an anti-poverty programme. While Klein does not doubt the general relationship between poverty and ill-health, he points out that social engineering lacks a precise knowledge of the causal relationship between socio-economic conditions and health, and it therefore advocates the blunt instruments of general solutions rather than specific policy tools. In short, it is ironic that while medical engineering has been criticized partly on the basis of the lack of scientific evaluation in the shape of RCTs, the social alternative has been even less subjected to them.

Within the NHS, resource allocation has often been decided on the basis of historical accident or professional power rather than any more rational mechanism. Some health economists have argued that the NHS should maximize the level of total benefits from a given level of expenditure by changing its pattern of treatments or priorities. In other words, the rational NHS must be a cost-effective service and must compare the return on society's investment achieved by putting money into different treatments. This requires a common currency of comparison. As we saw above, mortality rates are insufficient because they examine the length of life and not its quality. A basis for comparison must be able to compare such diverse activities as life-saving operations, cataract surgery and caring for long-term patients. Reisman (1993: chs 10, 11) explains that while cost-effectiveness examines the cost of reaching a specified goal by alternative means or squeezing the most out of a set budget towards a set task (operational efficiency), cost-benefit is more ambitious, in that it looks at competing ends or different ways of spending the budget on different treatments. Crudely, it asks if treatment is worth doing, bearing in mind that the money could be spent elsewhere. This is inevitably a controversial issue. One study examined the costs and benefits of neonatal intensive care: 'Solomon will tut-tut and Hippocrates will look askance, but what they found was that it would be an inefficient use of scarce resources to minimise the number of infants dying' (Reisman 1993: 237).

One method that has been proposed to compare the costs and benefits of different treatments is the 'quality-adjusted life year' (QALY) (Mooney 1994: chs 2, 4): the cost of delivering a year of life at some defined level of quality. In other words, the measure claims to capture aspects both of quantity and quality of life in a single index. While measures of operational efficiency can tell us whether we should treat varicose veins by drugs or by surgery, this wider measure of allocative efficiency can tell us whether we should be putting more money into varicose veins or heart transplants. Some procedures yield a QALY at relatively low cost: for example, neurological intervention for head injury costs £240 per QALY (all data from Allsop 1995: 348). However, neurosurgical intervention for malignant intracranial tumours costs £107,780 per QALY. Thus, the former is QALY-efficient, buying nearly 450 QALYs for the same cost of one QALY of the latter. A rational service would try to buy as many QALYs as possible for its money. This might mean a variety of changes, such as home rather than hospital haemo-dialysis, buying hip joint replacements rather than heart transplants and more 'advice' and prevention than treatment. By these means, the National Health Service should also become the Rational Health Service.

An experiment to purchase health care using similar 'rational' principles has been carried out in the state of Oregon in the USA. Cost-benefit data on treatments were collected and then, after some public consultation, a ranking was drawn up. Of the 709 treatments, there was money available to fund the most cost-effective 587. There was no money for the less cost-effective treatments, such as those for varicose veins and babies of extremely low birthweight (Baggott 1994a: 55; Honigsbaum *et al.* 1995). There has been no wholesale introduction of QALY principles in Britain, although some DHAs have announced that they will not purchase treatments such as tattoo removal and some fertility treatment.

TEMPORAL EVALUATION

In the 1980s the 'three Es' – economy, effectiveness and efficiency – gained wide currency at all levels of government. However, it has been claimed that economy and efficiency were emphasized at the expense of effectiveness, and a further 'alphabet of evaluation' has been proposed, including efficacy, electability and equity and acceptability and availability (Carter *et al.* 1992: 37–41). This section aims to examine changes in the NHS over time. First, indicators of inputs, outputs and outcomes are examined (compare Le Grand *et al.* 1990; Mohan 1995). Inputs include expenditure, staff and capital resources. Outputs (activity) focus on the number of patients treated, while outcomes refer to the state of health of the population. Then, relationships between these indicators are examined. In particular, the focus is on efficiency, effectiveness and consumer satisfaction.

Inputs

Expenditure

There can be little doubt that on almost any definition of input the NHS has expanded since 1948. The most obvious type of input is money (Table 5.1). In crude or nominal expenditure terms, NHS expenditure has increased from £437 million in 1948–9 to over £42,000 million in 1995–6, an increase of nearly 100-fold. It has increased its share of national wealth, accounting for 3.50 per cent of GDP in 1949 rising to 5.75 per cent in 1996. In terms of its priority within public expenditure, it rose from 11.8 per cent in 1949 to 14.9

Table 5.1 NHS expenditure, 1949 and 1996

	1949	1996
NHS expenditure (£m)	437	42,691
NHS adjusted expenditure (£m at 1949 prices)	437	2169
Index at 1949 prices (£)	100	496
NHS expenditure as % of GDP	3.50	5.75
NHS expenditure as % of public expenditure	11.8	14.9
NHS expenditure per person (£)	9	727
Index per person at 1949 prices (£)	100	422

Source: OHE (1995).

per cent in 1995, overtaking defence in 1986 to become the second largest component behind social security with 34.8 per cent in 1988 (Appleby 1992: 33). These figures need to be adjusted in two ways: first for changing population size, and second for changing prices, or inflation. In terms of total cost per head this translates into a rise from £9 in 1949 to £727 in 1996, or about 80 times the 1949 figure. However, prices have also risen since the 1940s and there is a need to adjust these raw figures to take account of inflation. When this is done the NHS spent over four times as much in 'real terms' in 1996 as in 1949. The general inflation figure is not really meaningful for the NHS since it refers to general price rises in the economy as a whole. The NHS buys a basket of health-care goods and services such as the wages of doctors and nurses, drugs and so on. In other words, a special figure for inflation, specific to the NHS, must be calculated. When this is done, the NHS spends a little over twice as much as it did in 1948. This translates into an annual increase of just under 2 per cent (Appleby 1992: 34).

The amount of NHS expenditure has always been an issue, whether in terms of under- or overfunding. However, in the 1980s it became both a crisis and a paradox. The government claimed that the NHS was improving, with record levels of expenditure and activity, while the opposition pointed to cuts and closures in the service. To some extent, both these accounts are correct. In 'objective' terms, NHS expenditure certainly rose in the 1980s in 'real' terms, whether this is measured by 'general' or 'health-specific' inflation. However, it is also true that the impact of closures and cuts were felt. This apparent discrepancy is partly explained by - disaggregating the expenditure figures. Expenditure for the cash-limited hospital and community health services (HCHS) increased more slowly than that for the demand-led family practitioner ser-vices (FPS) (see Ham 1992: 41–2). The areas that experienced the slowest increases in spending were the 'RAWPed' Thames regions (Mohan 1995: 80). Adding the geographical and sectoral trends together, the parts of the NHS that were under the greatest finan-cial pressure were the hospitals in the south east in general, and the teaching hospitals in inner London in particular. Thus, the greatest pain was felt in precisely those areas whose protests would be felt most – those near to the centre of the medical elite, the media and the heart of government.

Moreover, the issue was not really about whether the NHS was spending more, but rather about whether it was spending enough. In other words, the question was in terms of keeping pace with the changing level of need. Critics examined this issue in two broad ways. The first involved extrapolating past NHS expenditure. Last year's expenditure is used as a baseline, and adjustments are made for 'NHS inflation' (the increase of relevant prices such as staff salaries and the cost of drugs) and increases to account for demography (the 'greying' of the population) and technology (the introduction of new medical technologies). There are a number of problems with this approach. First, some of the factors are difficult to quantify. This applies particularly to new technologies, some of which may reduce costs (Ham 1992: 250). Second, the calculations build in expectations. Assuming that new technologies are beneficial, the measuring yard-stick is calibrated not for a static NHS, but for an expanding one: to incorporate expectations of the benefits of new treatments. While more money is needed with respect to demography in order to stand still, more money for technology is needed in order to move forward. Third, this method assumes that last year's budget is the appropriate starting point. Thus, it is assumed that at one time, presumably the default value of 1948, the NHS was fully funded. The second method involves comparing NHS expenditure with that of health services in other countries. This assumes that all other factors are equal and that expenditure (input) is the most relevant index of comparison. Both assumptions are problematic (see Chapter 7). To some extent, both approaches used the measuring rod as a stick with which to beat the government rather than an objective measure. If pursued consist-ently, both methods would tend to show that the NHS has always been underfunded.

Klein (1995a: 178–83) terms the 'underfunding debate of the 1980s' the 'dialogue of the deaf', between the 'inputters' and the 'outputters'. While the critics examined the input of expenditure, the government pointed to the output of the NHS: what it was actually producing. As the Prime Minister's Efficiency Unit argued, 'There is too little emphasis on the results to be achieved from resources . . . the Government is judged by what money goes in [to public services] and not what comes out' (quoted in Allsop 1995: 169). In one respect the government was correct: it is not cash, but the things bought with that cash that are important. What intermediate inputs did the NHS buy with this extra money?

Staff

The first intermediate input is staff (Table 5.2). There were some 15,000 hospital doctors in Britain in 1951, a figure which had grown to over 57,000 by 1995. In terms of a ratio per 100,000 population, the figures are 29 and 98, a rise of some 240 per cent. Over the same period hospital nursing and midwifery staff increased from 189,000 to 473,000, or 375 to 794 per 100,000 population, an increase of about 110 per cent. The NHS has also seen large increases in the number of professional/technical and administrative/clerical staff. Indeed, the latter group has grown by more than twice the rate of hospital doctors. There has been a fall in the number of domestic

Table 5.2 NHS staffing, 1951 and 1995

	1951	1995
Hospital medical and dental staff	14,777	57,419
per 100,000 population	29	98
Hospital nursing and midwifery staff	188,580	473,042
per 100,000 population	375	794
Professional and technical staff	14,110	125,119
Administrative and clerical staff	29,021	213,873
Domestic ancillary staff	163,666	100,648
Total hospital staff	410,154	970,101
Unrestricted GPs	20,179	32,865
per 100,000 population	40.1	56.1
Resident population per unrestricted GP	2492	1782
Dental practitioners	11,279	18,529
per 100,000 population	22.4	31.7
Optical practitioners	7334*	12,071
per 100,000 population	16.9	20.7

Source: Office of Health Economics (1995).
* 1949 figure.

ancillary staff after reaching a peak in 1982, as a result of the contracting out of 'hotel services'. In total, there are now over twice as
many NHS staff working in hospitals as compared with 1949.
Outside the secondary or hospital sector, staff numbers grew more
slowly. GPs (unrestricted principals) increased from some 20,000 in
1951 for Britain to nearly 33,000 in 1995, or 40 to about 56 per
100,000 population, a rise of 40 per cent. The increases for dentists
and opticians were about 40 per cent and 22 per cent, respectively.

However, critics have pointed out that figures such as these need
to be qualified (RSHG 1987). For example, the figures for nurses
refer to all full-time and part-time staff, and need to be translated
into full-time equivalents. The working week of nurses was reduced
from 40 to 37.5 hours per week in 1980, which meant that for the
same number of nurses 6 per cent fewer hours were available. It has
been claimed that nurses now perform some of the tasks formerly
carried out by ancillary staff (RSHG 1987: 51; Audit Commission
1991).

Qualitative issues are even more problematic than these quantitative ones. Many GPs now work in large partnerships and fewer
work alone. A parallel trend has seen the development of more
primary-care teams including GPs, health visitors, district nurses
and others. For many years it has been claimed that this increased
teamwork yields benefits both for doctors and patients. An even
more complex issue concerns the quality of training and of staff
themselves. Are doctors and nurses of the same quality as they were
50 years ago?

Beds

In contrast to the staffing figures, the number of beds has fallen
(Table 5.3). After reaching a peak in 1957 the number of NHS beds
has fallen almost continually. There are three basic reasons for this
decline. First, changing patterns of disease mean that the need for
beds has changed. For example, there is now less need for beds for
people with tuberculosis or other infectious diseases, as these diseases have declined over time. Second, fewer beds are needed as
the average length of hospital stay has declined (see Table 5.4).
Third, since the 1950s there has been a policy of closing long-stay
hospitals in favour of community care. This is shown by a sectoral
variation. For the period 1959–95, the number of total beds fell by
about 50 per cent. However, the numbers of mental illness beds
and mental handicap beds fell by 77 per cent and 78 per cent,

Table 5.3   NHS beds, 1959 and 1995

	1959	1995
Available beds	542,000*	285,000
Available beds per 100,000 population	10.8*	4.9
Average daily available beds:		
Acute care	183,000	130,000
Mental illness	178,000	40,000
Mental handicap	64,000	14,000
Geriatric care	62,000	52,000

Source: Office of Health Economics (1995).
* 1951 figures.

respectively. In particular, recent years have seen the continuation of a long trend of closing older, small hospitals. For non-psychiatric hospitals, 49 per cent of beds were in hospitals with fewer than 250 beds in 1959, as compared with 34 per cent in 1989. On the other hand, psychiatric hospitals have seen the opposite trend, with the disappearance of the old 2000-bed, remote asylums and the growth of smaller units. For example, in 1959, 7 per cent of psychiatric beds were in units of fewer than 250 beds and 71 per cent were in units of over 1000 beds; by 1989 the figures were 22 per cent and 4 per cent, respectively.

Not all closures of wards or hospitals are necessarily a bad thing (Social Services Committee 1988: 14). Many hospitals in Britain tend to be old and unsatisfactory in some ways. The government claimed that new facilities often replace old, outdated and inefficient hospitals, thereby providing a better health-care environment for patients and a more productive and efficient working environment for staff (DHSS annual report for 1985, quoted in RSHG 1987: 58). However, many closed hospitals were treasured by the local community as prized and accessible assets, and the substitutes are often seen as remote and inaccessible.

Tables 5.1 to 5.3 show a clear difference in the trends for inputs. Expenditure and staff have increased, but hospital beds have decreased. For staff, the pattern of growth shows the largest increases in the ordering of hospital doctors, hospital nurses and GPs. The allocation of the NHS budget has also varied over time. Hospitals have always been dominant in the NHS in the sense that they have always taken over half the budget. In fact, the 'hospital centredness' (Davies 1979) of the NHS has increased, hospitals taking 51.3 per cent of expenditure in 1951, rising to 67.2 per cent in 1972, although it had fallen to 54.2 per cent by 1995. Generally speaking, in terms of the rise in expenditure, the hospitals' poor relations have been the family practitioner and community services, although there are signs that this is now changing with the slogan of a 'primary-care-led NHS' (NHS Executive 1996). Similarly, capital expenditure has always suffered in comparison with revenue expenditure. The NHS was slow to build new hospitals and British hospitals were renewed at a slower rate than those of other countries.

There are two main problems in the data in tables 5.1 to 5.3. First, individual elements tend to be seen in isolation rather than as a part of the wider health-care system. Second, within hospitals, a similar isolated supremacy tends to be given to the number of beds as opposed to any other indicator of activity. In short, the symbol of health provision is the hospital, and the symbol of the hospital is the bed.

It is clear that health care is an interactive system: one component cannot be examined in isolation from the others. For example, government policy since 1959 has been to replace long-stay hospitals with 'care in the community'. In the capital, an official body set up to advise on changes in health care, the London Advisory Group (LAG), recommended that savings from the run-down of the acute sector should be used to develop neglected aspects of care. Thus, 'the proposed reduction in acute beds should free resources some of which could be used to develop services for the elderly, mentally ill and handicapped and a variety of community services' (London Advisory Group 1981: 10). This theme was repeated in a later official report: 'In inner London the overwhelming emphasis historically has been on hospital facilities; the potential scale of substitution between secondary and primary care is considerable. This trend requires a shift in the balance of expenditure between the acute, and the primary and community services' (Tomlinson 1992: 8). In its response to the Tomlinson report, the government accepted that 'There will be more cost effective care outside hospital. . . . The community is the future setting of much health care' (DoH 1993a: 6–7). It has been claimed that better and more accessible primary care can reduce the need for inpatient care and accident and emergency services. For example, London accident and emergency departments tend to receive many patients who, away from London, would have gone to their GP. Patients are kept in hospital longer than necessary because of inadequate local health and social services (DoH 1993a: 4). London's primary and community health services are often claimed to be of poorer quality than those of many other parts of the country (DHSS 1981; Eyles *et al.* 1982; King's Fund 1992; Tomlinson 1992). In short, it is claimed that the balance of care in London must change: as acute care is rationalized, primary and community care must be developed (King's Fund 1992; Tomlinson 1992; DoH 1993a).

Traditionally, the hospital and the community were seen as different parts of the NHS, with separate budgets. The patient ceased to be a drain on the hospital budget on discharge. However, the cost of the patient's future care would be transferred to the community budget of the NHS, the social services budget of the local authority, or often the financial and time budget of unpaid care by relatives, friends and neighbours in the shape of care *by* the community rather than *in* the community. As hospitals are usually the most expensive part of the health-care budget, this strategy was always likely to reduce total expenditure and certainly did so when it relied on the moral blackmail and enforced altruism of unpaid carers, possibly with detrimental impacts on their own health. Sometimes people were discharged to the very conditions that had contributed to their illness in the first place, but the problems of damp, over-crowded, cold housing or of lack of housing (homelessness) were not the responsibility of the NHS, even though there are obvious health consequences. There have been some creations in the 1990s of hospital and community trusts that should in theory reduce the problems of coordination and budgets, although coordination with local authorities may still be problematic. There is much talk of 'bed blocking', particularly with respect to the elderly, who often continue to occupy expensive hospital beds as they cannot be discharged because of the lack of suitable facilities in the community. In short, the 'joint approach to social policy' is still the exception rather than the norm.

There is some doubt as to whether such stress should be placed on bed–population ratios (Klein 1989: 52–3, 233). The debate is still conducted in terms of the extent to which an area is 'over-bedded'. However, some 40 years ago, George (now Sir George) Godber, at that time Deputy Chief Medical Officer at the Ministry of Health, stated:

Hospitals are commonly described in terms of the number of beds they contain, and in former times these figures would have given some estimate of the work that was done; but that is no longer true. A hospital is primarily a diagnostic and treatment centre at which some of the patients must stay. . . . Beds can be used in different ways and at different speeds

(Godber 1958: 4)

In an article entitled 'The Golden Bed', Robert Kemp, a hospital physician, attacked the bed as the sacred symbol of medicine and the equation of the bed with healing (Kemp 1964). With the development of outpatient departments and day surgery, the argument of these articles is probably even more valid today. When asked in 1985 about bed closures, Health Minister Kenneth Clarke replied, 'I see no sensible purpose in keeping centrally a full inventory of furniture in each of our hospitals' (quoted in RSHG 1987: 58).

Beds are therefore only one measure of input. Perhaps the quantity and quality of staffing is a more important input. Staff constitute the largest element of health-care expenditure, and it is arguable that in resource terms the question is more concerned with being 'over-staffed' than 'over-bedded'. There is some scope for substitution between 'new' and 'old' beds, beds and staff (resource or production mix) and between staff and other staff (labour or 'skill mix'). The new drugs of the 1940s substituted to some extent for prolonged labour inputs, especially from nurses. It is possible that the NHS has needed more staff because the fewer beds and shorter lengths of stay mean that patients are usually more sick and therefore need more labour input than in former times. The basic point of skill mix is that it is not economic to have a highly paid person do a job when a cheaper person can do it equally well. Recent years have seen a large rise in the number of practice nurses who, for example, can take blood pressure as well as the doctor. There is much talk of the 'nurse practitioner' occupying an intermediate position between the traditional roles of the doctor and the nurse.

Outputs

The outputs of the NHS have also seen large increases over time. However, there are conceptual and empirical problems with this. First, we do not know if it is 'good' or 'bad'. From one point of view, the NHS is treating more people. From another, it could indicate that the population is more ill, and the NHS is failing. It is probable that the first explanation is closer to the truth. More activity is probably due to two main reasons. First, increasing medical technology means that treatments are now available for conditions that were previously untreatable. Second, people tend to live longer, resulting in more elderly people, both in absolute terms and as a percentage of the total population: the 'greying of the population'. Crudely, the NHS increases demands for its services by extending life expectancy for the elderly, and by keeping alive those who would have died previously. In other words, increasing activity is necessary to respond to higher levels of need in the population, that, paradoxically, is 'healthier' in the sense of living longer, but is 'less healthy' than were earlier shorter-lived populations, in that the longer lifespans entail special needs for health care.

Patients treated

The empirical problems relate to how NHS activity is measured. For many years, NHS activity was measured in terms of deaths and discharges (D&Ds). This implied that, mathematically, a death was equivalent to a discharge, implying that 110 deaths were 'better' than 100 discharges. More recent measurement is in terms of 'finished consultant episodes' (FCEs). Activity in terms of D&Ds increased until the mid-1980s and FCEs have risen since then (Table 5.4). However, it is difficult accurately to chart the trend over the long term, because of this change in measurement. It has been claimed that FCEs tend to inflate the figures, as one hospital stay (one D&D in the old currency) may now contain treatment under a number of different consultants, for example casualty and a

Table 5.4 NHS activity, 1951 and 1995

	1951	*1995*
Available beds per medical and dental staff	37	5
FCE per medical and dental staff	258	179
Available beds per nursing and midwifery staff	2.9	0.6
FCE per nursing and midwifery staff	20.2	22.1
Average daily occupied beds (%)	87	80
Deaths and discharges per available bed	7.2	35.0
FCE per 1000 beds	18*	57
FCE per 1000 acute beds	64*	130
Average length of stay (days)	45	8

Source: Office of Health Economics (1995).
* 1959 figures.

number of different departments (RSHG 1994). Another problem is that the data do not separate new admissions from readmissions (RSHG 1987, 1994). In other words, increased activity may not be due to more new patients being treated, but to people being re-admitted to hospital. Indeed, if patients are discharged too early, there is likely to be an increased probability of a return to hospital for a further spell of treatment.

Waiting lists

Despite the large increase in the number of cases treated in hospital in the first 20 years of the NHS, the waiting lists for admission remained steady at around half a million people, or around 10 people per 1000 population. Moreover, the mean waiting time hovered around 14 weeks (Cooper 1975: 22–4). The waiting lists reached about 0.75 million in the 1970s and were generally below 0.7 million until they rose to 0.876 million in 1988, hitting the politically sensitive figure of 1.0 million in 1994 (Holliday 1992; Mohan 1995). As Holliday (1992: 30) argues, waiting lists are popularly held to be a clear indication of NHS underfunding. However, rather than being a reliable and objective measure of need, waiting lists are unreliable and in many ways subjective, an unscientific measure of NHS resource gaps (Yates 1987; Frankel 1989; Holliday 1992: 31). Frankel (1989) points out that waiting lists are largely accounted for by a few specialties and, indeed, a small number of conditions. In general, they tend to reflect conditions low in the list of priorities of professionals and the public. In many ways, more important than the size of the queue is the speed with which it is moving. Frankel (1989) calculated that for 1987 the number of waiting patients represented some 14 per cent of the inpatient throughput of the NHS. Put another way, the NHS was simply keeping, on average, six weeks' work in hand. The length of time on a waiting list has been declining lately and is featured in the Patient's Charter (see below).

Consumer satisfaction

The NHS, one of the most popular institutions in Britain, has had a relatively bad press in recent years. It has rarely been out of public and political debate, and at times has been at the centre of such debate (for example, Timmins 1988; Social Services Committee 1988: 5–7). Its popularity rating has dipped, albeit still retaining levels that other services might aspire to. While the British public remains strongly committed to the idea of the NHS, it has become increasingly dissatisfied with the current state of the service. Overall dissatisfaction levels as revealed by the British Social Attitudes surveys rose from 26 per cent in 1983 to 47 per cent in 1987 (Holliday 1992: 4; Judge and Solomon 1993), although there are signs of some increases in satisfaction in the 1990s (RSHG 1994). There has been a rise in the numbers of complaints. However, it is difficult to detect the main reason for this. Is it due to a deterioration in the service or due to an increased propensity to complain? It may be due to a more consumerist attitude towards the NHS in general, and to expectations associated with the Patient's Charter. It is possible that people feel that it is easier to complain nowadays.

There has been an increase in the use of consumer satisfaction surveys. However, their value is unclear, owing to problems of consumer sovereignty (can lay people judge good medical care?) and perhaps to an unwillingness to criticize doctors (Roberts 1990: ch. 6; Nzegwu 1993: 15–25; Phillips *et al.* 1994: ch. 6). Two anecdotes may illustrate this point. First, it is said that all consumer satisfaction surveys in health show that 70 per cent are satisfied. The second, concerning the 'research methods' of a member of a visiting party to an outpatient department in the 1930s, is given by Prochaska (1992: 126). One visitor argued that waiting did not matter. To prove his point he went to a long queue of miserable people waiting for the dispensary and seized a little man by the shoulder, swung him round and said, 'You like waiting, don't you?' To which the terrified man replied, 'Oh yessir, yessir, yessir!' He turned to the party and said, 'You see – they like waiting!'

The main problem associated with consumer dissatisfaction remains waiting lists for elective surgery, but the almost daily media coverage of closed beds and cancellations (e.g. Timmins 1988; Social Services Committee 1988) must have contributed to the feeling of dissatisfaction. It remains unclear whether this dissatisfaction is due to a personal contact with the NHS or merely a second-hand impression via the media. There always have been hospital and bed closures, but they appeared to have increased prominence in the 1980s. Moreover, there is a clear difference between planned closures and unplanned ones that are due to financial reasons (Social Services Committee 1988: 15–16). Responses to financial pressures included a range of measures including closures, temporary closures (now occurring in January or February rather than the 'traditional' closures in March, at the end of the financial year), five-day wards and newly built accommodation and newly installed equipment lying idle (Mohan 1995: 82–4) – all occurring while waiting lists lengthened. Many GPs pointed to the difficulties of getting patients admitted to hospitals, and many doctors seemed to spend most of their time not practising their clinical skills, but practising their telephone manner, trying to find an empty bed for patients. London, in particular, experienced many 'yellow alerts' (admitting only a certain proportion of non-emergencies) and 'red alerts' (admitting emergencies only). Patients had operations cancelled close to or on the day of admission, some more than once. Sometimes patients have been transported long distances by road or air to the nearest empty bed. On admission, some patients faced occupancy rates of over 100 per cent, resulting in their waiting for beds on trolleys and in corridors for prolonged periods, in addition to the mysterious practice of 'hotbedding': placing inpatients in a day room so that day surgery patients can use their beds.

Outcomes

In some ways, health in contemporary Britain is at its highest ever level. For example, infant and perinatal mortality rates have never been lower (DoH 1993b: 2). However, improvements are not uniform and there are some causes for concern, such as the marked rise in suicides among young males, levels of smoking, drinking, diet and exercise and the record levels of notifications of drug addicts (DoH 1993b: 3). As Jacobson *et al.* (1991: 9–13) point out, some areas of health are improving, in others progress has been mixed, in others there has been little change over the past decade, and in others it is getting worse.

If examining trends over time with respect to inputs, outputs and outcomes is difficult, then examining the relationships between these variables is even more so.

Efficiency

Measuring efficiency is a difficult task. Operational efficiency is concerned with the ratio between inputs and outputs. However, specifying outputs is difficult. In fact, some indicators of 'efficiency' are ratios between inputs, such as the cost per bed rather than the cost per patient. The fact that the number of hospital beds has declined while staff have increased means that hospital beds are now more intensively staffed. This has implications for measuring efficiency. The NHS is treating more patients in fewer beds and is, in these terms, more efficient. Table 5.4 shows that patient activity per bed has increased between three- and fivefold between the 1950s and the 1990s. This is largely due to a dramatic reduction in the average length of stay. However, as Klein (1982: 392) points out, it is staff rather than the beds themselves that cost money. If productivity is examined in terms of the ratio between staff and the number of patients treated, then a very different pattern seems to emerge. The number of staff has increased faster than the number of patients and so efficiency has decreased. Table 5.4 shows that between 1951 and 1995 hospital deaths and discharges per medical and dental staff decreased from 258 to 179, while the figures for nursing and midwifery staff were fairly similar.

However, these crude calculations make a number of assumptions that patient needs and treatments do not vary over time. First, uniform effectiveness is assumed. Treatments have improved in many areas and so the 'value added' to patients' health may be greater. Second, the increasing throughput with respect to beds has been achieved with shorter lengths of stay. One reason for this might be the changing disease pattern. For example, the length of stay in 1948 included many long stays for tuberculosis. Now there are very few cases of this disease and drug treatments introduced since 1948 mean that stays are much shorter. Similarly, for many years there has been a policy of 'de-institutionalization' or closing down many long-stay hospitals and treating people in the community. Moreover, new drugs and anaesthetics mean that stays are generally shorter for the same circumstances. There has been a trend towards day surgery and outpatient treatment. However, we do not know if there has been a human cost to offset the financial savings. There is much anecdotal evidence that people are discharged too soon – that is, before they should be in clinical terms – and the reason seems to be financial pressure. Moreover, it has been claimed that there is some degree of 'bounce': patients being re-admitted soon after discharge. With the available statistics it is very difficult to separate out new from readmitted patients.

Crude examinations of efficiency in the NHS can be made with the package of PIs. A more sophisticated approach may be found in the work of the Audit Commission (for example 1990, 1991). Its basic methodology is similar to medical audit. It involves examining indicators of efficiency between different units, which may be wards, hospitals or health authorities. It is usually seen that there is a large variation between the units that cannot be easily explained in terms of factors such as case mix. The implicit assumption appears to be that performance levels below those of the best units are due to 'inefficiency'. The Commission encourages all authorities to reach the levels of efficiency displayed in the best cases by spreading 'best practice', and gives estimates of money that could be saved or the extra number of patients who could be treated if all units performed as well as the best ones.

Effectiveness

The ultimate and most obvious indicator of NHS success is its impact on health status. The 1946 Act set the goal of securing 'improvement in the physical and mental health of the people'. More recently, Sir Kenneth Stowe, the Permanent Secretary at the Department of Health and Social Security, in 1982 said that the end-product of the NHS is whether it makes patients better or cured – 'that is the supreme performance indicator' (quoted in Klein 1982: 401). The Royal Commission on the NHS (1979) and Ham (1992) examine health trends over time. They compare recent death rates with those at the beginning of the NHS. There is certainly a significant improvement in mortality, but:

> the question arises how far these improvements can be attributed to the NHS. In one sense it is impossible to answer because there is no way of knowing what would have happened if the NHS had not been introduced in 1948. It is likely that mortality rates would have fallen, as they have in comparable countries whatever the organisation of health services.
> (Royal Commission on the NHS 1979: 21)

A more limited approach examines not all deaths but 'avoidable deaths'. These are deaths resulting from diseases for which mortality is largely avoidable given appropriate medical intervention (Charlton *et al.* 1983). These avoidable deaths have been almost halved in the period 1979–92, with the figures for individual conditions varying from 14 per cent of the 1979 value for chronic rheumatic heart disease for ages up to 44, to 68 per cent for cervical cancer for ages 15–64 and asthma for ages 5–44 (DoH 1993c).

'More of the same'?

It is often claimed that 'additional resources and more hospital beds are needed to meet the medicosocial needs' of deprived areas (Avery-Jones 1976: 1048). In other words, it is sometimes assumed that the existing package of services is the best available and improvements will result from increasing the size of the package ('more of the same') without a consideration of its structure or content. However, it is by no means clear that 'more of the same' is the best response to such needs (Mays and Bevan 1987: 71, 79). As a former Minister of Health has put it, the NHS is 'spending money in the wrong places and on the wrong priorities' (Owen 1988: 155). In particular, it has been said that the NHS is too much oriented towards cure as opposed to prevention, and to secondary as opposed to primary care. In this view, the balance of resources ought to be changed towards preventive measures, including expenditure on the social environment outside the NHS, such as improving housing, reducing levels of unemployment and pollution, and towards services outside the hospitals.

> The calculation of any input–output coefficients implies precise knowledge of the relevant technical production process, which may be fairly straightforward in the case of how much coal, iron ore, and limestone is needed for a ton of pig iron, but less so with respect to the most efficient way of ensuring that a newly-born child survives to its first birthday.
> (Eyles *et al.* 1982: 241)

In order to achieve this objective, should resources be put into more quantity or quality of GPs, health visitors, midwives, hospital doctors or hospital beds, or to reducing social deprivation? It is hardly surprising that we have few answers to such difficult questions, but it is surprising that they have rarely been asked. Inertia and vested interests have combined to ensure that resource allocation tends to be incremental, and the 'RCT' debate about the best way of spending money has hardly begun. There is much talk of 'effective health care' and 'evidence-based medicine', essentially talking the language of Cochrane (1972) some quarter century after publication, but it is too early to see if this new industry is producing much in the way of useful output.

Conclusion

So, by most criteria, the NHS has changed significantly since its creation in 1948. It now spends more in real terms, and employs more staff, but has fewer beds. The NHS's record on efficiency is unclear since it is more efficient in terms of patients per bed, but less efficient in terms of patients per member of staff. Its record on effectiveness is difficult to assess since while there has been a decline in mortality rates over time, the NHS's contribution to it is unclear. Moreover, the rate of change has not been constant over time. As Table 5.5 shows, the greatest growth rates of expenditure and staff (and lowest rates of decline for beds) were in the 1960s and 1970s, with slower growth in the initial period of the service and in the most recent decade. Indeed, the number of nurses has fallen in the period 1983–92, and the decline in the number of beds has been marked. However, 'efficiency' in the form of FCE per medical staff and the average length of stay has seen significant advances compared with earlier decades. The pattern of change in the period 1983–92 is clearly different from the preceding two decades.

'A break of slope'?

It is useful to compare the rate of increase of health indicators before and after 1948. Although the NHS has expanded since 1948, how does this rate of expansion compare with that of the system it replaced? Making the large assumption that other factors remained constant over time, we would expect a distinct 'break of slope' in the historical trend if the NHS made a significant difference in trends over time. If the rates of expansion are different, it should be possible to detect a 'break of slope' in (or around) 1948, with the period after that date showing either a faster or slower rate of change.

Table 5.5   Percentage change by decade, 1953–93

	1953/62	*1963/72*	*1973/82*	*1983/92*
NHS expenditure	46	60	51	37
NHS expenditure per person	38	52	51	33
NHS expenditure as % of GDP	11	16	31	12
Hospital medical staff per 100,000 population	32	39	42	19
FCE per medical staff	–8	–18	–18	+6
Hospital nursing staff per 100,000 population	25	40	27	–8
Beds per 100,000 population	–6	–11	–14	–36
Length of stay	–26	–26	–27	–48

Source: Office of Health Economics (1995).

During the interwar period the voluntary and municipal hospital sectors increased markedly in size (Pinker 1966: 71). In some ways, the increases were more impressive than in the early years of the NHS.

> Although the 'pessimistic' view of the 1930s still has powerful adherents. . . . it has been shown that public social welfare expenditure during the 1930s in fact grew at a faster rate than at any other peacetime period before the late 1960s; and that far from being a period of stagnation and retrogression the inter-war period was a time of experiment and innovation in many areas of social reform. In part, the exponential growth of health services in the hands of the local authorities and approved societies *before* 1939 was considerably higher than under central government *after* the Second World War.
>
> (Harris 1992: 30; see also Webster 1990; Berridge 1990)

This was the case for both revenue and capital expenditure, and the latter in particular presents a marked contrast with the early years of the NHS. It was later estimated that hospital capital expenditure was more than three times as high in 1938–9 as in 1952–3 and it is thought that this proportion would not be materially altered by choosing different years either towards the end of the 1930s or during the operation of the NHS (Guillebaud 1956: 33). As Webster (1988a: 8) states, 'in local cases capital investment in new hospitals and clinics easily outstripped the performance of the National Health Service'. For example, before the war Middlesex County Council was spending about £0.7 million annually on capital schemes on its municipal hospitals. In 1950, despite vastly increased costs, the total capital allocation for the whole North West Metropolitan Region, of which Middlesex was only a part and which included ex-voluntary as well as ex-municipal hospitals, was only about £0.6 million (Eckstein 1958: 258). Moreover, while no new hospital was built under the NHS until the 1960s, some seven were started during the 1930s, including ones in such depressed areas as Glamorgan and Gateshead (Powell 1997). According to the results of a hospital survey published by the Ministry of Health, estimated net additional bed accommodation known to the Department to be either under construction or contemplated, was in the order of 10 per cent of existing stock in 1938. Nor was this expansion confined to the richer and/or better-provided areas. Some of the largest expansions were in areas with low provision of municipal general beds, such as Cumberland and Westmorland (24 per cent), the

Lincolnshire area (18 per cent), South Wales (17 per cent) and the north-east (16 per cent). Middlesex had plans for three new hospitals as well as the reconstruction and extension of two others, while Essex had bought sites for five new hospitals. In addition, the surveyors note plans for new hospitals in a further seven local authorities, and extensions elsewhere were halted by the war (Powell 1997). Today the NHS still has a large stock of old hospitals. In particular, some hospitals condemned by the hospital surveyors in the 1940s as unfit for the purpose still perform the same functions (Powell 1992c).

However, it is important to focus on the outputs of this rise in expenditure, as these are in many ways more important than either expenditure *per se* or bricks and mortar. During the 1930s the number of beds in municipal hospitals for the 'general sick' varied little, but the character of bed usage appears to have changed. With a similar stock of beds the number of admissions grew at about 5 per cent per year, the number of operations grew at about 10 per cent per year, and the number of outpatient attendances grew by over 25 per cent per year (Powell 1997).

The number of doctors and nurses was increasing before the NHS. Waiting lists were often in terms of weeks rather than months, although waiting lists for many of today's routine procedures could not exist because of the limitations of medical knowledge. To some extent, it is difficult to isolate the influence of the NHS because its formation largely coincided with the 'drugs revolution', Many new drugs, such as penicillin, were discovered and introduced from the 1930s onwards and we cannot know how the old system would have fared in the new era of medicine.

The change in the state of health of the population in the 1930s is the subject of a prolonged debate between the 'optimists' and the pessimists (Webster 1982, 1985; Stevenson 1984; Laybourn 1990; Jones 1994). By most measures the aggregate state of health of the nation was improving. While it has been shown that the optimistic official reports of the 1930s painted too bright a picture (Webster 1982, 1985), the pessimistic case is probably also overstated.

If long-term trends are observed, for example for infant mortality or tuberculosis death rates, it is clear that there is no break of slope in, or soon after, 1948. Indeed, the rate of decline is greater before the NHS (see DoH 1992: pp. 6–8). Moreover, the early years of the NHS are associated with high rates of poliomyelitis notifications (DoH 1992: 9). This does not indicate that the NHS led to worse health, but it does illustrate the problems of making inferences about causation about complex problems from simple time series data. It also shows the difficulty of social as opposed to natural science experimentation: it would not be ethical to deprive a 'control group' of the NHS to examine its effects.

A major component of the pessimistic case is that there were large variations in health between different geographical areas and social classes, that the rate of improvement was slowing down and that improvements were slower than in many other countries (Jones 1994: 75). However, these criticisms can also be aimed at the NHS (see Chapters 6 and 7).

CONCLUSION

Temporal evaluation of the NHS shows that it has grown in terms of inputs, outputs and outcomes. The input variable of expenditure has increased over time, but the rate of growth varies depending on how expenditure is measured. Nominal expenditure is now roughly 100 times its initial level. When population growth is taken into account, this reduces to about an 80-fold increase. The general level of inflation reduces the real increase in expenditure to about four-fold, and 'medical inflation' (the price of the NHS basket of goods) reduces this to roughly double the initial level. So, we now spend about two 'health-care pounds' per person as compared with one in 1948. However, the answer to the question of whether we spend enough to keep pace with the demands of demography and technology is less clear. Increases in expenditure have allowed more intermediate inputs to be bought. Over time, the number of staff has increased, but the number of beds has fallen. There have been increases in outputs in terms of the number of patients treated, but conceptual and empirical problems make it difficult to determine the exact rate of increase. Finally, outcomes have increased in that mortality rates are now lower than 1948, but the trend for morbidity is more problematic.

So, it is clear that by most measures the NHS has grown considerably since its inception. The few exceptions are that there are fewer hospital beds and directly employed ancillary staff in hospitals than there were in 1949, and recent years have seen a decline in the number of nurses, although it is still well above the 1949 figure. Indeed, the NHS has an almost continuous record of expansion, regardless of the state of the economy or the political party in power. However, the rate has been very uneven, varying from temporary stops to periods of rapid growth. Moreover, the rate of expansion in some ways compares unfavourably with that before the NHS. It is much more difficult to address the issue of the adequacy of the NHS because the variables in the equation are problematic and their quantification is contentious. Nevertheless, the service has tended to treat more people with an ever expanding range of treatments, but waiting lists and public dissatisfaction hit record levels in the 1980s. To some extent this may be the inevitable result of expanding medical technology and public expectations. It has been said that expenditure can never be sufficient. According to Bevan, the founder of the NHS, 'Expectations will always exceed capacity . . . [the NHS] must always appear inadequate' (quoted in Foot 1975: 209–10). A later Minister of Health, Enoch Powell, wrote, 'There is virtually no limit to the amount of medical care an individual is capable of absorbing . . . the appetite for medical care *vient en mangeant*' (quoted in Timmins 1996: 261). The NHS is a 'financial treadmill' (Leathard 1990: 39). By extending life, it creates more need. From the purely financial point of view, the NHS created a vicious circle: its successes in extending life mean that it spends more. Linked to evolving medical technology, and expectations, it has an inbuilt expansion mechanism.

Examining efficiency and effectiveness over time is problematic. Operational efficiency in terms of beds (patients per bed) has increased, but it has decreased in terms of staff (patients per staff). However, the difficulty of the *ceteris paribus* assumption means that it is unclear whether the NHS is really more efficient (an equally good or better service for lower cost) or merely a cheaper service (lower cost per patient gives a worse service). As for allocative efficiency, we have just about got to the point of asking the right questions, and the relevant answers will be some time in coming. Despite the slogan of 'effective health care', we are probably at the question stage here too. Increasing emphasis is being placed on examining the effectiveness of individual therapies, but until all the pieces are put together, the jigsaw of effectiveness of the NHS will remain unclear. We simply do not know either the overall rate of health return on our health-care investment, or whether we should put more money into certain therapies and less into others. Even when the scientific answers are clear, such rationing will encounter many political and public obstacles.

Thus, while reasonable confidence may be placed on certain issues, questions such as the efficiency and adequacy of the NHS are more dificult to answer, partly because of the inadequacy of the measuring rods. While the measures of performance have improved, they still give answers to the wrong questions. Questions of throughput can be answered with the accuracy demanded by a supermarket manager, but questions such as effectiveness are much less clear. We have good answers to the wrong questions, but our answers to the right ones remain poor.

6

INTRINSIC EVALUATION

This chapter is concerned with intrinsic evaluation, which involves examining the extent to which the NHS has met its objectives. In other words, how well has the NHS done on its own terms? To what extent has it lived up to its principles? In particular, the degree of equity or fairness in the NHS is examined. As we saw in Chapters 2–4, equity was a major component of the criticism of health care before the NHS, of the debates of the creation of the service, and of the aims of the NHS. The NHS was to achieve an equitable distribution of health care through a free and comprehensive service.

It has been claimed by the political opposition and the medical profession that the Conservative government has eroded the principles of the service. In 1988 Labour's shadow Health Secretary, Robin Cook (1988: 6), argued that the government was taking 'a succession of Granny's footsteps tiptoeing away from a universal, publicly-provided comprehensive health service hoping that no one will be sufficiently alarmed by the noise to ask the questions of principle raised by each step'. The BMA (1991: 2) asserted that 'progressively the high principles of the caring services have been eroded'. Stephen Lock, then editor of the *British Medical Journal*, claimed that 'it is not fanciful to talk about the end of the traditional health service with . . . its decent principle of uniform access to a high standard of medical care' (1989: 1). The government has denied these allegations. The text of the White Paper, WFP claimed that 'The principles which have guided it for the last 40 years will continue to guide it into the twenty-first century. The NHS is, and will continue to be, open to all, regardless of income, and financed mainly out of general taxation' (p. 1). This message was endorsed by the Prime Minister, Margaret Thatcher, in her introduction to the White Paper. In the House of Commons statement on the NHS review, the Secretary of State for Health termed the proposals contained in the White Paper a 'change of pace rather than any fundamental change of direction' (Clarke 1989, quoted in Mohan 1995: x).

This debate makes two broad assumptions: first, that the principles of the NHS are clear and unambiguous; second, that the principles of 1948 were still intact up to the election of the Conservative government in 1979. However, as was shown in Chapter 3, the principles of the service are far from clear. The question of whether the NHS has met its objectives is extremely difficult to formulate precisely, let alone answer, because it presupposes that what the NHS is intended to do is fairly clear and well specified. However, there is a long history of debate about the principles and priorities of the NHS (Harrison *et al.* 1990: 118). Objectives should be explicit, specific, measurable, scheduled, prioritized, 'owned', related to each other and communicated. Objectives for the NHS generally do not satisfy these criteria (Phillips *et al.* 1994: 71–4).

It is unlikely that the principles of 1948 were fully preserved up to 1979. Thunhurst (1982: 9) considers that the promises of the NHS have been realized only in a highly piecemeal and diluted form. Iliffe (1988: 47) claims that 'the principles upon which the National Health Service was founded no longer apply. Successive governments of both parties have modified a medical service that was intended to be free at the time of need, comprehensive in scope and financed by the Exchequer.' Indeed, Timmins (1996: 158) writes that 'within three years of its birth, the completely comprehensive and free health service had ceased to be'.

This chapter examines to what extent the principles of the NHS have been applied in practice. To return to the analogy of granny's footsteps, it attempts to monitor her speed and acceleration. It uses the framework of three main principles identified earlier: free at the point of use, a comprehensive and an equitable service. The attention given to the three principles is far from equal. Much of the debate centres on the issue of equity, and within this issue much of the debate is concerned with social class.

FREE AT THE POINT OF USE

Charges have always been a central issue in debates about the NHS (Falconer 1996). The principle of the totally free health service can be argued either to have been still-born or died in infancy. In the

Parliamentary Standing Committee examining the NHS Bill, Mr Piratin pointed out the existence of charges relating to after-care, and moved that these should be removed. Bevan replied 'I really must resist this amendment. Does the Honourable Member think that all services should be free?' (*Hansard* 1946). Yet Bevan stressed the importance of the principle of a free health service in cabinet and in the House of Commons during the financial crisis of the latter period of the Labour administration (Webster 1991a). Nevertheless, he defended the NHS Amendment Act of 1949, which allowed for a prescription charge of a shilling, but resigned from the cabinet on the introduction of dental and optical charges (Webster 1991a). In the 1950s the Conservatives extended the charges. Prescription charges were removed by Labour in the 1960s, but quickly returned, to become a permanent feature of the NHS landscape (Timmins 1996; Falconer 1996).

A fundamental question is whether patients' charges are important as a deviation from basic principles in their own right, or only if they deter use (Foster 1983: ch. 9; Walsh 1995: ch. 4). It may be argued that the idea of services free of charge was a means to an end: to ensure that people did not go without health care for lack of means, as they did before the NHS. If the intention was to remove barriers to care, there would be no objection to charges that did not constitute a barrier. On this reading, a charge of, say, 1p would be unlikely to deter and would be of symbolic rather than real importance. Neither a nominal charge for all nor a higher one payable only by those who would not be deterred would prevent use. As things stand, many people are exempt from charges, which in theory are paid only by those who can afford them. The importance of charges is then an empirical problem: if there is evidence of deterrence, the principle is breached; if not, then there is no effective breach of principle. It appears that Bevan considered that prescription charges were more acceptable than other charges (Webster 1988a: 144), which suggests that the practical arguments outweighed the symbolic. Reisman (1993: ch. 7) examines the issue of charges and fees and presents one example of an RCT of charging. The RAND Corporation in the USA concluded that the quantity of medical care that was demanded was in inverse proportion to changes in out-of-pocket payments. In other words, charges were a deterrent. However, the impact of the charges was less clear: for the median consumer, it was found that more care did not appear to mean better health (Reisman 1993: 134–8; Birch 1986: 178–9).

The erosion of the principle of a free health service accelerated in the 1980s. After remaining at the same price since 1971, prescription charges increased from £0.20 in 1979 to £5.50 in 1996, an increase of over 2500 per cent in nominal terms. However, a majority of patients are exempt from charges (Falconer 1996) and about four-fifths of all prescriptions were dispensed free of charge to the consumer (Earl-Slater 1996). Nevertheless, many of those who pay now find it cheaper to buy their prescription over the counter. In other words, a process of re-commodification (Cook 1988) or privatization (Birch 1986; Earl-Slater 1996) appears to be occurring. Birch (1986) claims that while prescription rates for the exempt groups rose, they fell for the non-exempt groups, implying some deterrent effect. Increasing the proportion of private finance (substituting private for public money) has led to the development of a two-tier service and a backdoor privatization of the NHS, compromising the 'free at the point of use' principle (Birch 1986).

Moreover, the White Paper of 1987 entitled *Promoting Better Health* introduced 'a completely new principle' in the charging arrangements in the ophthalmic and dental services (Johnson 1990: 86). Free dental checks were abolished and those patients who paid for treatment faced higher charges, paying 75 per cent of the cost of their treatment. These measures were said to save the government some £85 million a year. The government's view was that it was right for those who could afford it to pay more for their treatment (Timmins 1988: 55–6). This caused a backbench revolt, with 22 Conservative MPs voting against the government (Baggott 1994a: 211). Later, in 1993, the Health Committee (with its Conservative majority) urged the government to restore free dental checks (Bayley 1993). Such charges clearly further undermine the original principle of a comprehensive service free at the point of use. In particular, critics pointed out that charges for preventive tests might discourage people from coming forward for check-ups. Routine tests can detect the early stages of conditions such as glaucoma and oral cancer (Baggott 1994a; Taylor 1990). If discovered later, delayed treatment would be less effective and more costly, leading to serious health consequences for the individual, and financial consequences for the NHS. It seems ironic that these policies had their roots in a document entitled 'Promoting Better Health'. Here was an action in which there was a clear contrast between the rhetoric of subscribing to the principle that 'prevention is better than cure' and applying it in practice. The decision to end free eye tests marked the end of any form of NHS optical services for non-exempt patients (Timmins 1988: 56). The withdrawal of these services from those other than the exempted groups suggests that effectively the NHS is giving up on bodily parts one by one: teeth, eyes – what next?

The most expensive part of the NHS, hospital inpatient treatment – 'the core of the NHS' (Walsh 1995: 87) – remains free, but there is talk of charges for GPs' domestic visits and the 'hotel' aspects of hospital care. However, politicians have been discussing charges such as these almost from the beginning of the service (Webster 1988a, 1994) and it seems unlikely that the NHS will return to being a totally free service (Falconer 1996). Nevertheless, there is at least one example of a charge upon patients for watching television: a sort of 'poll tax' on hospital beds. It has recently been announced that at Northwick Park Hospital in London, managers are to ban portable television sets from bedsides, and patients are to be charged £1.50 per day for 'smart cards' that will give them access to TV programmes (Revill 1994).

Although services remain largely free at the point of use, reaching that point is rarely without cost. In other words, people often have to pay transport costs to use NHS facilities and some may lose wages by taking time off work (Le Grand 1982: 32–3). Such costs may be especially significant for people in rural areas and for those who need to make frequent visits.

A COMPREHENSIVE SERVICE

The NHS has always been a universal service in the sense of covering all citizens and not formally excluding any groups. Whether it was, or could ever be, a comprehensive service in the sense of being all-inclusive is more debatable. Although the principle of a comprehensive service may appear to be in contradiction to the concept of rationing, it has been argued that rationing is unavoidable and has been practised within the NHS since its infancy (Ham 1992: 251; Harrison and Hunter 1994: 1; Health Care 2000 1995; New 1996). Harrison and Hunter (1994: 24–30) outline the 'five Ds' of mechanisms of rationing: deterrence, delay, deflection, dilution and denial. Such rationing or 'priority setting' is an international phenomenon (Honigsbaum *et al.* 1995). Deterrence suggests that demands for health care can be obstructed. The most obvious example is payments, but others include accessibility, psychological and social barriers. Delay in the form of waiting lists is perhaps the most obvious and common form of rationing. Deflection concerns the 'gatekeeping' function of GPs. Unlike in some other countries, patients do not generally have direct access to secondary care and may be deflected into the continuation of primary care or occasionally by referral to another agency, such as social services. Sometimes information (about outcomes or side-effects) acts to deflect patients from treatment. Finally, delay (waiting lists) may deflect people into going private. Dilution may refer to reductions of the quality of care, for example cheaper drugs. However, a less obvious, but more important, means of dilution is the exercise of 'clinical freedom' by clinicians. Essentially, doctors work within the budget set by politicians, cutting as many coats as they can from the political cloth that they are given. Doctors in other countries may be given more cloth, and this means that patients in these countries may be treated when patients in Britain with the same condition may not (Aaron and Schwartz 1984). Denial refers to exclusion by treatment (e.g. *in-vitro* fertilization), age (e.g. too old) or behaviour (e.g. smoking). There are various ways of discussing rationing (Harrison and Hunter 1994; New 1996), but the approach here is in terms of covering everyone (universality) and everything (comprehensiveness).

Although the NHS is a universal service, this does not mean that people have automatic and enforceable entitlements to treatment. The British courts, unlike those in the United States, are wary of challenging the rationing process when asked to rule on entitlement to treatment. They attempt to avoid questions of social policy, leaving decisions to medical paternalism: in effect, declaring that 'doctor knows best' (Brazier 1993). In other words, the Secretary of State's duty to provide a 'comprehensive health service' leaves considerable discretion, and does not lead to enforceable entitlements (Harrison and Hunter 1994: 30–1). The right to health care on the basis of clinical need is 'pure rhetoric' (Brazier 1993: 57). Rights are collective rather than individual. People have only the right of access to a professional assessment of their needs. In this sense, patients are more like clients than customers. There appear to be two reasons why access may not lead to treatment. First, a patient's self-perceived need for treatment may not receive clinical legitimacy. In other words, everyone has a right of entry into the system, but some may get no further than the gatekeeper: to this extent the NHS rations by 'clinical need' rather than by 'patient demand'. A patient's felt need will lead to no further action if it does not correspond to a GP's concept of normative need. Second, needs legitimized by health-care professionals may not be treated. A patient may be referred to secondary care, but fail to reach the top of the waiting list, possibly being bypassed by those with greater priority. A patient may decide to 'go private', and join the queue where rationing is by money rather than need.

In some ways the NHS has never been comprehensive. Some forms of health care have been effectively excluded from the NHS. For example, it has never covered some alternative therapies. Many medicines continue to be sold over the counter. However, it is generally accepted that its degree of comprehensiveness has been squeezed over time. Some writers have argued that medical advances have widened the gap between what is medically possible and what is delivered. Butler argues that the impossibility of satisfying everybody's need for health care was realized some 20 years ago: 'The pretence that a tax-funded health-care service can (and should) provide everything from cosmetic surgery to life-extending treatments must sooner or later be confronted for what it is. The NHS, financed as it is, cannot deliver all forms of health care of an acceptable standard to all who could benefit from them' (Butler 1992: 125; see also Health Care 2000 1995).

If the original concept of comprehensiveness is correctly read as meaning all-inclusiveness, and if Butler's analysis is accepted, then it follows that a major breach of the founding principles was acknowledged before 1979. On the other hand, the IHSM (1993: 37) argues that in practice a 'comprehensive service' is impossible to define, but clearly cannot mean every possible treatment for every possible patient, as that would imply infinite resources. In practice, it is generally agreed that the NHS should provide satisfactory treatments to meet reasonable expectations at any given time. The obvious problem is then defining 'reasonable expectations'. It follows that rationing takes place not merely by the familiar device of the waiting list, but also by exclusion: not responding to 'unreasonable expectations'. The IHSM (1993: 37) accepts the inevitability of rationing or priority setting and argues that the government should publicly concede this. The resulting rationing process should be as transparent as possible and priorities should be based on the values of the NHS. This, of course, begs the question of defining such values (New 1996).

There was very little debate about the NHS's level of comprehensiveness before 1979. Rationing was the word which dared not speak its name. Delay was the only 'D word' mechanism of rationing (Harrison and Hunter 1994) that was discussed. The others were certainly not mentioned in polite NHS company, although it is unlikely that everything that was medically possible was done for everybody. Some people no doubt got treatment that people in other areas in the NHS, or in other age groups, went without. Some people in Britain probably went without treatment that was available to the more fortunate in some other countries (Aaron and Schwartz 1984; Griffith *et al.* 1987: 227–33). The NHS may not have been totally comprehensive in the fully inclusive sense, but rationing – certainly in terms of exclusion – did not emerge as such a prominent political issue.

In the 1990s the NHS's *de jure* comprehensiveness remains unchanged, but its *de facto* comprehensiveness may have been reduced in a number of ways. Some parts of the NHS have been floated off. The easiest pieces to dislodge are those that have always been rather semidetached from the main structure of the NHS (Griffith *et al.* 1987: ch. 6). In many parts of the country it is impossible for adults to be registered with a dentist as an NHS patient. As Levenson (1992: 28) states, NHS dentistry is on its way to becoming an endangered species. Griffith *et al.* (1987: 125) write that, in a way, the general ophthalmic services have never seemed part of the NHS at all. For the general population, both dentistry and optical services appear to be more in the realm of the 'high street' market than part of the NHS. Bayley (1993) reports that only 59 per cent of the population use the general dental service. If current trends continue, dentistry will be well on the way from a universal towards a residual service. Similarly, Timmins (1996: 505) claims that bits have fallen off the edges of the NHS, with the result that some parts of the service are means tested, residualized and made invisible to the middle classes.

Perhaps of greater long-term significance are the moves towards separating acute from chronic care. The 1980s saw a large expansion of private nursing homes, and some areas have more private than NHS beds for the elderly (Mohan 1991: 44–5). According to Williams (1989: 107) the NHS is surreptitiously pulling out of free long-term inpatient care for the chronically sick via a process which he terms 'charitarization'. There is some state funding available to patients in the independent non-acute sector. However, 'NHS responsibility, not only for providing care, but also for funding it has continued to decline' (Whitehead 1994a: 232). 'The most disturbing erosion of the principle of entitlement to a comprehensive range of free services has been in continuing care' (Whitehead 1994b: 1285). Tudor-Hart (1994: 70–2) writes of the 'abdication from continuing care'.

Vickridge (1995) explains this as a redefinition of health care in general and hospitals in particular. This has involved stripping down to a leaner acute/curative clinical model of hospital treatment and shedding 'continuing' and non-acute health care. The latter is redefined as 'social care' and is therefore not part of the free NHS, but part of means-tested social service provision under the local authorities. In short, it is 'means-tested health care masquerading as consumer choice'. The boundaries of what constitutes 'health care' as opposed to 'social care' shrink. In the opposite of the traditional 'medical model', where doctors lay claim to everything as 'medical', financial pressures mean that conditions usually associated with 'health care' such as malignant carcinoma or Alzheimer's *disease* are redefined as 'social'. Patients are sometimes discharged into private nursing homes, implying that nursing care is not part of the NHS. Vickridge (1995) illustrates the extreme frailty of people with such conditions by claiming that up to a quarter of patients discharged into private nursing homes will die within the first four weeks.

This is similar to hospitals in the USA that seek to discharge uninsured patients as soon as possible. In 1994 Leeds Health Authority discharged from hospital a man who, after a severe stroke, was doubly incontinent, unable to communicate, walk or feed himself. The NHS ombudsman found in favour of the patient and a health minister admitted that DHAs had a clear obligation to pay for continuing care 'for seriously ill patients' (Tudor-Hart 1994: 71–2; Timmins 1996: 506). As Tudor-Hart (1995: 72) points out, the decision to reaffirm what must have been assumed was the traditional responsibility of the NHS since 1948 depended on the continued independence and integrity of just one man (the ombudsman).

A 1995 guideline from the Department of Health stresses locally defined eligibility criteria, which reinforces the continuing erosion of national rights of entitlement to free health care and deepens geographical inequalities (Vickridge 1995). This means that people in similar situations are likely to receive a different service response depending on where they live. As the Alzheimer Society has noted, it is difficult to justify people with similar conditions having differential access to free health care because they live in Bury, Manchester, rather than Bury St Edmunds (quoted in Wistow 1995: 84). This entire process of defining eligibility criteria is something of a novel departure in British health policy, since it asks DHAs to lay down explicit criteria for rationing access to 'free' NHS long-term care services, something the NHS has so far studiously avoided doing for acute medical care (Saper and Laing 1995: 22). Many have seen this as a betrayal of the promise of 'cradle to grave' NHS care (Tudor-Hart 1994: 72; Timmins 1996: 506), essentially – at the price of mixing metaphors – moving the goalposts after the tax-paying horse has been put out to pasture. There is an understandable sense of anger, particularly among those property owners who had been promised by Prime Minister John Major that wealth would cascade down the generations. They now discover that their houses may have to be sold to fund their care, with their wealth cascading to the local authorities to pay – via means testing – for services they had assumed would be free. Many eligibility criteria are far from clear, leading to the accusation that you are entitled to NHS continuing care if a doctor says you are (Saper and Laing 1995: 23). The number of continuing-care beds is likely to fall, and some DHAs have planned to reduce contracts with the private sector (Saper and Laing 1995: 23).

Many critics saw the NHS funding crisis as undermining the principle of comprehensiveness. In 1987 the Presidents of three Royal Colleges took the unprecedented step of publicly declaring that the government's parsimony was putting the ideal of a comprehensive health service at risk. Although expenditure was rising in real terms, it was not keeping pace with the spending need associated with demographic 'pull' and technological 'push'. In short, the gap between what was possible and what was done increased. As the boundaries of a comprehensive service widened, patients' expectations were dashed. For example, the North East Thames Regional Health Authority has identified five procedures, including *in-vitro* fertilization, operations for varicose veins and tattoo removal, that it will generally no longer offer (Dean 1991: 351; Woodman 1993). Dean identifies this decision as the end of a comprehensive NHS, although it may also be the start of a more honest NHS. It is possible to point to 'specious waiting lists where, unknown to the patient, there was no chance of being treated. There were plenty of districts with "never-never" lists' (Dean 1991: 351). In the reformed NHS, rationing, or its 'Department of Health-speak' priority setting (Woodman 1993), may become more explicit and visible (Pearson 1992; Ham 1992). Decisions made behind closed doors, often in an individual, *ad hoc* manner, may be replaced by more explicit, and possibly more rational, policy decisions on rationing.

There are recent examples of people being denied treatment because of their behaviour, like the smokers who have not guaranteed to comply with some doctors' requirements that they give up the habit. Others, admitted to waiting lists, found the queue moving very slowly; some of these people took the exit option and went private. The 1980s saw a large increase in the number of people covered by private health insurance, and a significant proportion of some types of elective surgery was undertaken privately. In one sense, neither the existence of a private sector nor its increased size breaks the principle of comprehensiveness: the choices to work in or be treated in the private sector were enshrined in the settlement of 1948. However, a policy-led increase in private medicine, which has a selective impact on the population, may be a different matter. Mohan (1986: 337) has pointed out that the rise of the private sector has at least as much to do with the highly visible hand of the government as with the hidden hand of the market. The growth in private medicine has been encouraged by planning decisions, changes in consultants' contracts and tax relief. It has also been claimed that the NHS has been run down in order to increase the incentive to 'go private' for those who are able to afford it. The private sector has benefited from health authorities' use of 'Waiting List Initiative' money to purchase care. In the internal market, health authorities are encouraged to purchase care from private hospitals.

AN EQUITABLE SERVICE

While the NHS remains largely free at the point of use and reasonably comprehensive, its record on equity is more open to debate, largely because of the problems of defining such a complex concept. Both sides of the equity coin can be examined: equity of funding and equity in distribution. In other words, there are questions of who pays and who benefits. Bevan saw the redistributive side of the NHS as compromised by the Conservatives in the 1950s. To raise extra revenue they increased the amount of funding from National Insurance (NI) contributions, a 'poll tax' rather than income tax, transferring the burden from the shoulders of the rich to those of the poor. This was inimical to the redistributive principle (Webster 1991a: 211). However, the proportion of total NHS funding from National Insurance did not increase significantly, and it later became a graduated rather than a flat-rate tax. Taxation has never accounted for less than 70 per cent of NHS expenditure, while the largest contributions from NI and patients' payments were 16 per cent and 5 per cent, respectively (Appleby 1992: 47). In other words, the NHS remained largely financed from progressive taxation.

Perhaps the most contentious debate about the NHS is whether it has achieved equity in distribution. In spite of the work of Le Grand (1982), Mooney (1986, 1994) and Rae (1981) on the different interpretations of equity (see Chapter 3), many studies continue in the line of abstracted empiricism. It is possible to examine different groupings and different conceptions of equity. We can focus on two main issues: distribution of what, and distribution among whom? The 'what' question has been examined in terms of inputs, processes and outcomes, while the 'who' question has been examined in terms of socio-economic groups, age cohorts, gender, ethnic groups, diagnostic categories, and geographical groups. Thus, this simple classification yields 18 different tests (that is, 6×3) for equity (Harrison and Hunter 1994: 55). Perhaps a better classification of the 'what' question is given by Le Grand (1982: 14–17), who examines five distinct types of equality: equality of public expenditure, equality of final income, equality of use, equality of cost (access) and equality of outcome. A further problem concerns the difference between equality and equity. In the case of health care, the vital distinction is whether distribution should be equal or according to need: for example, should there be equal use of the NHS *per se* or equal use per unit of need? Thus, all but the equality of outcome category can be divided into equality and equity. So a more complex categorization based on Le Grand's five types of equality gives 90 test statistics ($5 \times 2 \times 6 + 5 \times 6$). This multiplicity of possiblities means that there is a large range of possible 'test statistics' of equality/equity, although some will be more important than others (e.g. Mooney 1994: ch. 5). Most studies have examined only one or at best a few of these categories, meaning that any conclusions about equity in the NHS are likely to be limited. In other words, the topic of equity and the NHS covers a large field that writers have usually selectively cultivated. Many studies are partial: for example, Ham (1992) examines social class, geography and client group, Nettleton (1995) focuses on health status with respect to social class, race and gender, while DoH (1996b: 9–10) uses the examples of occupational class, sex, geography and ethnic group. This review examines social class, gender, race, client group and geography.

Social class

Social class is the most common way of slicing British society in terms of occupation, providing a crude measure of affluence and lifestyle, ranging from social class I (professionals, e.g. doctors) to social class V (unskilled manual workers, e.g. cleaners) (see, for example, Townsend *et al.* 1992). As Le Grand (1982: 31) sums up, 'The NHS ... along with other systems of public health care, appears to favour the better off'. In short, the 'Strategy of Equality' (Le Grand 1982) has failed. As Abel-Smith (1984: 169) states, 'no one now seriously tries to argue that the coming of the post war "welfare state" went very far to create greater equality between social classes.' These broad statements need to be broken down into a more specific set of issues. The conventional wisdom is neatly summarized by Stacey (1977: 898):

> There is evidence, first, of continuing and perhaps increasing class differentials in death rates; second, of more illness in lower than in higher classes; third, that the health services are more available to the middle classes than to the working classes; fourth, that the middle classes use the health service more than the working classes; and, five, get more out of them when they do use them.

The evidence regarding the first two issues of inequalities in health is firm: there are inequalities in mortality and morbidity between social classes. There is a clear social-class gradient affecting most conditions and for most ages (Townsend *et al.* 1992). In 1981, of the 66 major causes of death among men, 62 were more common among social classes IV and V than for all men. Similarly, of the 70 major causes of death among women, 64 were more common among women married to men in social classes IV and V (Jacobson *et al.* 1991: 108). The expectation of life for a child with parents in social class V is over seven years shorter than for a child whose parents are in social class I. The order of magnitude of the ratio between mortality rates for most age and sex groups of classes V and I is approximately two to one. The concept of excess mortality – the number of deaths in the manual social classes, IIIm, IV and V, over and above the rates pertaining to non-manual classes, I, II and IIInm – illustrates the point. Excess mortality of the manual classes was greater than the total number of deaths from stroke, infectious disease, accidents, lung cancer and other respiratory diseases combined. There would have been 42,000 fewer deaths per year for the age range 16–74 had there been no excess mortality. If all ages are considered, the excess mortality amounts to the equivalent of a major air crash or shipwreck each day (Jacobson *et al.* 1991: 107–8). Although it is more difficult to measure morbidity, it is generally accepted that similar class gradients exist (Blaxter 1990; Townsend *et al.* 1992).

In addition to inequalities in health, it has been claimed that there are inequalities in health care. The conventional wisdom is that there are social-class inequalities both in quantitative aspects of use, when related to need, and in qualitative aspects of the consultation. However, most of the evidence is for the use of GP services, leaving a great deal of ignorance about hospital care. Many of the studies are dated, and great reliance is put on a limited number of them. Warnings given about the use of social class as a classificatory device are often not heeded.

It is convenient to divide the studies into 'quantitative' studies of utilization rates, usually presented in terms of 'use–need' and expenditure ratios, and 'qualitative' studies of the content of consultations. Most of the quantitative studies claim that, allowing for 'need', working-class people consult GPs less frequently than middle-class people (Townsend and Davidson 1982). The most influential analysis is by Le Grand (1982), who uses the criterion of expenditure per person, standardized for differences in need. The group in the highest social class is found to receive over 40 per cent more expenditure per person than the lowest group. It is this finding – Le Grand's 40 per cent – that has attracted most comment (see Powell 1995a).

There are a number of problems with the calculation of these ratios. First, many studies use data for a single year. Some results were not statistically significant and there was some variation from year to year. Second, the indications of both need and use are problematic. The Black report, often cited as a source of firm evidence, acknowledged uncertainties in connection with the evidence of inequalities with respect to GP consultation rates and hospital care: '*The data are limited and further analyses remain to be carried out*' (Townsend and Davidson 1982: 79–80, my emphasis).

The apparently contradictory conclusion of Collins and Klein (1980) is sometimes introduced centre stage, only to be subjected to critical scrutiny, to be found wanting, and to be dismissed (e.g. Le Grand 1982; Townsend and Davidson 1982; Morgan *et al.* 1985). This work is important, as it was mentioned by the then Conservative Secretary of State for Social Services, Patrick Jenkin, to counter the conclusion of the Black report that there was social-class inequity in access to health care (Townsend and Davidson 1982: 18). Although Collins and Klein's work is far from definitive, it is an advance on earlier studies, and most of the criticisms to which their work has been subjected apply with greater force to previous analyses. So, the conventional wisdom before Collins and Klein should not be restored to the throne, as implied by Morgan *et al.* (1985: 219), but should be subjected to even greater scepticism: to be buried rather than praised.

As regards the content of medical consultations, many sources cite the study of Cartwright and O'Brien (1976). It is based on data over 20 years old and examined one GP practice; generalizations from it to the whole population should be made only with extreme caution. Moreover, a study that challenged some of Cartwright and O'Brien's conclusions, published as long ago as 1986, is generally overlooked: Boulton *et al.* (1986: 328–9) point out the reasons why such evidence needs to be interpreted with caution. The measures used in the study were somewhat limited: counting the number of units of expression says little about the effectiveness of such activity. Many of the social-class differences reported are small, not statistically significant and in some ways point to a fundamental similarity in the experience of all patients (see Tuckett *et al.* 1985: 4). Boulton *et al.* (1986) show that although patients from the higher social class were more active in consultations, the consultations were not longer; nor were there clear class differences in the cognitive outcomes of the consultation. Boulton *et al.* conclude that their results do not support the thesis that middle-class patients were getting a better service from GP consultations than were working-class patients. Wilkin *et al.* (1987), in a study of general practice in Manchester, found that patterns of care seemed to be associated more with doctors than with the social class, age or area of residence of patients. In other words, 'patterns of care depend far more on who your doctor is than on who you are' (p. 158).

If satisfaction with the consultation is used as a valid indicator of care, there is some limited evidence to suggest that working-class patients are more satisfied with the consultation (Cartwright and Anderson 1981: 177–8; Wilkin *et al.* 1987: 129). This may be due to lower expectations, but should third-party researchers force their standards on to other groups, implicitly taking for granted their 'false consciousness'?

There are a number of studies that have not found significant social-class inequality in the NHS. The first piece of counter-evidence appeared in 1980 (Collins and Klein 1980). This study has been reinforced by a subsequent study of General Household Survey data for the period 1974–6 (Collins and Klein 1985) and by other writers (Crombie 1984; Puffer 1986). More recently, a number of contributions have criticized the original Le Grand study, and have concluded that the distribution of NHS expenditure across income groups, controlling for need, is either uniform or slightly in favour of lower-income groups (Wagstaff *et al.* 1991; O'Donnell and Propper 1991; Propper and Upward 1992). Le Grand (1991) accepts that there is some temporal pattern, with earlier studies suggesting inequity and later studies indicating equity. In other words, it is possible that accusations of inequity are outdated. It has been noted that the NHS has seen some moves towards equalization since the 1970s (Le Grand *et al.* 1990). By 1991, one of the main witnesses for the prosecution was arguing that 'the jury is still out' on the issue (Le Grand 1991: 244). Speaking of inequalities in health, Klein (1988: 3) argued that the post- Black consensus depended on 'filtering out dissonant evidence and excommunicating those who offer more optimistic interpretations'. Klein (1988: 12) has vigorously defended his minority view:

> The Black Report's assertion that access to the NHS is biased against the working class . . . has been shot down. There is little evidence of bias in access to general practice, the gateway to the rest of the NHS [reference to Collins and Klein]. Perhaps the most interesting aspect of this study is that . . . it prompted an immediate avalanche of attempted rebuttals: inequalities were something to be cherished and defended as political ammunition, and not to be surrendered to the first critic. . . . In the event, this finding has been fully supported by subsequent studies [references]. And the strategy of those who continue to support the original Black thesis has switched to arguing that while, just conceivably, quantitative equity in access to the NHS might have been achieved, this tells us nothing about the quality of care given once access had been obtained.

Klein is being a little unfair: the Black report examined evidence of both quantitative and qualitative aspects of care, and his 'new conventional wisdom' is not beyond dispute. However, it does illustrate that the topic of social-class inequalities in health care should be regarded as a debate rather than as a firm conclusion.

Gender

The Black report devoted about one page to sex differences in mortality. However, 'in the past few years, the once-neglected area of inequalities in women's health has been given more attention' (Townsend *et al.* 1992: 242). The general conclusion is that women live longer than men, but are more likely to be ill and to use the

NHS more (Miles 1991; Doyal 1995). This seems to represent something of a paradox (Doyal 1995: 11) because in mortality terms males are disadvantaged, while in morbidity terms females appear to be disadvantaged. This apparent feature of male disadvantage was often dismissed in a few lines by writers on gender and health en route to discussing female morbidity. However, recently the field of gender and health has seen two developments. First, there has been an interest in men's health (Sabo and Gordon 1995; Griffiths 1996). However, this tends to be restricted to specific areas (Griffiths 1996). Moreover, much of the material has been behaviouralist, in spite of problems that the Black report (Townsend and Davidson 1982) saw in this approach. It is but a short step to 'blaming the victim', as it is pointed out that men have unhealthy lifestyles, drink too much alcohol, smoke too much tobacco, eat a less healthy diet, and indulge in risk taking and aggression (Sabo and Gordon 1995; Griffiths 1996). It seems that writers who probably would not dream of criticizing out of context unhealthy behaviour of the poor have declared open season on men! Second, the conventional wisdom that women consistently report higher levels of illness is being reassessed. For example, Macintyre *et al.* (1996) see the field of women's health as more complex than was thought. They claim that the direction and magnitude of sex differences in health varies according to condition and age. It appears that the conventional wisdom of a relatively unproblematic model of sex differences was maintained by a combination of oversimplification, overgeneralization, and overlooking inconsistencies and complexities in patterns of gender differences. Indeed, in some cases aberrant findings were not reported when they did not fit the 'expected pattern'!

Increased life expectancy for women of all ages has been a feature of twentieth-century Britain (Miles 1991: 5). 'Mortality rates of males are higher at every age than of females and in recent decades the difference between the sexes has become relatively greater' (Townsend *et al.* 1992: 66). The ratio of male to female deaths ranges from 1.11 for ages 1–4 to 2.47 for ages 15–24. The importance of looking within age groups and groups defined by other characteristics cannot be stressed too strongly, as looking only at overall rates can lead to incorrect interpretation (Macfarlane 1990: 41; Macintyre *et al.* 1996).

In general, the mortality differential favouring women is reversed as regards morbidity, although there are complex interactions with age and disease type. Studies have shown that the self-assessed health of women is significantly worse than that of men (Miles 1991: 7–8). Men have higher rates of serious illness, while the excess ill-health among females appears to be largely in relation to non-life-threatening physical conditions, various measures of mental illness and poor subjective perceptions of health in general. Women are more likely than men to report ill-health on two types of measures: subjective measures and measures of restricted activity (Popay 1992). There are three main problems in the debate on women's morbidity: first, conditions associated with reproduction; second, the classification of women by social class; and third, the effect of employment. It has recently been claimed that when conditions associated with reproduction are excluded, the difference in hospital admissions of men and women between the ages of 15 and 44 years and for GP consultations for all women virtually disappears (Macfarlane 1990: 45). This may fit in with General Household Survey data that show that women consulted GPs twice as much as men for ages 16–44, but at a more similar rate for those aged 45–64 (DoH 1993b: 89).

Married women are classified by their husbands' occupation. Macintyre (1986) has noted that class gradients in some diseases disappear if women are classified in terms of their own occupations: for example, cancers of the reproductive system were more common among professional than manual women workers. Findings are inconclusive, but in general employed women have better health than women outside the labour market (Doyal 1995: 154). It is a consistent research finding that housewives have more health problems than are experienced by women with paid jobs outside the home and this appears to apply both to mortality and morbidity (Miles 1991: 15–16). However, the best levels of health tend to be found in non-manual women workers who worked part time. This may be due to a direct effect: part-time work seems to combine the best of both worlds, gaining self-esteem, wider social contacts and financial rewards from employment while avoiding some of the stress and overwork of full-time employment. However, it may be an indirect marker for social advantage: the choice of working as opposed to the necessity of contributing to the family income. Yet again, it may represent a selection effect: women who work are more healthy than women who are unfit to work. In other words, health determines work rather than work determines health – the selection effect of employment. Thus there are some some positive and some negative effects of waged work on women's health. 'Thus the key question is not whether paid work in general is good for all women, but rather which types of work will be harmful or beneficial for which women and under what circumstances' (Doyal 1995: 155). 'In summary, the familiar statement that men have higher mortality than women, but women suffer more illness is obviously an over-simplification' (Townsend *et al.* 1992: 247; Macintrye *et al.* 1996).

Doyal (1979: 228, 237) has claimed that 'the practice of medicine within the NHS remains basically sexist' and 'Indeed, that sexism is often more overt and apparent in medicine than elsewhere'. However, the evidence on consultation process and gender and doctor–patient interaction is unclear (Miles 1991: ch. 6): do doctors treat males and female patients differently and do female doctors treat female patients differently to male doctors? The issue of differential treatment for patients of different gender 'is contentious and difficult to resolve, partly because the evidence is contradictory and partly because the implications are unclear' (Miles 1991: 159).

Race

'Ethnic minorities are only rarely mentioned in significant documents: for example two pages with no recommendations in the Black Report and four sentences with no recommendation in the Royal Commission' (McNaught 1988: 60–1). However, McNaught does go on to admit that there have been some national and local initiatives and developments since then.

The Chief Medical Officer claimed in 1993 that 'the rise in interest in the health of people who are from ethnic minority communities has led to a substantial increase in the quantity of health research which uses the concept of "ethnicity" or "race"' (DoH 1993b: 148). Moreover, there has been more official recognition of ethnic minority health issues in recent years (Balarajan and Soni Raleigh 1993; Hopkins and Bahl 1993). However, Ahmad (1993: 24) has pointed out that the health-inequalities debate generally either ignores 'race' or marginalizes it to a few paragraphs. A spate of papers and special issues of journals on the tenth anniversary of the Black report failed to notice that Britain is no longer all white.

Part of the reason for race and health being an under-researched area is problems with data. There are no universally agreed definitions of 'ethnic' or 'racial' groups. Aggregate headings such as 'Asian' tend to conflate a wide range of factors that might include skin colour, place of birth, religion, language and so on (Nettleton 1995: 185). Generally, researchers have been forced to use place of birth as an indicator of race. In other words, much of the research tells us more about migration than the health of black people born in Britain. Overall, the mortality experiences of migrant populations are generally better than both in the country of birth and for the population born in England and Wales (Smaje 1995: 37). This has been explained in terms of the selective effects of migration: 'Men and women prepared to cross oceans and continents in order to seek new occupational opportunities or a new way of life do not represent a random cross-section of humanity' (Townsend and Davidson 1982: 59). However, this favourable health experience appears to apply only to the lower social classes. Immigrants in the higher social classes tend to have higher mortality than people of the same social class born in England and Wales, and it is difficult to see why this 'favourable selection' hypothesis does not apply to them. Smaje (1995: 87) argues that although selection is often invoked to explain patterns of migrant health, the empirical evidence for it is rather scarce.

It is important to disaggregate the overall data on migrant health, as for some groups and causes the death rate is higher than for those born in England and Wales, while for other groups and causes it is lower. Generally, for many immigrant groups, deaths from lung cancer are lower but deaths from coronary heart disease and accidents are disturbingly high. There is strikingly high mortality from hypertension and strokes among people of Caribbean and Asian origin, and markedly higher mortality rates for babies of mothers born in Pakistan and, to a certain extent, for babies of mothers from the Caribbean (Grimsley and Bhat 1988: 179–80). Most groups have higher mortality than the general population, except for Carribean men and for those aged 70 and above, where there is a general narrowing or reversing of advantage. Infant mortality and perinatal mortality are generally high for migrant groups. For diabetes, mortality is more than four times as high for Caribbean women. There is generally lower mortality from cancer, often of the order of 30 per cent; there is a lower rate for respiratory disease for men from the Caribbean and the Indian subcontinent, but this is 10 times as high for women from the Indian subcontinent, although this is based on a small number of total deaths (Smaje 1995: 36-9).

It is more difficult to assess the situation as regards morbidity, and there is much reliance on local studies (Grimsley and Bhat 1988). Much attention has been focused on ill-health specific to black people and conditions with much greater prevalance for them, such as rickets (Grimsley and Bhat 1988: 188–92) Consequently, evidence of ethnic patterns for 'common diseases' is patchy and local, and it is impossible to draw any general conclusion about the state of ethnic health with respect to 'common disease' (Grimsley and Bhat 1988: 193–4). As a result of examining specific diseases rather than the overall pattern, knowledge about the general health status of minority ethnic groups remains rather fragmentary (Smaje 1995: 33). There are problems of measuring morbidity at a national level, but a number of local studies suggest poorer health status (Smaje 1995: 43–7). As for mortality, 'we need more information about the health of ethnic minority groups born in this country' (Townsend *et al.* 1992: 263).

'Much less is known about race-specific than about class-specific access to health care' (Balarajan and Soni Raleigh 1993: 51). Consultation rates with GPs tend to be higher among ethnic minorities, especially in Asians in general and Pakistanis in particular. It is not possible to determine whether these patterns reflect differences in morbidity, varying thresholds and perceptions of illness, differential uptake of services, or a combination of these factors. There is less variation for inpatient admissions, and a more complex picture of outpatients appointments varying with race and age (Balarajan and Soni Raleigh 1993: 51–3). Nzegwu (1993: 210) concludes that, although there are some complex interactions with class, age and gender, the black population appears to be less satisfied with GP, outpatient and inpatient services.

The evidence on whether Britain's black population has a higher admission rate to psychiatric hospital is equivocal. Some groups such as Caribbean men have higher admission rates while those born in India, Pakistan and Bangladesh have lower rates. Afro-Caribbeans have higher rates of admission to psychiatric hospitals and are diagnosed as schizophrenic three to six times more often than the white population. Rates of schizophrenia are higher than the rates in Jamaica and are reported to be even higher in second-generation British-born black people than in the first generation. This group is more likely to come to hospital on a compulsory admission, and police and social workers are more likely to be involved. The little available evidence on treatment shows also that they tend to be on harsher forms of medication than equivalent white groups and seem to be viewed differently once in hospital (Grimsley and Bhat 1988: 199; Balarajan and Soni Raleigh 1993; Smaje 1995).

Differences of opinion exist as regards access to health care. Grimsley and Bhat (1988: 201) claim that 'For the black population inequality also exists in the utilization of health services, particularly preventative ones, and they may receive less good care'.

However, Smaje (1995: 99) argues that evidence on health-care access and utilization is based on a relatively small body of evidence. 'Ethnic patterns in health care utilisation are clearly complex. On the face of it, there is no compelling evidence that people from minority ethnic populations do not in general receive adequate levels of care.'

Although there is a growing recognition and policy response in recent years, ethnicity merits barely a mention in textbook accounts of health policy in Britain. There are initiatives at central and local levels, but their impact is unclear. An extensive literature has developed, but some quite fundamental questions remain unclear (Smaje 1995: 115–31).

Client groups

The term 'client group inequality' is used here in a broader sense than its common usage in the literature. In its normal narrow sense, it refers to the 'priority' or 'Cinderella' groups. However, this is a symptom of a broader problem of the relative statuses of different care regimes. Generally, hospital care has taken priority over primary and community care and, within hospitals, teaching hospitals have precedence over general hospitals and 'high tech' has more kudos than services for the priority groups. This situation is usually explained in terms of the hierarchy associated with the 'medical model' (Ham 1981, 1992; Morgan *et al.* 1985).

The wartime hospital surveyors (Chapter 2) exposed the grim state of institutional services for the elderly in the 1940s. In the early years of the NHS a great number of chronic patients were consigned to hospitals that the surveyors had condemned (Webster 1991b). About 100 public assistance institutions (workhouses) became NHS hospitals and conditions remained poor, with reports echoing those of the wartime surveys (Townsend 1964: 20–1). For example, a report on Birmingham geriatric hospitals in 1961 stated that there were at least six hospitals 'whose conditions were so deplorable that I have recommended replacement. . . . Many of our hospital buildings were never designed to be anything more than human warehouses' (quoted in Townsend 1964: 21; see also Means and Smith 1994: ch. 2).

Urgently needed radical changes for the chronic sick were not forthcoming. In some respects the position under the early NHS compares unfavourably with the interwar period. For the chronic sick as a whole, the NHS failed to bring about a revolution in their hospital care. In retrospect it is difficult to be impressed by the effort made to improve standards of hospital care for the elderly. Although most Ministers of Health since Bevan had warned about the possibility of scandals in long-stay institutions, it was not until the 1960s that scandals about the treatment of the elderly in hospital brought the horror of the situation to public attention (Watkin 1978: ch. 5; Martin 1984; Webster 1991b).

As Doyal (1979: 196) shows, in the 1970s costings varied between different types of hospitals: mental illness and mental handicap hospitals spent roughly a third of the amount per inpatient week as did acute hospitals. Part of the explanation may be that these hospitals may not need such intensive medical and nursing inputs, but other categories, such as catering, cleaning and domestic, showed a similar gradient. The Secretary of State for Social Services in the Labour government in the late 1960s, Richard Crossman (1972: 13), argues that it might be thought that the same amount of money should be allocated for food for each patient. He asked his civil servants to defend this discrimination. They replied that the mentally handicapped would not appreciate better food.

> Now what was appalling about this reply was that it was totally untrue and yet the civil servants had come to accept it as true ... you have this astonishing situation that civilised people in Regional Hospital Boards allocate vast sums to their kitchens in their new district hospitals and are perfectly content to see that a third of what they are paying in their 'crack' new hospitals is allocated to an old fashioned, out of date ex public hospital for the mentally handicapped. ... In fact we are running a two class system in the Service. We are treating the patients in these long stay hospitals ... as second class citizens. Although they live there often for years and therefore need their creature comforts more, they are given less resources, less skills, less nursing staff, less food than those who spend ten days or three weeks in one of our luxury marble palaces. We, the healthy, who go there for a short time and come out after the operation are magnificently looked after. They who may spend the rest of their lives in these places are treated in an infinitely inferior way.
>
> (Crossman 1972: 14)

Later he added that: 'For the desperately ill we have the best Health Service of the world. ... If you just have piles, it's a bit different' (Crossman 1972: 26). Crossman's Conservative successor as Secretary of State, Keith Joseph, made a similar point: 'This is a very fine country to be acutely ill or injured in, but take my advice and do not be old or frail or mentally ill here' (quoted in Timmins 1996: 291).

Such inequalities are often explained in terms of professional power (Ham 1981, 1992; Wilding 1982). Medicine has a clear 'pecking order', with high-technology medicine at the top of the pyramid of power and specialties such as geriatrics lagging behind. Moreover, areas such as the latter also rank low on the public's list of priorities (Frankel 1989). Consequently, such areas have little power in the struggle for resources. George Bernard Shaw saw medicine as a conspiracy against the laity; the Cinderella groups appear to reflect a conspiracy of both the profession and the public.

In an important but neglected paper, Eyles and Woods (1986) proposed 'an inverse interest law', which suggested that the more commonplace the problem and the more people affected, the less will be the medical interest. Frankel (1989) reinforces this view. He shows that the most common medical conditions, such as varicose veins, tonsilitis and inflamed adenoids, inguinal hernia and haemorrhoids, generate little interest in the medical press. For example, 'slow virus disease', accounting for 40 deaths and discharges in 1987, attracted over 3300 times as much 'interest' per case as varicose veins, with nearly 50,000 D&Ds. Moreover, the conditions that attract little medical interest all have long waiting lists. Eyles and Woods (1986) noted that the Cinderella services illustrate the 'inverse interest law' well, with little sign that relative hospital expenditure was improving. In short, Cinderella never went to the ball, and this is unlikely to change now that the ball game has shifted to the community.

> The major structural problem of the National Health Service is to redistribute resources from the hospital sector to the community sector. The subsidiary problem is to redistribute resources from hospitals caring for the acute sick to those caring for the chronic sick. . . . And both strategies must involve a shift of emphasis from professional supervision and treatment to prevention and community health education and involvement.
>
> (Townsend 1981: 71–2)

Geography

There are still large variations in mortality and morbidity rates on a number of scales of analysis: north–south, regional, district and local levels (Haynes 1987; Eyles 1987; Blaxter 1990; Mullen 1990; Reisman 1993: ch. 5; Curtis and Taket 1996). Different diseases have a distinctive geography (Jones and Moon 1987). Sometimes this is associated with features such as water hardness, but sometimes with the socio-economic environment, particularly poverty (e.g. Townsend *et al.* 1988).

Studies for more than a century have shown that poorer areas tend to have lower levels of health. The Black report noted that there were regional variations in mortality, with a broad north–south divide appearing (Townsend *et al.* 1992: 51). However, it has been argued that 'the "North/South divide" has little importance in itself . . . it is the "local" environment that matters' (Blaxter 1990: 86–7; Townsend *et al.* 1992: 247–52). In the 1970s and 1980s, work on area inequalities in health burgeoned (Townsend *et al.* 1988: 3; Blaxter 1990: 236; DoH 1996b: 9). There has been a flourishing of small-area analyses or 'local Black reports'. Often, the entire national gradient of health can be found in one region or even one city. It has been claimed that such area variations in health have been increasing in recent years (Phillimore *et al.* 1994; McLoone and Boddy 1994).

It is relatively easy to demonstrate that the geographical inequalities inherited by the NHS have been been modified only slowly by the largely incremental pattern of resource allocation (Webster 1988a). On a variety of indicators, regions like Sheffield were significantly worse off than regions such as Oxford (Culyer 1976: ch. 9). At the regional level there has been a significant narrowing in expenditure levels (Mohan 1995: 75–80), but regional inequalities in expenditure and inputs such as staffing remain (Ham 1992: 192–4). A similar point can be made at more local levels. The variability in distance from revenue targets for health authorities was much greater within regions than between them, but there has been some narrowing at this level also. For example in the North East Thames Regional Heath Authority the gap between the most 'overfunded' and 'underfunded' districts closed from 44 percentage points in 1983–4 to 27 in 1987–8 (Mohan 1995: 81). Change was rapid during the 1980s: some districts lost over half their beds (Mohan 1995: 81–3), but large variations remained. For example, revenue expenditure per capita at DHA level for 1987–8 varied from £79 in Chorley and South Ribble and £118 in East Hertfordshire to £1,076 in Bloomsbury (data from *Hansard* 1989). Outside London, the highest figures are Preston with £582, central Birmingham with £521 and Newcastle with £514. Thus, the variation between DHAs is of an order of 7.4 outside London and 13.6 including London. The coefficient of variation for per capita expenditure is 49 per cent for all authorities and 36 per cent for authorities outside London. In particular, London is still said by some to be relatively over-supplied (Tomlinson 1992, King's Fund 1992, but see Jarman 1993). Similar inequalities exist in the distribution of GPs (Benzeval and Judge 1996). Moreover, variation is also found at the small scale, for example between different parts of a town.

The accessibility of services remains a problem. 'Differences in sheer availability and, at least to some extent, in the quality of care available in different localities provide one channel by which social inequality permeates the NHS' (Townsend *et al.* 1992: 81). In other words, there is still a clear geography of health services in Britain and where you live has an influence on the service you get (Haynes 1987; Eyles 1987; Jones and Moon 1987: ch. 6; Curtis and Taket 1996: ch. 6). Indeed, it is possible that this effect will increase as health authorities set different priorities: for example, some authorities will not fund tattoo removal and some forms of fertilization treatment. In this sense, it has been questioned whether we are moving away from a *national* health service (Mohan 1995; Mohan and Powell 1996).

It has been claimed that inequity exists in addition to inequality. In other words, there is an inverse correlation between need and provision, as asserted in the famous 'inverse care law' (Tudor-Hart 1971). However, the evidence to support this assertion remains inconclusive (Powell 1990). Thus, there are clear geographical inequalities in provision of health care, but the extent to which these inequalities are also inequities is less clear. Moreover, areas with similar levels of provision may see different levels of activity: 'One of the most fascinating and almost certainly inefficient and inequitable aspects of modern medicine is the extent and nature of variations in medical practice. It is a blight on the medical landscape. Yet the extent to which policy has moved to deal with variations is surprisingly small' (Mooney 1994: 113).

'Doctors of medicine, it would appear, have much in common with doctors of economics, in that the advice one obtains depends significantly on the expert one consults' (Reisman 1993: 213). In other words, medicine is an inexact science: faced with the same symptoms, one doctor may decide to operate, another may treat with chemotherapy, while a third might observe. This, if for no other reason, suggests that full equality in the NHS will be impossible. The existence of variations in medical practice is clear, but the reasons for them is less so (Reisman 1993; Mooney 1994). McPherson *et al.* (1981) summarize a number of possible explanations: random, morbidity, supply, clinical, and demand. The morbidity explanation is the most attractive because a systematic, invariant and appropriate response to illness is what is generally expected of health-care provision. Thus, a threefold variation in the rate of hysterectomy between countries could, and perhaps should, be a manifestation of a threefold variation in morbidity. However, it is difficult to obtain comparative morbidity rates, with the exception of incidence rates for cancer. The usual second best solution is to standardize the data for age and sex variations, since these factors are known to be associated with many disease patterns. It is vital to exclude artefactual reasons for variation. For example, high rates of intervention for previous years may give rise to low rates for current time periods. In other words, rates must be related to the estimated population at risk. Once epidemiological factors based on illness rates, age and sex variations, and artefactual reasons have been excluded, the observed variations are taken to be manifestations of practice variation (and, in large part, the level of professional uncertainty concerning appropriate treatment) until demonstrated to be attributable to something else (McPherson 1990: 20).

Variations in medical practice exist both within and between countries (for the latter, see Chapter 7). 'Considerations of effectiveness, efficiency and equity lie behind the interest in health service variations' (Ham 1988b: 9). Large variations have been found in countries such as the USA (Ham 1988a), but such variations go against the concept of a national health service, which should provide a uniform response to illness – horizontal equality, - the equal treatment of equals, irrespective of area of residence. The variation in factors such as the number of operations per doctor, the length of stay and the admission rate is striking. Clearly, standard practice is remarkably non-standard, despite the long-standing commitment to universalizing the best within the unitary matrix of the NHS (Reisman 1993: 215–16). The problem is the question of an appropriate level of intervention. Until there is consensus, it is impossible to conclude whether services are rationed in Trent and over-utilized in London. McPherson *et al.* (1981) conclude that supply variables are a crucial factor in variations in surgical rates, with some evidence of a 'Parkinson's law of surgery': the more surgeons, the more operations. 'Whether you choose to measure the size of waiting-lists, the length of waiting time, the throughput of patients, the success rate of operations, or even the hospital death rate, you will find the most unnerving variations from one part of the country to another. . . . Variety is the spice of NHS life!' (Yates 1987: 4–5). Put less charitably, inequity is the poison of NHS principles.

Interaction effects

The above dimensions have tended to be studied in isolation, but there are likely to be significant interaction effects. In statistical terms, the important point is whether the effects of each dimension on health are direct or indirect. For example, do black people have poorer health because of racial or ethnic factors, or because black people in Britain tend to be disproportionately represented in social classes IV and V, which in general have poorer health experience? If the latter, then social class is the 'real' effect, which is mediated through race.

A similar example can be produced for geography. It has been pointed out that poor areas could have poor health for two very different reasons. The first can be termed compositional: the area is populated by people with poor health, for example those in the lower social classes. In this case, social class is the direct effect. The second may be termed contextual: the place *per se* does have a direct effect (Jones and Moon 1993; see also Macintyre *et al.* 1993; Duncan *et al.* 1993). It has been found that geographic variations cut across social class. For example, social class IV and V women in East Anglia have a lower (i.e. better) standardized mortality ratio (SMR) than social class I and II women from Scotland for 1979–83 (Townsend *et al.* 1992: 249; see also Blaxter 1990: 75). Not only do areas such as East Anglia have the lowest SMRs, but also the least social-class gradient: the gap between the best and worst SMR for women is 17 per cent, as opposed to 70 per cent in the north.

It is also necessary to be aware of possible interaction effects for health-related behaviour. There is clearly a geography of smoking in that the smoking rate varies in different areas. However, is this merely a reflection of the class composition of different areas, or is there a geographical effect independent of social class? Duncan *et al.* (1993) conclude that the apparent geography of smoking is largely due to compositional effects, which plays down the importance of geography.

One final example indicates that a social class V owner-occupier has a similar SMR to a social class I local authority tenant

(Townsend *et al.* 1992: 52). All this means that examining one dimension in isolation can lead to misleading conclusions. If possible, a number of dimensions should be examined, and the independent effect of each should be statistically produced.

Inequality in the reformed NHS

One of the most significant criticisms of the reformed NHS of the 1990s is that it is associated with more inequality (Whitehead 1994a, b). A major area of concern is associated with GPBHs. Two main problems have been noted. Many critics point out the danger of 'cream skimming'. Patients can now be seen as costs or benefits in financial terms. However, patients could always be seen as assets or liabilities in workload terms. There is plenty of past *anecdotal* evidence of high-need patients finding difficulties in being accepted on a GP's list. 'Some patients have always been more trouble to GPs than others. . . . Thus, to some extent cream skimming is not a new phenomenon' (Glennerster *et al.* 1994a: 179). The currency may have changed from time to cash, but the strategy of exclusion has always existed. Some newspaper headlines have provided anecdotal evidence of selection, but the fears that fundholding would sharply increase selection were based on the American literature. As fundholders have been funded on a historic cost basis and a limit has been placed on the costs associated with individual patients, these fears have not been substantiated to any noticeable extent: 'There is no hard evidence of cream skimming' (Glennerster *et al.* 1994a: 179).

The most controversial assertion is that patients of GPBHs have shorter waiting times for hospital treatment than other patients, which has been termed a 'two-tier' service (Mohan 1991: 52; Pearson 1992: 243; Whitehead, 1994a; Coulter 1995) or 'fast-tracking' (Baggott 1994b). In other words, treatment is not delivered solely on the basis of clinical need. As Baggott (1994b: 41) writes, early anecdotal evidence has since been supported by surveys that indicate fast-tracking to be fairly widespread. However, there are many difficulties of evaluation and few studies containing empirical evidence have been published (Coulter 1995). Coulter's (1995: 238) conclusion is that 'Claims that GP fundholding has proved to be a success are premature'. A similar verdict is given by the Audit Commission (1996), which argued that, on average, the benefits of fundholding do not substantially outweigh the costs.

On the other hand, Glennerster *et al.* (1994a: 178) remain unconvinced by the equity argument against fundholding. Furthermore, it is possible that early inequalities may be ironed out by the spread of fundholding, the development of consortia of non-fundholding GPs and by district purchasers flexing their muscles. The evaluation of the OECD (1995: 22–3) is positive:

> What research there is gives increasingly encouraging results. . . . There is no evidence that inequity has risen with the emergence of General Practitioner fundholders. If there were to be any transitory rise in inequity of this kind, it should be tolerated, as it would largely reflect efficiency gains . . . the answer should be sought by 'levelling up'.

In the absolute sense, the claim of a two-tier service is nonsense insofar as it implies that a state of perfect equality has been transformed into a dichotomy. The NHS has always been a multi-tier service (Glennerster *et al.* 1994a; OECD 1995) and the reforms may merely have made old inequalities more visible, whether or not they have added to them. Previously, the most obvious inequalities were found in waiting lists between different areas (Yates 1987), and few people knew that someone with the same condition was being treated more quickly in a different area. Now, the most obvious inequality may be between patients of fundholding and non-fundholding GPs in the same area: Mr A with Dr X may get treated a lot more quickly than his next-door neighbour, Mr B with Dr Y. Instead of the unknown wait in bus queues in another area, a taxi now stops and picks up selected people from the same queue in full view of those remaining.

However, the evidence for inequity remains limited. This is hardly surprising, for a number of reasons (Le Grand 1994; Appleby 1994; Coulter 1995). The NHS reforms were not accompanied by a governmental system of monitoring and evaluation. Early unofficial evaluations have only recently been reported, and it is inevitable that they are partial rather than complete. The debate on equality in the 'old' NHS is still continuing after over 40 years. So it is clearly too soon to expect definitive conclusions. Appleby (1994: 357) claims that, as Mao Zedong was alleged to have said of the consequences of the French Revolution, it is too early to draw any firm conclusions (see also Le Grand 1994: 259; Carr-Hill 1994: 1189). Many early analyses examined the first 'steady-state' period of the reforms, and evaluations of later periods may vary. Many data are no longer collected centrally. Finally, it is difficult to distil out changes resulting from the reforms from those associated with other major changes in the NHS.

CONCLUSION

The main focus in this chapter has been on the degree of equity or fairness in the NHS. There have been no obvious clean breaks of NHS principles: any fractures have been multiple and compound. Robin Cook's 'Granny's footsteps' arguably started at the beginning of the NHS, and with his own party. However, Granny has not become enfeebled with age; her footsteps have lately become more like giant strides. On the principle of free services at the point of use, she is almost running as prescription charges have spiralled and new charges have been introduced.

Nominal universalism in the sense of 'open to all' remains, but real universalism has been reduced as more people have 'gone private'. On paper, *de jure* comprehensiveness remains unchanged. However, *de facto* comprehensiveness has been reduced: first, as the boundaries of the NHS and the private sector have been blurred, and parts of the NHS have been floated off; and second, as the gap between actual and possible activity has increased. But is this an inevitable result of medical progress?

It is more difficult to come to a clear conclusion on equality, partly because of the difficulty of defining such a multifaceted term and partly because the NHS's record is disputed. The greater inequalities that have been identified with the reformed NHS may partly be old ones rendered more visible. Moreover, the concept of a two-tier service is far too simplistic to capture the complex and often subtle multi-tier nature of NHS inequalities, before and after the reforms.

There is little in the health reforms of the 1980s in general and in WFP in particular that *necessarily* breaches the principles of the NHS, although assurances on the principles of the service are less than convincing. The commitments of WFP are to the continuation of funding 'mainly' (51 per cent?) from taxation, and to the service remaining 'open to all', rather than to the original principles of the service, and any deeper sense of comprehensiveness. Commitments to services free at the point of use and an equitable service are conspicuous by their absence.

7

EXTRINSIC EVALUATION

Extrinsic evaluation involves examining how well the NHS compares with other health-care systems. How well does it compare on
issues such as efficiency, effectiveness and equity? Is or was the
NHS the 'best in the world'? Are the problems of the NHS unique
or common to other systems? Are the recent trends in the NHS a
British or an international phenomenon? Can we learn anything
from other health-care systems?

International comparisons are difficult for a variety of reasons
(Maxwell 1981; Schieber and Poullier 1990). The first reason is defi-
nitional: countries may define health care in different ways. Some
may include items such as spa treatment, residential homes and
occupational (work) facilities, while others may not. There are two
main aspects to this problem (Webster 1993: 178). First, there is the
difficulty of separating 'health' from 'social' services. Second, the
boundary between formal and informal or lay health care is often
unclear. It is particularly difficult to measure private inputs such as
travel, non-prescription drugs and alternative therapies (Reisman
1993). The groups that often straddle such boundaries include physically and mentally handicapped people, elderly people in residential homes and people who are addicted to drugs.

The second reason is that data are often not comparable. For
example, in countries such as Germany the expenditure associated
with salaried hospital physicians will be treated as part of in-hospi-
tal physician services, while in countries such as the USA most hospital physicians are paid on a fee-for-service basis and expenditure
will be reported separately as physician expenditures. It is particularly difficult to compare quality. For example, is a British doctor
the same as an American doctor? Is a British nurse of equal quality
to a German nurse?

A third problem concerns comparing countries with different geographical, cultural, social, demographic, political, and economic structures. Although some factors such as age differences can be controlled for statistically, many other factors, such as attitudes about health, cannot (see Payer 1990). In short, 'International comparisons are clearly limited by the methodological state of the art' (Schieber and Poullier 1990: 13).

This chapter encounters similar, but more difficult, problems to those found in Chapter 5. Instead of examining the same system (the NHS) over time, this chapter compares different systems. The main variables in health-care systems are analysed in a framework of inputs, outputs and outcomes, with the relationships between the variables examined in terms of efficiency, effectiveness and equity. However, the 'flow chart' linking inputs, outputs and outcomes is more problematic than for a single system. This is because at the international level there are 'inputs' into the system apart from expenditure, which may exert more influence on outputs and outcomes than the expenditure variable. These are, first, the structural features of a system – the way the system is organized – and second, and linked to the first factor, variations in medical practice – the way in which doctors treat patients. A particular emphasis is placed on three countries, which are then examined in more detail. After that, Great Britain is viewed in the wider comparative context, leading to the search for lessons from other countries.

MEASURING HEALTH-CARE SYSTEMS

During the twentieth century the health-care sector in most countries has grown in terms of expenditure, staff, beds and activity. Moreover, the state has become increasingly involved in the coordination of medical care over the last century in most countries of the world, but when, how, and to what extent the state has intervened have varied from one country to another (Hollingsworth *et al.* 1990). Most systems in the Organization for Economic Cooperation and Development (OECD) claim to seek similar ends, but rely on different means (OECD 1987).

International patterns of health care may be described in the same terms as were used for the NHS in Chapter 5. Health-care systems convert inputs such as expenditure into intermediate inputs such as beds and staff and output in terms of patient activity. In turn, the objective is some positive impact on outcome in terms of the health of the nation. However, the international production process of health is more complex, as there is a wide variety of structural features of systems as well as variations in medical practice in different countries.

Inputs

As in the case of the NHS, there has been excessive preoccupation with describing health-care systems in terms of the single variable of expenditure. However, international comparisons of expenditure are fraught with difficulties (Parkin 1991; Appleby 1992: 72–3; Webster 1993; Donaldson and Gerard 1993). In particular, there is no consensus on the 'correct' level of spending.

> The interpretation of high or low levels of spending by a country differs between commentators according to their purpose. Does low expenditure imply a low volume of health care or simply low levels of cost? Are high spending countries buying more health care or do they simply have an inefficient system? It is extraordinary that the same measure is used for so many different purposes.
>
> (Parkin 1991: 180)

In other words, the expenditure variable, in spite of its popularity, appears to be of little value by itself, and this suggests either that it should be abandoned in favour of other variables or that it should be used in conjunction with others, for example to examine the impact of a system given its level of cost.

The usual procedure in comparing differences in spending in different countries is to convert prices into a common currency (usually dollars), using market exchange rates. However, prices vary between countries. Therefore, often purchasing power, the amount needed to buy a common basket of goods, is examined. For cost-of-living comparisons, this could be a 'weekly shopping basket' of goods, but in the case of health care it should reflect the prices of health-care goods and services. There are two types of conversion using purchasing-power parities (PPPs). The first, GDP PPPs, allows for the differences in the level of general prices between countries. The second is concerned with PPPs specific to health care. This shows the volume of health-care services provided (in monetary terms), allowing for differences in health-care prices between countries, and takes account of the fact that in the USA, for example, physicians' fees and incomes are generally higher than in, say, Britain. Although PPPs are not as 'accurate' as exchange-rate conversions, it is better to use an inaccurate measure of a correct concept than an accurate measure of a concept known to be wrong (Parkin 1991: 185). 'Without taking account of such medical care price differentials any comparison of health care spending is meaningless' (Appleby 1992: 74). By implication, this means that most (non-specialist) comparisons for public consumption are meaningless. Different conversion methods – exchange rates, GDP PPPs and health-care PPPs – yield different conclusions (Parkin 1991; Appleby 1992: 72–6; Oxley and MacFarlan 1994: 82–3). The USA slips from being the highest spender in terms of exchange rates to the eighth highest in terms of health-care PPPs. In contrast, Britain improves its position from thirteenth to tenth. Comparing the figures for average health-care spending for 18 OECD countries, the US value changes from 56 per cent above average to 14 per cent above, while Britain moves from 21 per cent below average to 5 per cent below (calculated from Appleby 1992: 74). In other words, in terms of health-care prices, UK spending is near the average OECD level.

Table 7.1 compares different indicators of expenditure. The OECD countries show large variations, usually between high-spending Norway and Switzerland and low-spending Greece. The USA is one of the largest total spenders, but its public expenditure is not as high as that of other countries. Britain is a low spender, but its relative position varies between the indices. For example, it spends 60 per cent of the OECD average for total expenditure, compared with 72 per cent for the total/GDP measure, 82 per cent for public expenditure, and 98 per cent for the public/GDP measure. The difference between the total and public measures is because Britain's public expenditure as a proportion of total expenditure is about 40 per cent above the OECD average.

Moreover, Britain is not as wealthy as other countries. It has been found that a country's spending on health care can be fairly accurately predicted using regression techniques from its national wealth (OECD 1987). In general, a 10 per cent increase in GDP tends to produce a 10–15 per cent increase in per capita health spending (Appleby 1992: 38–9). Per capita GDP statistically explained over 80 per cent of the variation in health expenditure in 1970, and this rose to 95 per cent in 1980 and 1990 (OECD 1993: 15). In other words, as countries become richer they tend to spend a higher percentage of their national income on health care. There is no expected norm for health spending, although the regression line

Table 7.1 Health-care expenditure in selected OECD countries, 1992

	Total expenditure per capita (£)	Total expenditure as % of GDP	Public expenditure as % of total	Public expenditure as % of GDP	Public expenditure per capita (£)
Germany	1395	8.7	71	6.2	998
Sweden	1304	7.9	88	6.8	1117
Britain	732	7.1	85	6.0	618
USA	1860	13.8	48	6.3	850
OECD average	1229	9.9	61	6.1	754
OECD maximum	1883	13.8	96	7.7	1280
	(Switzerland)	(USA)	(Norway)	(Norway)	(Switzerland)
OECD minimum	238	5.4	48	4.1	181
	(Greece)	(Greece)	(USA)	(Greece)	(Greece)

Source: Office of Health Economics (1995).

is often implicitly taken as one and there are some signs of a convergence towards the line. However, in an examination of 'outliers' – countries at some distance from the level of spending predicted by the regression line – if it is said that Britain spends too little, then by the same logic, Sweden and the USA spend too much. Indeed, one calculation shows that Britain is spending slightly above its expected level (Oxley and MacFarlan 1994: 82).

Moreover, this refers to total health-care expenditure. If public expenditure alone is examined, Britain's level of spending does not appear to be particularly deviant. Thus many of the conclusions drawn from the association between GDP and per capita health-care spending are changed or even overturned if, instead of using exchange rates to convert different countries' health-care spending to a common unit, PPPs are used. First, the association becomes weaker, and second, Britain appears to spend about the right amount on health care given its wealth, but gets more inputs for its money than many other countries (Parkin 1991: 187–8; Appleby 1992: 75). The tremendous difficulties inherent in the exercise of comparing health-care systems across countries would appear to render such exercises less than useful in the context of gaining some practical handle on the right level of funding for Britain's health-care system (Appleby 1992: 75–6). Donaldson and Gerard (1993: 182) go further: international comparisons of expenditure are naive and unhelpful.

To some extent, it is not surprising that the expenditure variable has achieved such dominance. As some 90 per cent of international health-care expenditure per capita is explained by national income, at first sight it appears that very little is left to be explained by any other factors (Maxwell 1981). However, this is misleading, for two main reasons (Donaldson and Gerard 1993; Webster 1993). First, there are still significant expenditure variations between countries with similar levels of GDP. Second, other factors combine with expenditure to influence what and how much can be bought with any given sum of money. As argued in Chapter 5, it is misleading to evaluate health-care systems in terms of inputs.

It is important to examine what is bought with health-care expenditure: the problem of transforming expenditure inputs into intermediate inputs. This section concentrates on hospital services. Institutional expenditures are the largest component of health expenditures, accounting for nearly half of all expenditure in 1990, ranging from 19 per cent in Turkey to 70 per cent in Norway (Oxley and MacFarlan 1994: 73). The clear picture from Table 7.2 is that

Table 7.2 Health care in selected OECD countries, *circa* 1990

	Germany	Sweden	Britain	USA	OECD average
Doctors per 1000 population	3.1	2.9	1.4	2.3	—
Beds per 1000 population	10.3	11.9	5.9	4.7	8.4
Nurses per bed	0.5	—	0.7	—	0.8
Doctors per bed	3.2	2.9	1.4	2.2	2.5
Bed occupancy rate (%)	86.7	84.7	80.6	69.0	75.0
Bed days per capita	3.3	3.4	2.0	1.2	2.5
Admission rate as % of population	21.1	19.9	19.3	13.7	16.2
Average length of stay (days)	16.1	16.8	14.0	9.1	14.4
Doctor contacts per capita	11.5	2.8	5.7	5.6	6.1

Source: Scheiber *et al.* (1994); Oxley and MacFarlan (1994).

Britain has fewer intermediate inputs, such as beds, than other countries. However, it is closer to the OECD average than it was for indicators of expenditure.

It is often assumed that, in examining a single health-care system, the most important single variable is that of expenditure. It follows that the best way of increasing outputs and outcomes is to spend more. We have seen that even in a single system that this assumption is too simplistic. However, in comparing international health-care systems, there are other sources of variation beyond expenditure. The first is concerned with structural factors. The second is concerned with variations in medical practice. In other words, outputs and outcomes are affected by factors beyond expenditure.

Structure

Differences in specific features of health systems can have important effects on utilization, prices, efficiency, outcomes and quality. Unfortunately, isolating the impacts of specific features on health systems' performance is quite difficult (OECD 1987: 31).

One structural feature is the degree of population coverage or degree of universalism. The growth in coverage is relatively recent.

In 1960 universalism, or something approaching it, was the exception, not the norm. However, most systems now have almost universal coverage (OECD 1987: 25; Moran 1992: 80). However, in no country are citizens entirely exempt from charges, obliging us to revise the notion that the health-care state in Europe can be described in the language of universalism (Moran 1992: 80–1). The evidence suggests that the farther the patient gets from the institutional heart of the modern health-care system – the hospital – the more important does the market as a regulator of access become. In other words, while inpatient hospital care is largely free, patients usually contribute a higher proportion of the total cost of treatment for ambulatory care. For example, for inpatient care, patients pay 10 per cent or less of the total bill in 14 of the west European states, but ambulatory-care patients contribute similar levels in only four countries. Some countries impose charges for visiting the primary physician, and virtually all impose charges for pharmaceuticals, but most exempt the poor from these charges and payments are generally nominal (OECD 1987: 25). Thus, total public expenditure figures do not tell us who the money is spent on: the whole population, as in Britain or a minority of the population, as in the USA. Moreover, they do not tell us which parts of the system are free at the point of use, or the level of charges.

There are differences in funding health services. Money can be raised by taxation, national health insurance, private insurance or direct payment (Donaldson and Gerard 1993; Webster 1993). This will have implications for the degree of equity in financing the system.

There may be variations in the public–private mix in the finance and in the production of health services. It is important to separate production or ownership from finance. The first issue is concerned with who owns the facilities, while the second is concerned with who pays for the care. In the case of hospitals in Britain, the two are linked: the government owns the hospitals and pays for the care. However, Britain is the exception; it is more usual for a government to ensure that people have access to health care through paying for care in hospitals not actually owned by the government. Moreover, for general practice in Britain, the care is provided by self-employed doctors who receive most of their income from the public purse (Donaldson and Gerard 1993).

There are differences in remuneration in terms of paying the doctor and paying the hospital. Some doctors are paid on a fee-for-service (piece work) basis, others by capitation and others by salary

(Abel-Smith 1976; OECD 1987: 26–30; Donaldson and Gerard 1993; Webster 1993). Hospitals may be paid on the basis of annual global budgets that are set prospectively or refunded retrospectively, usually on an item-of-service basis (Webster 1993; Donaldson and Gerard 1993; Oxley and MacFarlan 1994).

Finally, in some countries, people may have direct access to hospitals while in others, such as Britain, access to hospitals is generally by referral from GPs (Oxley and MacFarlan 1994).

So, two systems can have a similar level of expenditure, but can be different in virtually every other respect and be two very different systems. In other words, it is misleading to describe the structure of a health-care system in terms of merely one ingredient of that structure.

Outputs

There are large variations in medical practices both between and within countries (Ham 1988a; Reisman 1993: 212–19; Mooney 1994). Variations between countries can be typically three- or fourfold for operations such as exploratory laparotomy and inguinal hernia repair, sevenfold in the case of hysterectomy, over 16-fold for tonsillectomy, over 60-fold for coronary bypass and over 100-fold for cholecystectomy (McPherson 1990: 22). In general, some countries such as the USA tend to do most, while countries such as Britain tend to do least (McPherson 1988; Payer 1990).

International surveys show that in terms of satisfaction, the NHS is far from the 'best in the world'. A study by Blendon *et al.* (1990) showed that Canada is regarded by its own population as having the most popular health-care system in the world: 56 per cent of its population considered that the system needed only minor changes and only 5 per cent thought that it needed to be rebuilt completely. Similar levels of satisfaction were found in the Netherlands and West Germany. On the other hand, the Italian and American systems were the least popular: 40 per cent of Italians considered that the system should be rebuilt completely, with only 12 per cent thinking that only minor changes were needed. The respective figures for the USA were 29 per cent and 10 per cent. Britain and Sweden had similar levels of satisfaction. For Britain, 27 per cent thought that minor changes were needed, 52 per cent said that fundamental changes were needed and 17 per cent thought that the system should be rebuilt completely. The respective figures for Sweden were 32 per cent, 58 per cent and 6 per cent. There were two main conclusions. First, a national health system (as in Britain and Italy) does not guarantee satisfaction. Second, with the exceptions of the USA and Sweden, satisfaction tended to be associated with higher levels of spending. The OECD (1993: 36) presents a graph that suggests that there is a weak trend of satisfaction increasing with expenditure. However, it appears that there is more satisfaction with the NHS than its level of expenditure would predict.

Outcomes

In spite of the diversity in their health-care systems, there is little difference in terms of overall life expectancy among the countries in Table 7.3. There is more variation in terms of young deaths. Sweden and Germany have the lowest mortality, and Britain has lower mortality than the USA. Indeed, the USA appears to have a poor reward in terms of outcomes for its heavy health-care investment, although it is unclear whether this is primarily due to failings of the system or to wider socio-economic factors.

Efficiency

On a crude level, it appears that Britain is efficient as it squeezes more intermediate inputs and activity out of any given level of expenditure. Conversely, the figures for the USA tend to be below the OECD average, suggesting that it is less efficient in converting expenditure into other inputs and activity. Overall, in spite of some

Table 7.3 Mortality indicators for selected OECD countries, 1992

	Germany	Sweden	Britain	USA	OECD average
Female life expectancy (years)	79.3	80.8	79.0	79.0	79.2
Male life expectancy (years)	72.9	75.4	74.0	72.3	72.9
Perinatal mortality rate (%)	0.56	0.56	0.81	0.87	0.80
Infant mortality rate (%)	0.60	0.53	0.66	0.85	0.91

Source: Oxley and MacFarlan (1994).

moves towards convergence, international patterns of medical inputs and activity in the OECD countries remain remarkably diverse.

Explanations linking inputs with outputs are very tentative. The first explanation is concerned with the supply of health care. In very broad terms, countries that spend more on health care have higher levels of intermediate inputs and higher levels of activity. Nations with a greater supply of health care will treat people who would not be treated in other nations. In other words, the threshold for treatment varies with available supply: if beds are in short supply, the condition has to be advanced or severe before the patient is admitted. On the other hand, if there are many beds, patients with less severe or advanced conditions get treated. There is a strong statistically significant and positive relationship between number of beds per capita and bed-days, with a correlation coefficient of 0.94, which lends credence at an international level to 'Roemer's law' or a clinical version of Parkinson's law, that the number of patients expands to fill the available beds. Hospital admission rates have been steadily increasing, but average length of stay has been steadily falling (OECD 1987: 67–70). Again, there is a statistically significant correlation of 0.48 between beds per capita and average length of stay.

However, there are exceptions to this pattern. There is no obvious relationship between the number of physicians and health-care costs per capita across the OECD countries. For example, Greece, with the second lowest expenditure, has the third highest number of doctors. It appears that extra revenue may go into higher income for doctors as opposed to purchasing more doctors, as there is a clear relationship between physicians' income and per capita health-care expenditure (OECD 1992b: 25–7). Moreover, the data in Table 7.2 show that the high-spending USA does not have particularly high levels of activity. In other words, countries will transform inputs into outputs with differing levels of efficiency.

This 'supply side' explanation has been examined at the level of individual treatments. Some large variations are associated with relatively expensive technologies (Hollingsworth *et al.* 1990: 141-6). Kidney dialysis is more common in the USA than in Britain, and patients aged over 45 appear to be denied treatment in Britain. On the other hand, Britain appears to carry out more kidney transplants. The US had in the late 1970s five times as many computerized tomography scanners per million population as Britain. Griffith *et al.* (1987: 227–33) argue that the NHS provides less extensively than other countries for two main categories: high-technology care and routine surgery. In relation to life-and-death emergencies, the NHS tends to provide as much care as the American system, for example bone marrow transplant. Second, the NHS devotes far fewer resources to relieving pain: for example, the Americans do 10 times as much coronary artery surgery. Third, the NHS spends far less on diagnostic procedures. However, it is claimed that there is wasteful use of resources for operations such as tonsillectomy in the USA. As Tudor-Hart (1994: 24) puts it, in the USA there exists for some procedures gross overprovision for the rich and underprovision for the poor.

It has been claimed that structural features other than expenditure have an impact on levels of activity. The first concerns the payment of physicians. In general, fee-for-service payment provides strong incentives for the provision of additional services, high quality and increased expenditure. Payment by salary contains incentives for reduced service provision, potentially lower quality, and reduced expenditure. Capitation provides incentives to reduce quantities and expenditures while maintaining the patients' health status. But salary and capitation contain strong incentives for referral (Abel-Smith 1976: ch. 5; OECD 1987: 28). Each of the three ways of paying doctors can have perverse incentives (OECD 1994: 46–7), but fee-for-service medicine tends to attract most criticism. It is claimed from both the comparative and historical evidence that this feature is associated with a wasteful investment in equipment, unnecessary intervention, an incentive not to refer, and the lack of specialization in the form of the 'part-time surgeon' and an unequal distribution of doctors. For example, Enthoven (1990: 57) states that in the USA it is well established that there is a pronounced negative relationship between the annual volume of cases in a hospital and mortality for complex surgical procedures such as open heart surgery. Moreover, many interventions have been deemed by expert evaluation panels to be 'inappropriate'. For example, 14 per cent of coronary artery bypass surgery has been deemed inappropriate, with a further 30 per cent equivocal. If doctors are paid per item of service, this will encourage them to do more than if they were paid by salary or capitation. This is essentially an ideological argument reflecting a distaste for the market in health care: 'the highest financial rewards go not to the best doctor but to the quickest and to the doctor with the least professional scruples about responding to the financial incentives of the payment system' (Abel-Smith 1976: 63; see also Griffith *et al.* 1987).

Abel-Smith (1976: 63) presents some supporting evidence. For example, he cites a study that shows that the rate of appendectomies in Germany under fee-for-service was 40 per cent of the weekday rate for Saturdays and 25 per cent for Sundays, which is surprising for an operation normally regarded as an emergency.

Sandier (1990) claims that there is no simple relationship between fee-for-service medicine and overconsumption in treatment or contacts. She suggests it is difficult to separate out the effect of payment from other factors, but it appears to be secondary to factors such as the behaviour of patients. For example, Germany, with fee for service, has high physician contact rates, but Britain with capitation and salary, has a similar low rate to the USA, with fee for service. The level of consumption may be determined more by its free nature rather than the method of payment. Payer (1990: 78–9) points out the effects both of physicians' and patients' behaviour. She compares Britain and Germany. Patients in both countries pay few out-of-pocket expenses (unlike in France) and so have no incentives to economize on medical costs. However, German doctors, as they are paid by fee for service, are unlike British doctors in having little incentive to economize. In particular, they are rewarded by use of technology such as electrocardiograms. In Britain, GPs are paid largely by capitation and specialists are paid by salary. So in contrast to other countries, where GPs and specialists often fight over patients, in Britain – to exaggerate a little – they fight over not having patients, so as to keep the workload down. 'More patients do not mean more money, and they can only cut down on civilized institutions such as the tea break' (Payer 1990: 105–6). Mooney (1994: 116) states that the evidence for greater variation associated with fee-for-service medicine is scant, and much will depend on the nature of the fee schedule rather than on the existence of fee for services *per se*. 'The crude "FFS means overservicing" reaction of health economists is far too simplistic' (Mooney 1994: 122).

It is claimed that whether patients have direct access to specialists or must be referred by GPs or 'gatekeepers' has implications for expenditure. There is some suggestion that countries that allow free choice of primary-care physician for each service and pay primary-care physicians by fee for service, such as Germany, have higher consultation rates, longer consultation times and higher prescribing rates than countries such as Britain that pay most physicians by capitation or salary (OECD 1992a: 133). No particular model of the organization of health service delivery and financing seemed to have a clear advantage in controlling costs but there are some indications that countries with capitation or salaried payment and a strong referral system tended to keep costs down (OECD 1994: 43; Oxley and MacFarlan 1994: 43–4).

Effectiveness

'The crucial yardstick by which all aspects of medical care will come to be measured will inevitably be outcome and, in particular, the improvement in outcome consequent upon the particular intervention' (McPherson 1990: 17). The important question, then, is do variations in medical practice matter? Is Britain doing too little or the USA too much? What impact does this have on patients? How are outputs linked to outcomes? In other words, what is the 'value-added' of health care? We would expect the impact of health care on health to be positive. However, some have claimed that in some cases it is marginal or even negative. Despite the popularity in Canada of hysterectomy and mastectomy, the death rates from cervical, uterine and breast cancer were very similar to those in England and Wales, while for diseases of the gallbladder, the mortality rate in elderly women and men was twice as high in Canada although the cholecystectomy rate was five times higher. Some of the excess mortality may be attributed to the increased surgery (Vayda 1973: see also Illich 1975).

There are a number of difficulties in determining the effect of health care on health. The first is the problem of defining health. Mortality rates are often used as a proxy for it; and a high level of spending does not necessarily ensure high health status (Maxwell 1981: 51). For example, West Germany ranked highest and the USA ranked second (of 10) for expenditure as a percentage of GDP, but they ranked tenth and ninth (i.e. worst) respectively on a composite mortality ranking. Conversely, Britain ranked tenth on expenditure, but fourth in terms of mortality. On the other hand, countries such as Sweden and the Netherlands did well on both expenditure and mortality (Maxwell 1981: 52). This early study is dated and limited by the utility of correlation and regression techniques for 10 countries. However, the broad relationship has been confirmed by other studies: there is a statistically significant inverse correlation of 0.68 between health spending per capita and the IMR (OECD 1987: 43-4). In other words, expenditure statistically 'explains' about half the variation in IMRs, and countries that spend more on health tend to have lower IMRs. In general, aggregate mortality measures are only weakly related to health-care spending (Oxley and MacFarlan 1994: 19-21, 72). Moreover, such associations do not necessarily indicate causality, since higher spending on health is also associated with higher levels of national wealth, and the lower rates of infant mortality may be due to the greater wealth rather than to the health care. The correlations between *per capita* health spending and life expectancies tend to be statistically significant for females but not for males. This may be because the morbidity pattern for women is more amenable to intervention than for men: life expectancy for men may be linked more to occupational factors, while for women it may be linked to factors specific to the health system (OECD 1987: 42). There appears to be little association between health spending and deaths from malignant neoplasms and diseases of the circulatory system (OECD 1987: 45), implying that deaths from such causes may be linked more with social rather than medical factors.

Equity

Of the two yardsticks used by economists to judge the performance of health-care systems – equity and efficiency – the latter has dominated cross-country comparisons. In contrast there are few international studies of equity. As a result, little is known about the equity characteristics of alternative health-care financing and delivery systems. This is despite the apparent importance attached to equity as a policy objective in most OECD countries (Wagstaff *et al.* 1993: 2). Equity is one of the key objectives of most health-care systems – at least in terms of various policy documents and policy statements it appears to be so. However, the reality, in terms of the extent to which equity is pursued in practice, is not always what one might conclude from reading the policy documents (Mooney 1994: 65). There is a broad measure of support for the idea that health care ought to be distributed according to need and financed according to ability to pay: in other words, equity in distribution (who benefits?) and equity in finance (who pays?) (Wagstaff and Van Doorslaer 1993a: 15). Equity in finance concerns the sources of income: taxation, social insurance, private insurance premia and out-of-pocket payments. Finance from taxation is the most progressive, followed by social insurance; and the countries with private insurance or out-of-pocket payments are the most regressive. Britain is one of the few countries that finances health care progressively, while the USA has one of the most regressive structures (Van Doorslaer and Wagstaff 1993). On the two criteria for equity in distribution – equality of health and equal treatment for equal need – Britain and the USA tend to score badly, while countries such as the Netherlands, Switzerland and Denmark do well. With the exception of the USA, it appears that countries that spend a lot on health care tend to have smaller inequalities in morbidity. 'Thus higher health care spending in Europe seems to "buy" some reduction in health inequality' (Wagstaff and Van Doorslaer 1993b: 56), although this may be due to factors external to the health-care system, such as the degree of income inequality. Moreover, the picture is complex: while some countries such as Sweden, Norway and Finland have low differentials both for mortality and morbidity, Germany and the USA have differentials that are high for morbidity but low for mortality, while the reverse is true in Britain (Power 1994).

In terms of differences in the delivery of health care, Britain and Spain emerge poorly, while Denmark and Switzerland have the least inequity. Thus, there appears to be inequity favouring the rich in some countries where public cover is universal and comprehensive, notably Spain and Britain. Conversely, health-care systems that do not have universal and comprehensive public cover are not necessarily those with the highest degree of inequality. Indeed, inequity appears to be less in countries such as the Netherlands (where public cover is income-related) and in Switzerland (where public cover is virtually non-existent) (Wagstaff and Van Doorslaer 1993b: 82–3). There is some difference, then, in equity of finance and distribution: Britain does well on equity in finance, but poorly on equity in distribution, whereas the reverse is true for Switzerland.

HEALTH-CARE SYSTEMS

Many people think of the NHS in an ethnocentric manner: either the NHS is the only possible type of system or it is at least the 'best in the world'. In the 1940s Britain decided for the 'NHS model' and against developing the earlier routes of social insurance and local government, although these options had their supporters at the time and other countries did develop along these lines. There have been recent calls that the NHS route is a cul-de-sac and that we ought to return to the other roads (for example, Whitney 1988; Green 1993). However, the only thing we tend to know about other health-care systems is that they spend more on health care than we do. There are a number of different models of health care, although variations within them mean that there are as many systems as there are countries.

Health-care systems can be characterized in a variety of ways, none of which is mutually exhaustive or wholly analytically satisfying. The most frequent approach categorizes systems according to one of three basic models (OECD 1987; Timmins 1988; Leathard 1990). The first is the national health service or Beveridge model: universal coverage is funded out of general taxation, with provision administered by the state, as in Britain. The second is the national health insurance or Bismarck model: compulsory health insurance is funded by employers and individuals, largely through state schemes. Substantial private provision exists on a fee-for-service basis, as in Germany, France and Japan. Third, there is the voluntary private insurance or market model: voluntary private insurance and provision exists, underpinned by a safety net for selected groups of the population. In the case of the USA, the public systems are Medicare (for the old) and Medicaid (for some of the poor).

Sketches of three countries are presented. First, Germany is a model of and pioneer of NHI. As the British NHS established a new policy model, the German NHI influenced the set of policy alternatives in other nations (Immergut 1992: 65). Second, Sweden is usually regarded as a *de jure* NHI but *de facto* NHS model, covering all citizens with high-quality care and an emphasis on equality. Moreover, the Swedish system appears to achieve good results in terms of the level and degree of inequality of health status. Finally, it offers a localist model of health-care. Some on the political left point to Sweden as a model to follow. Third, the USA is a market-based model, one of the few industrialized countries that does not cover the vast majority of its citizens. It is generally regarded by the political right as having desirable features that the NHS should copy.

Germany

'Rarely, if ever, in modern history has a single piece of legislation had such a profound worldwide impact as the German Sickness Insurance Law of 1883' (Leichter 1979: 110). Germany represents the prototype of the social insurance model, which has survived, virtually unscathed, a number of political, military and social upheavals for over a century (Appleby 1992: 115). Following some earlier legislation in Prussia, the German Chancellor Otto von

Bismarck introduced social insurance in 1883. The basics of the scheme were fairly simple. It provided for compulsory participation by all industrial wage earners. Workers were to pay a maximum of 3–6 per cent of their wages, representing two-thirds of the total premium, with the employers contributing the remaining third. Initially the scheme covered less than 10 per cent of the population, but it has gradually come to cover almost all of it. In return, contributors were to have access to health care and sick pay when ill. The scheme was to be administered by insurance funds, which were based on existing trade unions and guilds.

After the Second World War, Germany was divided. The Federal Republic (West Germany) broadly continued with the scheme, while the Democratic Republic (East Germany) adopted a 'socialist' health-care system. Since reunification, the system for the whole of Germany has once again been based on social insurance.

However, there is more to the German system than social insurance. Moran (1995: 86) states that the German system rests on three principles: compulsory insurance, federal organization and the segmentation of ambulatory and institutional care. If the key principle of funding is compulsory insurance, the dominant principle of organization is the federal structure based on *Länder*. The third principle is the clear separation, embodied in law, between ambulatory and institutional care. The law more or less prohibits hospitals from providing the kind of care delivered to day patients by outpatient departments in Britain. This leads to increased prestige of ambulatory care, and a wider range of it. The patient can consult a specialist simply by walking in off the streets, rather than by referral, as in Britain.

Although the system is insurance-based, non-contributors such as the retired and the unemployed are covered. Almost all German workers are obliged to join a health insurance fund. Some highly paid employees are allowed to opt out of the compulsory scheme and take out private insurance cover. In practice, many choose voluntarily to join the scheme, which covers about 90 per cent of the population (75 per cent by compulsion and 13 per cent by choice). Sick funds are private, not-for-profit organizations responsible for paying for the health care of their members. Currently, there are over 1100 sick funds, with membership usually based on people's employment or area of residence. Each fund manages its own affairs and representatives of trade unions and employers play a major part in this process. One change from the original scheme is that contributors and employers now each pay half the total income of the scheme, with the employees' contribution being based on a fixed percentage of income. The sickness funds can be separated into 'RVO-kassen' (State Insurance Regulation) funds, covering about 60 per cent of the population, and 'Ersatzkassen' (substitute funds), which cover about 28 per cent of the population. The former cater for both blue- and white-collar workers. Some are organized on a local basis, some on an occupational basis and some on an enterprise basis. The latter, which already existed as mutual aid societies, when the state scheme was set up, cater mainly for white-collar workers and, because of a certain amount of risk selection, are in a strong position to compete for voluntary members. There is some element of a two-tier system, as about half of all members, mainly white-collar workers, can choose their sickness fund, while some RVO-kassen, catering mainly for blue-collar workers, are obliged to act as a safety net for disadvantaged individuals who do not belong to any group of employees. The sickness funds are obliged by law to offer a basket of benefits, but they are also able to offer additional, optional benefits. Premiums may vary within a given range, but they average about 12 per cent of gross income, varying from 8 to 16 per cent. Generally the funds that are organized on a local basis have the highest rates. There is considerable competition between the funds for voluntary members, largely on the basis of offering higher optional benefits rather than by lowering premiums (OECD 1992a: 60).

In terms of sources of funds, about 60 per cent of health expenditure is derived from compulsory and voluntary contributions to statutory health insurance, about 21 per cent is derived from general taxation, about 7 per cent is derived from private insurance and about 11 per cent is represented by unreimbursed, out-of-pocket expenditure. Patients pay only minor, direct charges for health services under the statutory insurance system. For example, in 1988, these included prescription charges of about DM 2 per person, hospital charges of DM 5 per day for the first 14 days in hospital and charges of DM 5 for non-emergency patient transport. However, these charges were subject to ceilings on total payments and to exemptions, mainly for children and for people with low incomes.

There are three main types of hospital: public hospitals, which may be owned by federal bodies (*Länder*) or local governments, accounting for 51 per cent of beds; private voluntary hospitals, which are often owned by religious organizations, accounting for 35 per cent of beds; and private proprietary hospitals, which are often owned by doctors, accounting for 14 per cent of beds.

In 1995 Germany introduced a statutory insurance scheme for long-term care. Contributions are 1.7 per cent of earnings, and benefits cover cash benefits for home and institutional care (excluding board and lodging) (Chadda 1995). Germany has the problems of dealing with the 'lamentable legacy' of the former East Germany. It is likely that there will be more freedom and competition between funds from 1997. Imbalances will be reduced by transfer payments between funds in deficit and those in surplus (similar to a recommendation of the Royal Commission on National Health Insurance in Britain in 1926). There will be incentives to increase the level of treatment outside hospitals (Moran 1995: 99).

Moran (1995) considers that the German system achieves universal coverage, freedom of choice and high-quality care with relatively short waiting times, comparatively economically. Indeed, 'Germany before reunification was probably the best country in the world in which to be treated for ill health, regardless of whether a patient was rich or poor' (Moran 1995: 92). Nevertheless, the German system is said to suffer from a number of problems. First, paying clinic doctors fees for each item of service has generated huge investments in high-technology equipment, often little used but acquired to attract patients and generate fees. West Germany, it is said, has enough lithotripters to smash every kidney stone in Europe (Timmins 1988: 76). As in many other advanced capitalist nations, Germany suffers from a 'bed mountain' – an overprovision of beds relative to need. However, while there is a gross surplus of doctors, there is a shortage of nurses (Moran 1995: 95–6). There is also the problem of equity. The highest rates of contribution tend to be associated with the poorest funds (Moran 1995: 96–7): a situation very similar to the criticisms of the NHI scheme in Britain before the NHS (Chapter 2). Thus, Germany has some elements of a 'two-tier' service.

Sweden

The Swedish health-care system is comprehensive and based on the regional authorities of elected county councils. It is nominally an NHI scheme, but coverage is not restricted to those who have contributed. In other words, it is a *de jure* national insurance scheme, but *de facto* a health service, based at the local rather than the national level. It typifies, to some extent, the municipal health service that Britain had before the NHS, and which early plans for the NHS were based on. It serves as a model for a localist health service.

Sweden was relatively laggardly in developing health insurance. As in other countries, the end of the Second World War was seen as the time to enlarge the scope of social citizenship. In 1943 a commission was set up to study the existing health system and to make recommendations. The resulting Hojer report of 1948 called for a national health service, whose ambitions surpassed those of the British NHS. Hospital inpatient services would be delivered at virtually no cost and all forms of outpatient care would be integrated into the service. Private patients' fees would be eliminated and all doctors would be paid a government salary. The proposals were seen as too radical and they were dropped. In place of a national health service, a new NHI law was introduced in 1953 and went into effect in 1955. The 'seven crowns' reform of 1969 eliminated private practice from public hospitals entirely and replaced fee-for-service payments to hospital doctors with full-time salaries. These measures introduced several of the more controversial points of the Hojer reform. As Immergut (1992: 220) puts it, 'With the enactment of the Seven Crowns reform, the Swedish health system moved a decisive step towards becoming a national health service'. According to some critics, it represented the total socialization of Swedish health care overnight. A further reform in 1985 – the 'Dagmar reform' – restructured NHI payments for visits by ambulatory physicians. Nominally, it was designed to reinforce existing long-term policy objectives by consolidating all primary-care services into the publicly operated county health system. In practice, it established 26 separate county-led planned markets for ambulatory-care services, several of which soon developed in rather different policy directions (Saltman and Von Otter 1992: 42). The reform distributed government subsidies to hospitals according to the number of inhabitants in their areas rather than by each hospital visit. This was meant to produce greater equality in funding rather than rewarding the areas with high provision and high use. Dagmar changed the fee-for-service mechanism into an annual capitated payment (age- and sex-adjusted) for visits by primary care physicians. There was also some further restriction on private practice. Private practitioners could continue to deliver publicly insured visits only with the explicit permission of, and only up to the volume agreed by, the county councils. Thus, with the responsibility for planning and financing for primary care consolidated in county hands, the private sector became fully dependent on the public sector for its survival.

The Dagmar reform of 1985 fulfilled a dual role. On the one hand, it was the capstone in the creation of a primary-care-based, county council operated health system. On the other hand, however, the Dagmar reform began the unravelling of national planning policy, facilitating the emergence of planned markets and organizational pluralism as the dominant policy perspective in the late 1980s.

(Saltman and Von Otter 1992: 43)

The pluralism and diversity resulting from the Dagmar reforms have, to some extent, undermined the Hojer scheme, which had eventually 'come to form the core of Swedish health policy for more than a decade' (Saltman and Von Otter 1992: 42). The Swedish health system is in the midst of substantial structural and organizational reform. The Hojer-based policy period, with its emphasis on an allocative planning system and prioritization of publicly produced primary health care, appears to be approaching its end. A period of experimentation with elements of greater choice and pluralism is now in progress, and is likely to lead to greater diversity (Saltman and Von Otter 1992: 55–6). Some counties did reduce the volume of private visits, but others contracted out new segments of primary-care provision to the private sector. This pluralism is also seen in secondary care. There is greater use of private hospitals, including one case of a round trip air fare to a London AMI hospital for coronary bypass operations (Saltman and Von Otter 1992: 44–7).

Like many other countries, Sweden has embraced the purchaser–provider split. There is anecdotal evidence of small changes that show providers to be more aware of their marketing activities, such as one hospital where patients rather than staff have the most convenient car parking spaces, and coach tours in Stockholm to help expectant mothers (and fathers to be) to choose maternity units (Anell 1995). The reforms are in their early stages, but it appears that there have been gains in accessibility and productivity.

Responsibility both for inpatient and outpatient services belongs to the 23 county councils and three large municipalities: Goteborg (Gothenburg), Malmo and the island of Gotland. These counties range in population from 60,000 to 1.7 million, with an average of about 300,000. About 80 per cent of county council activities are devoted to medical and health-care services. Much responsibility is devolved to the county level. In effect, this means that there are 26 different health-care systems in Sweden (similar to those of the states in the USA).

The financing and provider arrangements in the Swedish system are largely under the same ownership and management. The major insurers and sources of finance are the county councils, which are also responsible for producing health services. Local democratic legitimacy is associated with variations of about 45 per cent in the per capita cost of health care, with the variation for municipalities being more than 60 per cent (OECD 1992a: 274). About 70 per cent of the cost of health care is covered by the tax levied and administered by the county councils, with grants from the national government covering a further 20 per cent. 'The existence of what are, in effect, elected health authorities accountable to their communities and with the ability to raise money through taxes is one of the major differences between the UK and Sweden' (Ham *et al.* 1990: 23).

The patient pays a standard fee set by each county council for public outpatient services; it costs about Skr 100 (£5) to consult a physician. The standard fee entitles patients to laboratory tests, X-rays, sickness benefit certificates and referrals to specialists. There are charges also for prescriptions (Skr 90), direct access services such as physiotherapy (Skr 50) and hospital inpatient care (Skr a day 60-70) (OECD 1994: 271; Glennerster and Matsaganis 1994: 243).

The health standard of the Swedish people is unquestionably one of the highest in the world. Maxwell (1981) ranked it first (i.e. best) on composite mortality index, although the relative effect of health care as opposed to living standards is unclear. Inequalities are comparatively low (Ginsberg, 1992: 63; Townsend *et al.* 1992). For example, socio-economic differentials in the IMR have all but disappeared.

A number of criticisms have been aimed at the Swedish system. It has one of the highest levels of hospital beds in the world and is very 'hospital centred'. The other side of the coin is that until recently primary care was given much lower emphasis. Primary physicians have relatively low status. For example, about half of the 4000 posts in health centres are unfilled (Glennerster and Matsaganis 1994: 244). Unlike GPs in Britain, Swedish GPs do not act as gatekeepers to the hospital service and many patients refer themselves directly to hospital. A further feature is the lack of integration between primary care, hospital care and social services (Ham *et al.* 1990: 25–6). Indeed, it has been claimed that:

> Health services in Sweden exhibit many of the same problems that exist in the UK. The parallels are not exact, but the existence of waiting lists, the lack of incentives for efficiency, failures of coordination between sectors, and too heavy an

investment in institutional care mirror widely-recognised weaknesses within the NHS.

(Ham *et al.* 1990: 34)

USA

The US system is large, complex and heterogeneous. Indeed, some commentators regard the term 'system' as a misnomer. It represents a potentially bewildering patchwork of institutions – private and public; local, state and federal (Robinson 1990: 33). Health care, unlike education, is essentially a private matter. Of industrial democracies, only the USA and South Africa have a substantial population without any health insurance (Regan 1992: 13–15). The US system is generally associated with a number of myths, or at best partial truths. It is often said to be characterized by profit and competition, with the poor totally lacking access to care. However, non-profit hospitals represent some 59 per cent of 'community acute care' (general) hospitals, with local government hospitals accounting for a further 27 per cent. The 'classic' private hospitals, run for profit, account for a mere 14 per cent of all beds, although this sector is growing rapidly. In other words, the majority of hospitals are privately owned, but this conflates private 'not for profit' with investor-owned, 'for profit' hospitals. Most doctors and hospitals operate on a fee-for-service (or piece-work) basis. However, the actual level of competition between doctors is said to have been low until fairly recently. Some provision was made for the poor and the elderly in 1965 during the 'Great Society' reforms, but it is true that health care does remain largely a private rather than a public matter.

About three-quarters of the population is covered by private health insurance. Those under 65 years of age and their dependants obtain private health insurance either through their employers (61 per cent) or by direct purchase (13 per cent), with a further 13 per cent having multiple coverage (e.g. both public and private) and 14 per cent having none. This means that an estimated 30–40 million people have no insurance. Health care is an example of occupational welfare (OECD 1992b: 36–9), but the best packages are for those in large companies or with strong trade unions, as in the automobile industry, whereas service workers, such as those in the restaurant trade, may have little or no coverage. In 1983, a survey of large companies found that the costs of health benefits accounted for nearly a quarter of their pre-tax profits. In 1984 it was estimated that health benefits added about 10 per cent to the price of a cheaper model of a Chrysler car (Ham *et al.* 1990: 62–3).

Most private health insurance covers inpatient hospital services and physician services but, like motor insurance in Britain, the breadth and depth of the coverage varies and patients often pay something towards the total cost (the 'deductible'). Few packages are fully comprehensive and it has been estimated that some 55 million Americans with private insurance are underinsured (OECD 1992a: 319). While out-of-pocket payments represent only 6 per cent of hospital care, they represent 44 per cent of total nursing-home spending (OECD 1992a: 320).

Most insurance policies have benefit ceilings that are not sufficient to cover serious, long-term illness, and many people supplement their normal health insurance with 'major medical expense' or 'catastrophic illness' policies, but even these usually have ceilings and typically cover 80 per cent of the full amount. This means that there are very few people who, for reasons of losing their job or suffering from an 'expensive' illness, may not be thrown upon their own resources, those of the state or city government, or charity.

There are two public packages. Medicaid is a health insurance programme for certain groups of the poor, covering preventive, acute and long-term care services for 25 million people or 10 per cent of the population. It is jointly financed by federal and state governments and is administered by the states under broad federal guidelines governing the scope of services, the level of payments to providers, and population groups eligible for coverage. The largest client groups for Medicaid are mothers and dependent children, accounting for 68 per cent of recipients, with the elderly accounting for a further 13 per cent and blind and disabled people for a further 15 per cent. Childless, non-disabled adults under 65 years of age, no matter how poor or how high their medical expenses, are not eligible. This means that about 60 per cent of the poor below the federal poverty line are excluded from the programme (OECD 1992a: 320). In other words, although Medicaid is intended for poor people, it serves only a minority of them (as defined by the federal poverty line). Moreover, the holes in the safety net are growing. Medicaid covered 76 per cent of the poor in 1965 but only an estimated 38 per cent in 1991 (Regan 1992: 42).

As individual states have a degree of flexibility in setting income eligibility levels, the range of services covered and the duration of coverage, there are considerable variations between the way individuals in identical circumstances are treated in different states

(Wood 1995). Generally, poorer states such as Alabama are more restrictive than richer ones such as New York (Regan 1992: 20–21). In other words, poorer people tend to be better served in richer states.

Medicare is a national health insurance programme for the aged and the disabled, and is more uniform than Medicaid. It is administered by the federal government and covers about 13 per cent of the population, including virtually all the 31 million people aged 65 or over. The programme is financed by a combination of payroll taxes, general federal revenues, and premiums. It comprises two parts: coverage under Part A is earned through payment of a payroll tax during one's working years; coverage under Part B is voluntarily obtained through payment of a premium once eligibility for Medicare is established. Coverage under Part A (hospital insurance) includes inpatient hospital care, very limited nursing-home services, and some home health services. The Part A payroll tax is paid by virtually all employed individuals, with 1.45 per cent of income being matched by the employer. Part B (medical insurance) includes physician and other ambulatory services. Premiums account for 35 per cent of the costs, with the remainder coming from general federal revenues. Medicare patients must pay co-insurance and 'deductibles', which account for an average of 17 per cent of the services covered by Medicare and consume an average of 6 per cent of patients' per capita income (OECD 1992a: 319). About two-thirds of Medicare beneficiaries have private insurance (known as 'medigap' policies) to cover these out-of-pocket costs and the costs of uncovered services. The major gaps in Medicare are in long-term care (nursing homes) and prescribed medicine. By paying towards excluded services and cost sharing, the elderly now spend nearly 20 per cent of their income on 'out-of-pocket' health-care expenses (Regan 1992: 45).

The uninsured resort to a mixture of public hospitals or to 'charity care' or 'uncompensated care' by other providers. It was estimated that charity care and bad debts represented 5 per cent of hospital expenses in 1988. In other words, the uninsured are not likely to go without care at all, but generally receive care regarded as inappropriate (e.g. in hospital emergency rooms) and inferior in quality (OECD 1992b: 39–40). They tend to delay care, so that early prevention is a casualty of the system.

There were many changes in the US system during the 1980s, reflecting two contradictory trends: towards greater competition and greater regulation. There has been greater cost sharing.

Although the US system is generally seen as a market system, it was not until the 1980s that much competition was evident. The 1980s were termed a 'competition revolution' in that some anti-trust legislation was applied to doctors. Doctors were viewed not as a 'profession', but as a business or service in the market. The removal of restraints on trade has influenced the development of competition in two main ways. First, there has been a substantial growth in the number and variety of health insurance plans on offer, associated with intensive advertising and marketing techniques. Second, hospitals are now competing in terms of price and quality, and again advertising and marketing activities are prominent. The trend towards regulation was based on a desire to contain costs. In 1983 Medicare introduced a new form of price control: the prospective payments system. Before this, Medicare reimbursed hospitals on a retrospective cost basis. This gave hospitals an incentive to spend more, but under the prospective payments system they are given allocations based on a fixed amount per patient. The precise amounts are determined by allocating patients to one of approximately 470 diagnostic related groups. These groups seek to separate patients into clinically homogeneous categories that can be used as a basis for measuring different levels of resource use.

Health maintenance organizations (HMOs) were seen as the antidote to the incentives to increase costs that are traditionally associated with fee-for-service medicine. They are essentially capitation based. Members pay a set fee and receive all the health care deemed necessary. HMOs are similar to earlier British friendly societies before the NHI of 1911 (Green 1985, 1986). The incentive is now to minimize cost. In 1970 there were fewer than 30 HMOs, serving under 3 million people. Since then their growth has been dramatic. There were some 250 HMOs, with nearly 11 million members, in 1981, and some 550, with nearly 40 million members, in 1990. However, some commentators argue that the increase was too rapid. There were 700 HMOs in 1987 and some merged or disappeared in the late 1980s (Raffel and Raffel 1994: 65). There has also been a large increase in preferred-provider organizations. According to Robinson (1990: 23) these represent a modified form of insurance-based, fee-for-service response to HMOs. The preferred-provider organizations are a 'halfway house between a HMO and traditional fee-for-service' (Green 1986: 71). In essence, they are insurance plans that are able to offer lower premiums because they negotiate fee-for-service discounts with specified doctors and hospitals in return for guaranteeing them a given volume of work. If members use the preferred provider, they tend to face lower direct costs: for example, 10 per cent as opposed to 20 per cent of the total bill. This is similar to some motor insurance schemes in Britain that seek to persuade policy holders to use their recommended networks of repair agents. Part of the reason for the popularity of preferred-provider organizations is that patients have more choice between doctors, rather than being locked in and having limited scope for changing doctors in the event of unsatisfactory service. Their numbers have grown almost fivefold since 1983, so that by 1987 there were over 600, with an estimated 31 million enrolees, rivalling HMOs in size. Regulatory mechanisms such as HMOs and diagnostic related groups reverse the incentives: they contain costs rather than increase expenditure (Regan 1992: 23–7). In spite of these measures, total costs have continued to increase.

There are some signs that advances in the 1960s and 1970s are halting or even reversing, since the financial retrenchment of the 1980s. The number of uninsured steadily rose throughout the 1980s from about 29 million to about 37 million. There were increases in the IMR in 11 states during 1981 and 1982. In 1983 the maternal death rate increased for the first time in decades (Ginsberg 1992: 136). Moreover, Medicare will enter the next century on the brink of insolvency (OECD 1992a: 319). There is a clear multi-tier service, with the overworked and underfunded public hospitals at the bottom. Some of these closed in the 1980s, while those remaining are likely to become 'the twenty-first century version of the workhouse hospital' (Ginsberg 1992: 129–30). Financial crises in some large cities such as Los Angeles, Washington, Boston and New York may be leading towards 'the end of public healthcare' (Berliner 1995). Health-care workers have been laid off, beds closed and there are calls for hospitals to be closed.

Assessments of the US system are very varied. A minority view is that it works well on the whole. While many criticisms of health care in the US are associated with an excess of competition, writers such as Green argue that the defects in US medicine are due to too little competition. He argues that the increased competition in the 1980s led to benefits. 'Competition works in America to the benefit of the consumer' (Green 1986: 99).

On the other hand, the majority view is that the US system produces poor results. Some commentators have argued that the system is at the edge of moral and financial bankruptcy. There is the problem of 'rationing a surplus':

Millions are denied care, while hospitals beds lie empty and medical personnel are too often idle – or even making mischief. Of coronary artery operations in the United States, one-seventh do patients more harm than good, a proportion that may be modest compared with procedures such as tonsillec-tomies, prostatectomies, and caesarean sections. Redundant investments in technology sometimes actually worsen care – one third of the California hospitals performing heart surgery don't do enough to be good at it. Meanwhile, a growing army of administrators fights to keep the uninsured patients away from the empty hospital beds.

(Woolhandler *et al.* 1993: 194)

The OECD (1992b: 53) has termed the situation 'a worsening paradox of excess and deprivation', while a similar description is 'opulent splendour and shocking deprivation side by side' (quoted in Regan 1992: 3). According to Tudor-Hart (1994: 64–5), it is the world's most costly, most inefficient, most irrational and most unjust health service.

The USA does poorly on mortality, ranked ninth out of 10 indus-trial countries (Maxwell 1981), but this hides a large variation, or 'health gap' (Ginsberg 1992: 135–6). There are large variations in cover, utilization and outcome by income and race. Indeed, measures of inequality are rising. For example the black–white ratio in the IMR rose from about 1.8 in 1980 to over 2.1 by the end of the 1980s. Men in Harlem can now expect shorter lives than men in Bangladesh (Woolhandler *et al.* 1993: 200). In other words, almost the whole world of variation in health and health care can be found in the USA, sometimes within one city. In general, and on a variety of scales, correlations between income and the provision and use of health care are negative while those between income and health care are inverse – perhaps the best illustration of the 'inverse care law' (Tudor-Hart 1971).

The reform of health-care systems

After a long period of expansion – 'more of the same' – health-care systems have undergone a period of reappraisal. Cost containment is firmly on the agenda. To oversimplify: high levels of health-care expenditure are seen as a vice rather than a virtue. 'An emerging paradigm' of health-care reform is evident in many countries (Chernichovsky 1995). In northern European systems there has been a trend away from the relatively rigid 'command-and-control' planning model towards varieties of public competition (Saltman and Von Otter 1992, 1995; OECD 1992a, 1994). Many of the reforms are aimed at limiting health expenditures to an acceptable share of national resources, with two countries making an absolute reduction in health expenditure between 1982 and 1992: Denmark and Germany (OECD 1994: 37–9). Tight budgets rather than cost sharing has been the major weapon to achieve cost containment (OECD 1994: 27). The development of alternatives to hospital inpatient care is seen by many countries as an important way of using resources more effectively, particularly, but by no means exclusively, for the aged (OECD 1994: 21). In a study of 17 countries the OECD (1994: 45) concluded that 'The most remarkable feature of the health care system reforms . . . is the degree of emerging convergence,' with the most significant change being the movement away from the public integrated model towards the public contract model, which appears better suited to the pursuit of micro-efficiency and macro-efficiency (OECD 1994: 50).

BRITAIN IN INTERNATIONAL CONTEXT

The NHS tends to be viewed favourably in the international context. Its supporters point out a number of strengths: the GP service, tight cost control, a high degree of equity and its relative efficiency. On the other hand, it suffers from a lack of consumer control, the size of its waiting lists and underfunding (Timmins 1988: 79). Mechanic (1995: 57) finds a number of impressive features, such as cost control and equity, but that the NHS has become rather set in its ways, somewhat inefficient and unresponsive, and not particularly receptive to innovation or to patient preferences – 'the consultant always knows best'.

There is no dispute that the NHS is a relatively low-cost system, but it is more difficult to say whether this is primarily due to efficiency or economy: whether it is a good system or just a cheap one. It spends a low proportion of its budget on administration (Maxwell 1981: 93). One estimate put this at about 5 per cent, compared with about 10 per cent for France and Germany and over 20 per cent for the USA (RSHG 1987: 102). However, it is less impressive on other estimates (Oxley and MacFarlan 1994: 76). The explanation is relatively simple: revenue is collected as part of general taxation rather than by a dedicated insurance scheme, and no one is employed to produce bills and check eligibility. The NHS also manages to squeeze a great deal of value out of its money. It is practically a monopoly buyer or monopsony for medical goods and services (Griffith *et al.* 1987: 234–5). This means that it gets drugs and staff at comparatively inexpensive rates and gets more health care for its money. Doctors are paid by salary and capitation rather than by fee for service and there is little incentive for over-treatment.

> Perhaps the most important single strength of the British National Health Service is the pattern of general practice and the convention of referral from primary and secondary to tertiary care. . . . Over 80 per cent of episodes of illness reaching the National Health Service are dealt with from start to finish by general practitioners who account . . . for well under 20 per cent of total expenditure.
>
> (Maxwell 1981: 87)

Owen (1988: 3) has claimed that 'Our concept of the family doctor is unique'.

Rationing tends to be tighter in Britain than in the USA. 'The most striking characteristic of British medicine is its economy. The British do less of nearly everything: shorter consultations, fewer examinations, fewer X-rays, fewer prescribed drugs and less high technology medicine (Payer 1990: 101–3). This means that people with some conditions would get treated in the USA, but not in Britain. In general, some life-saving treatments such as bone marrow transplantation are carried out at roughly the same level in both countries. However, Britain does poorly on kidney dialysis, especially for those aged about 45 and over, and on intensive-care beds, coronary artery surgery and expensive equipment such as computerized tomography scanners. Ironically, the NHS, with its strong commitment to equality, has allowed less egalitarian access to dialysis machines than the market-orientated American system, which historically has had a relatively low commitment to equality of access to care (Hollingsworth *et al.* 1990: 143). In the case of chronic renal dialysis, 'the result of rationing is clearly death' (Mechanic 1995: 58). However, the problems of potential 'under-doctoring' must be set against those of 'overdoctoring' elsewhere.

The main negative features in Britain are seen as queueing and lack of consumer responsiveness. In the USA, if someone with insurance is told today that open heart surgery or a knee replacement is needed, then he or she expects to begin treatment within a few days. To wait months or more than a year would be unthinkable.

Or if diagnosis might be even marginally more certain by use of a magnetic resonance scan, the American patient would not accept being told that there are not enough machines and he or she will have to wait or go ahead without the assurance of further testing (Regan 1992: 87–8). As Regan (1992: 158) points out, Britain and the USA have different forms of rationing: all are eligible but wait in queues in Britain, while in the USA there is little waiting for most but some do not have the right to get into line.

The political right tend to see more faults in the NHS than in the US system. For example, Goodman (1980) claims that US health services are superior because they have been shaped by private citizens making choices as individuals in what is, for the most part, a free market for heath care whereas, in Britain, health-care decisions are made through the political process. At root, this is an ideological judgement, but Goodman does present some evidence for his assertion. He claims that Britain wastes money on ambulance journeys that are little more than 'free taxi services', and on primary care that offers little more than comfort and reassurance, while acute services are starved of resources. Much of this evidence is disputed: for example, general practice is cited by Goodman as a weak point, but for many it is a major strength of the NHS (Griffith *et al.* 1987; Maxwell 1981; Owen 1988). Conversely, many writers see much waste, overinvestment in technology and much unnecessary surgery in the USA.

Britain does only moderately well on indicators such as the IMR and life expectancy, ranking ninth and about eleventh respectively in Europe. Britain is not alone in experiencing inequalities in health. Every country to a greater or lesser degree experiences differences in health associated with geographical, socio-economic, racial and gender factors. Comparative studies lend support to the suggestion that the Nordic countries experience less social inequality in health than other European countries, including England and Wales (Townsend *et al.* 1992: 310). On most indicators, Britain has a more equitable distribution of health and health care than the USA (Hollingsworth *et al.* 1990: ch. 7).

Griffith *et al.* (1987: 239–40) conclude that the NHS is a moderately effective system for rationing health care, with low costs and facilitating a relatively humane form of medical practice. They continue that the NHS is one of the best systems in the world, and that it has the potential to become genuinely first rate. Tudor-Hart (1994: 64–5) termed the unreformed NHS 'the least costly, least inefficient, least irrational, least socially unjust health service in the world'. The Royal Commission on the NHS (1979: 356) concluded that 'we need not feel ashamed of our health services and that there are many aspects of it of which we can be justly proud'. The NHS may not be the best in the world, but given the caveat of its relatively low expenditure, it may be the best value for money in the world: a bargain buy of health-care systems – the envy of the world's finance ministers if not its health ministers.

LESSONS FROM ABROAD?

It is now accepted that it is desirable to learn lessons from abroad (Timmins 1988; Owen 1988; Ham *et al.* 1990), but it is not possible simply to transfer policies. Saltman and Von Otter (1992: 7) suggest that concepts such as diagnostic related groups and HMOs, which were designed to reduce expenditure within an insurance-based, fee-for-service delivery system, may be inappropriate within the context of the tax-based, globally budgeted health systems of northern Europe.

No perfect method of finance has been found. There have been a number of calls to move towards insurance. Social insurance offers a middle way between tax financing and private insurance. Social insurance is an earmarked tax, and gives greater visibility. However, it suffers a number of disadvantages. First, inequities can arise when social and private insurance operate in tandem, as in the Netherlands, where the income limit for private insurance sometimes gives higher earners lower payments in the private scheme, and in Germany where the sick funds set different contribution rates for a similar range of services, generally with white-collar workers doing better than blue-collar workers. Historically, this was seen as a major defect of the NHI scheme in Britain, before the autonomous approved societies were replaced by the unified NHS. Many other remedies have been tried – and found wanting (Whitehead 1988; Powell 1996). Finally, social insurance tends to be more regressive than taxation as a mechanism of funding (Ham *et al.* 1990: 93–5).

There are a number of themes in the delivery of services (Oxley and MacFarlan 1994; Chernichovsky 1995). Many countries are moving in the direction of pluralism and competition, and regulation in the shape of the management of clinical activity, for example audit and peer review. A second theme is concerned with shifting resources away from institutional care towards primary and community care. There has been a trend towards global budgets, for example diagnostic related groups and HMOs or variants such as GPBH (Ham *et al.* 1990: 96–101). Finally, although there is much rhetoric in support of public health policy, the reality is that the financing and delivery of health services continue to dominate health policy debate in all countries (Ham *et al.* 1990: 101).

Green (1986: 102) claims that the NHS could learn lessons both from contemporary America and the pre-NHS period in Britain. He summarizes his argument:

> without competition, consumers will continue to be poorly served and second-class treatment will remain the NHS norm. Private funding, with government subsidies to protect the poor, is preferable to taxation; competition is better than a doctors' monopoly; and the trial-and-error of the free market is superior to the bureaucracy of the NHS.
>
> (Green 1986: 117)

However the response of the American Alain Enthoven (1990: 57) to the question, 'What can Europeans learn from Americans about the financing and organization of medical care?' is 'The obvious answer is "not much". . . . We have much to be humble about.'

There are no quick-fix solutions to the problems faced by health-care systems. All methods of funding have their weaknesses, and a number of problems recur almost regardless of the method and level of funding. They include an overemphasis on hospital services, evidence of inefficiency in the use of hospitals, the relative neglect of primary care, a lack of incentives for GPs to deal with patients in primary care and poor integration between hospital services, primary care and social care.

CONCLUSION

It is clear that the NHS is not the only health-care system possible, nor may it be the best in the world. There are three main system types, but there are many variations on a theme. At the extreme, every system is unique. Some systems are based on social insurance and others on local government, both of which models Britain eschewed in 1948. Systems exhibit many differences in structure. Although access to hospitals is largely free and universal, some financial barriers exist outside the hospitals. No health care system – or private insurance scheme – offers fully universal and comprehensive cover. Every system has some gaps, although in the USA these are chasms. Similarly, although there is no bottomless pit of health-care expenditure, the pit is deeper in some countries than others.

Different incentive structures exist for doctors and patients. Some structures, such as fees for services for doctors and free access for patients, are said to lead to overconsumption of health care. Conversely, salary and capitation payment for doctors, systems of referral rather than direct access to hospital and cost sharing for patients are said to lead to cost containment. However, the evidence on these issues is unclear. Moreover, the tendency to suggest that the evident variations in medical practice amount to 'under-doctoring' in countries such as Britain and 'overdoctoring' in countries such as the USA and Germany (Payer 1990) is problematic, since the 'correct' level of activity is difficult to establish.

Differences in structure are associated with differences in system performance. There are wide variations in inputs such as expenditure and intermediate inputs such as beds and staffing, and the relationship between these is not straightforward. Similarly, outputs or medical activity vary widely and, again, it is not simply the case that countries with higher expenditure have proportionately higher levels of medical activity. Finally, the link between outputs and outcomes is far from clear. Putting these links in the chain together, this means that there is no simple linear process linking expenditure to health: 'buying' better health is not merely achieved by spending more money on health care.

In short, the common tendency to judge a health-care system by its level of expenditure is too simplistic. Expenditure is merely one input, albeit an important one, and two systems with similar levels of expenditure may be very different in other respects. Systems should be evaluated on the basis of their efficiency, effectiveness and equity rather than on their level of financial input. In these terms, the NHS could be judged as, at worst, a moderate success and, bearing in mind its relatively low level of expenditure, one of the bargain buys of international health-care systems.

The only easy lesson from abroad is that there are no easy lessons. The NHS certainly has problems of varied efficiency, limited consumer responsiveness and particularly long waiting lists. It is unclear whether these problems can be solved by more money or by structural changes. A further issue is whether such structural changes can simply be grafted on to the NHS or whether the medicine to solve its problems will have negative side-effects. The international remedy for health-service ills appears to be planned competition. The NHS is on this path and, in some ways, is in the lead, but it is too early to say whether the new NHS will be the best in the world or even better than the old NHS.

8

CONCLUSION

It was warned in the Introduction that definitive conclusions on evaluating the NHS should not be expected. This reflects three main problems, which have run through this book: first, we lack sharp conceptual and methodological tools of evaluation; second, even these deficient tools tend to have remained in the toolbox rather than being used and, third, different technicians may use the tools to different effect – that is, they may draw different conclusions from similar information.

REVIEW OF THE MAIN CONCLUSIONS

The main concepts to be used were set out in Chapter 1. The broad framework examines inputs, outputs and outcomes. The relationships between them gives concepts of efficiency, effectiveness, equity and acceptability. The emphasis placed upon these, both by academics and by governments, has varied over time. These concepts were to be examined within three broad frameworks of temporal, intrinsic and extrinsic evaluation.

Chapter 2 examined the health-care system before the NHS. It was stressed that the mirror of hindsight often distorts the picture: to criticize the previous system for its failure to fulfil later objectives is of limited value. For example, the delivery of health care used to be in the hands of individual local authorities for municipal hospitals, and of governing bodies for voluntary hospitals. In particular, the levels of local authorities' provision was a matter between them and their local electorate. In this sense, differential levels of provision could be seen as the success of local democracy rather than the failure of national uniformity. In other words, there was little reason to expect uniformity, and few mechanisms to achieve it. Equality may be a goal of the NHS, but it could not reasonably be seen as a goal of the previous system. Moreover, much of what may now be seen as shortcomings of that system may be attributed to the limited state of medical knowledge rather than to any weaknesses of the system.

This historical critique is important, as it has been claimed that in some ways the NHS of the 1990s resembles health care of the 1930s (Powell 1996) and there have been calls for earlier mechanisms such as localism and social insurance to be re-examined. The evaluation of the earlier system suggests that while it did not have all the virtues claimed by its supporters, neither did it have all the vices claimed by its critics. Moreover, criticisms of the practice of insurance and localism in the 1930s should not be equated with a rejection of these concepts.

Chapter 3 examined the creation of the NHS. In many ways, nobody would create the NHS from a blank sheet of paper. The service clearly bears the marks of compromise and constraint. Indeed, some of its problems may stem from these compromises. The NHS was, and continues to be, an imperfect vehicle for achieving its set goals, which in any case are not as clear as many have assumed. In particular, the principles of the NHS bear the marks of political rhetoric that could never be fully translated into reality. To some extent, then, the failure to achieve unrealistic objectives results more from false expectations rather than from any inherent fault of the service.

Chapter 4 outlined the main features of the operation of the NHS. The incrementalism of the early years illustrated the enormity of the task of operating the service with so little experience and information. Concern about economy emerged almost with the birth of the service, reminding us that the NHS has always been seen to be in crisis. The early incrementalism ended with the initiatives of hospital planning in the 1960s, of administrative reform in the 1960s and 1970s, and of equity in the 1970s. The 1980s saw a vigorous quest for efficiency. Initially this took the form of a general tightening of belts, closer managerial scrutiny and a limited contracting out of hotel services to the private sector. As the crisis deepened, stronger medicine was administered by the government, very much against medical advice. Essentially, the competition enforced on hotel services was widened to clinical services, in an internal market where providers would have to compete for the money of purchasers: the new or reformed NHS was born.

Chapter 5 was concerned with temporal evaluation, and examined NHS trends over time. On almost every case of inputs and activity the service has grown substantially since 1948. The NHS spends about 100 times as much as it did in 1948, over four times as much in terms of general prices, and about twice as much in terms of 'NHS-specific prices'. It employs more staff than in 1948, although there have been recent falls in the number of ancillary workers and nurses. The number of NHS beds has fallen gradually over time, but NHS activity has increased in terms of the number of patients treated. In spite of this greater activity, the long-term trend in waiting lists is for them to have lengthened and people appear to be less satisfied with the service. Both these tendencies may be the almost inevitable consequences of increasing medical technology and public expectations. In short, temporal evaluation tends to clash with expectations. There is a clear parallel with the absolute versus relative poverty debate. While it is clear that the NHS is, in almost every way, better than it was in 1948, for most people the appropriate reference point is how well the service compares with their expectations today. Indeed, an 'iron law of welfare expectations' may be tentatively advanced: that people's expectations tend to grow faster than the means of satisfying them.

The relationships between the indicators show that efficiency in terms of beds has increased (that is, shorter lengths of stay), but that efficiency in terms of staff has decreased (that is, fewer treatments per staff). Health outcomes, primarily defined in terms of mortality rates, have increased since 1948. However, it is unclear whether this is due to the effectiveness of the NHS or to external factors such as living standards. It should not be forgotten that the function of the NHS is more than preventing mortality and that its effectiveness may be seen more in determining the quality rather than the quantity of life – adding life to years rather than years to life.

Chapter 6 examined intrinsic evaluation: the extent to which the NHS has reached its objectives. It is widely agreed that the main principles of the service are concerned with free services at the point of use, comprehensiveness and equity. However, precise specification, let alone measurement, of these principles is difficult. The NHS has always been largely free at the point of use. The early years saw some charges imposed in the area of primary care. In recent years these have increased markedly and new charges have been imposed, yet the most expensive part of the health-care system – hospital care – remains free at the point of use. The boundaries of a comprehensive service have been under pressure from the factors of technological push and demographic pull. The NHS remains largely comprehensive, but pieces are being dislodged at the margins. These are largely items that arguably have always been marginal to the NHS: dentistry, optical services and, perhaps of greatest significance, continuing care. However, the most obvious rationing device in the NHS remains the waiting list. The NHS record on equity is most open to debate. There are many different definitions of equity and most analyses have concentrated on a limited range of dimensions. In general, analyses have centred on social class; solutions have centred on geography; and the factors of race, gender and client group have been relatively neglected. Very crudely, the degree of success in achieving equity depends on the degree of realism of the definition. It would generally be safe to say that in terms of equality of entitlement, the NHS is a success; in terms of equality of outcome, it is a failure. There is much scope for debate on definitions within these extremes. Over time, the tendency has been towards greater optimism, but the recent reforms in the NHS introduce new considerations. There appears to have been little *direct* effect on the principles of free services at the point of use and of comprehensiveness, although both are increasingly under threat. There is much prediction of, and anecdotal evidence for, increased inequality, but, as yet, there is little firm evidence to back up assertions about it.

Chapter 7 concentrated on extrinsic evaluation, or comparing the NHS with other health-care systems. The NHS represents one model of health care, but others are based on social and private insurance: Germany and the USA are respective examples. Brief outlines of these countries were presented, along with Sweden, representing a localist system. Problems of definition and measurement between countries are more difficult than those encountered in comparing one system over time (Chapter 5). Health-care systems exhibit structural differences. There are relationships, albeit unclear, between structure and performance. It appears that the NHS is at least the equal of most other systems in terms of its efficiency, effectiveness and equity. Two important conclusions can be stated. First, more activity does not necessarily equal a better service: there may be risks of overdoctoring as well as underdoctoring. The main problem here is the one of establishing the optimal level of activity. Second, more expenditure may mean more services, but does not necessarily buy better health. There is some association between higher expenditure on health care and lower mortality, but this may be due to greater levels of affluence rather than to health services *per se*. Moreover, mortality rates are by no means a sufficient measure of health outcomes.

The search for the perfect health-care system may be fruitless, but this does not mean that lessons cannot be learned from other countries. No country has a service that is fully comprehensive or totally free at the point of use. Many of the features of the NHS have international admirers, although some point to the need for incentives making for greater efficiency and to a general lack of consumer responsiveness. Moves to address these problems have seen many countries using planned competition within a purchaser–provider framework. It remains to be seen whether these initiatives can address weaknesses without compromising strengths.

TOWARDS AN EVALUATION

The question of the success of the NHS has a seductive but deceptive simplicity, for it begs the much more difficult and complex question of what criteria should be used in assessing the success, or otherwise, of the service. Any attempt to draw up a balance sheet involves disentangling the different possible criteria of success. The record of the NHS cannot be assessed in terms of a single currency of evaluation: all that an attempt at evaluation can hope to achieve is to expose the nature of the trade-offs between different values and the conclusions that follow from different ways of looking at the achievements of the NHS (Klein 1989: 145). Different evaluative criteria yield different conclusions: for instance, if the NHS's record in moving towards geographical equity is disappointing when measured against the expectations of its architects, it is a striking success story when measured against the achievements of other countries (Klein 1989: 150). The NHS's services for the old, the chronically ill and the disabled may be an indictment of Britain's claim to be a caring, civilized society, but other countries have worse records (Griffith *et al.* 1987: 230). The NHS has major defects when measured against an 'ideal' system rather than compared with other actual systems (Griffith *et al.* 1987: 239): its failures to live up to expectations is at least to some extent due to those expectations being unrealistic. As Klein (1989: 177) warns, to set up utopian expectations is to invite nihilistic disillusionment.

Thus, it is necessary to examine the performance of the NHS

from different perspectives: using different currencies of evaluation leads to different figures at the end of the balance sheet. But this is inevitable: as evaluation stems from different values, different people will use different exchange rates between the different currencies of evaluation.

> If the aim of the NHS is defined to be to eradicate disease and disability, then it is self-evidently a failure; if, however, its role is defined as being to minimise human suffering, then it can be reckoned as being a reasonable success story. If the aim is defined to be to limit public expenditure, the NHS is a triumphant success story when measured against other health care systems in the Western world; if, in contrast, the aim is defined to be to maximise the total supply of health care, the NHS's performance is distinctly less impressive. If the aim is defined to be to ration scarce resources in an equitable fashion, then the NHS is at least a comparative success; if the aim is defined to be to achieve responsiveness to consumer demands, then the NHS fails to meet it.
>
> (Klein 1989: 177–8)

There can, then, be no definitive evaluation of the NHS. This makes it vital that the criteria of evaluation are specified clearly. In terms of temporal evaluation, the NHS is better now than in 1948 on most counts of input, output and outcome. Questions of efficiency and effectiveness are more difficult to answer. Efficiency has increased or decreased depending on whether activity is examined in terms of beds or staff, respectively. There is little firm evidence on effectiveness over time, although increasing medical knowledge and technology suggest that existing therapies have improved and new therapies have appeared.

On the criterion of intrinsic evaluation, the NHS has largely achieved its generally ascribed, but imprecisely defined, objectives. It is mainly free at the point of delivery, and largely comprehensive in the sense of covering everyone and all treatments. Its record on equity depends on the definition of the term, as the NHS delivers equality in terms of eligibility, but fails on the more demanding definition of equal outcomes.

Lastly, considering extrinsic evaluation, the NHS ranks low on inputs and outputs, and mediocre on outcomes. However, bearing in mind its level of expenditure, the service compares well in terms of efficiency and effectiveness.

A NEW CONSENSUS ON THE NHS?

There appears to be a new international consensus on health systems. The emphases are on cost containment, public competition by means of the purchaser–provider split, the necessity of rationing, increasing interest in primary care and public health, public participation and effective health care in the form of health gain (OECD 1992a, 1994). Most of these concerns are mirrored in a political consensus within Britain. After earlier vociferous opposition, the Labour Party has come to accept many of the Conservative government's reforms. The Labour Party claims that its policy rejects both the 'old' NHS and the 'new' NHS of the Conservatives, and represents a 'third way' (Beckett 1995). However, in many ways, this 'third way' has much in common with the coalition White Paper of 1944 (Powell 1995d). Indeed, in some ways, such as the stress on elections, Parliamentary accountability and national planning, the 1944 document fits more easily into traditional Labour health policy. 'Future generations may learn that Aneurin Bevan did not make the National Health Service; he inherited it from that much underrated social visionary Sir Henry Willink' (Foot 1975: 215). Foot clearly hoped that his tongue-in-cheek prediction would be false, but Labour appears to be rejecting Bevan in favour of Willink, who was 50 years ahead of his time.

THE ROLE OF THE NHS

In some ways, the new consensus on the NHS is more important for what it does not say than for what it says. The NHS has always been a political football in that a major emphasis has been to score political goals. Political oppositions criticize governments over policies that they do not change when they come to power. It is easier to state empty slogans that have little chance of becoming reality (such as to 'democratize the NHS') and to tell the public what it wants to hear (to restore the NHS to the best in the world) rather than dare to speak the hard truth. In many ways, a government's room for manoeuvre regarding the NHS is limited. In spite of rhetoric, it is unlikely that some of the main features of the NHS will be changed.

First, its very name is a misnomer. It has never been a health service. At best it is an illness service, and at worst a hospital service. Considerations of effectiveness and cost containment may suggest a reallocation of priorities from secondary care towards prevention and primary care, and there have been some moves in these directions. However, the political constituency for the status quo among professionals and the public remains strong. In particular, prevention remains a long-term, uncertain, blunt instrument of health engineering, easily overshadowed by the pressure for facilities that allow immediate response to road accidents or heart attacks.

Second, the NHS will always be professionally dominated. It was built to address professionally defined needs rather than to satisfy consumer demands. 'If the language of demands is that of the market, the language of needs is that of paternalism' (Klein 1989: 153). How far can consumerism be grafted on to the NHS? In some ways, it is possible in terms of some hotel elements such as facilities and private rooms, booking systems and appointments, information, courtesy and respect. The NHS can be made more consumer friendly in the form of the 'supermarket model'. In other words, it can accommodate much of the peripheral, but no doubt welcome, aspects of consumerism. However, a more full-blooded consumerism or empowerment may be incompatible with the NHS. The customer may have greater choice among the goods on offer on the supermarket shelves of the NHS, but cannot in the full market sense influence the choice of the goods that are set out there. Public and professional preferences vary. If the NHS listens to 'local voices' it may neglect priority groups and prevention to an even greater extent than paternalism did, and place greater emphasis on heroic intervention. 'The logic of adopting consumer preferences as the guiding principle for the organisation of health care is to abolish the NHS and to replace it by a market-based system' (Klein 1989: 158). Even in its more modest form, greater consumerism may lead to greater inequalities as more articulate and knowledgeable people insist more forcefully and successfully on their entitlements.

Third, governments may drip feed extra millions or billions of pounds into the NHS. They may even bring the UK's expenditure on health up to its 'appropriate' level. However, the pressures of demography, technology and public expectation mean that it is unlikely that such extra resources will achieve a fully comprehensive health service with no waiting lists. While the slogan of 'infinite needs and finite means' overstates the case, it is nevertheless likely that health-care needs will outstrip expenditure. In other words, some mechanism of rationing will always be present (New 1996).

The NHS has a number of strengths: cost-effectiveness, a monopoly buyer of staff, goods and services, the gatekeeping of general practice, a relative absence of fee-for-service medicine, low administrative costs and a lack of the duplication that results from competition. On the other hand, its weaknesses include a lack of choice, and rationing. Are these remediable within the structure of the NHS, simply by more money? Could the NHS be the best in the world simply with a cash transfusion? It is possible to classify the problems in five ways.

First, some problems may be solved with more money spent in the same broad pattern, or 'more of the same'. For example, Klein (1989: 150) argues that 'There is nothing wrong with the policy instruments for promoting progress towards the achievement of geographical equity which could not be cured by a faster economic growth rate'. Second, other problems may require a reallocation of resources inside the NHS. For instance, the rhetoric of the 'priority groups' may eventually be matched by hard cash. Third, there are problems that are unlikely to be solved by increasing the money to the NHS, but that may be addressed by increased expenditure elsewhere such as on housing or job creation. Fourth, some problems that are not essentially financial in origin may be settled by changes in patterns of expenditure rather than increased spending. For example, the variations pointed out by the reports of the Audit Commission (1990, 1991) may be so addressed: day surgery could be increased or the existing skill mix varied in some areas. This category of problems with possible solutions that do not entail extra spending may extend to some that are amenable to changes outside the NHS, such as pollution controls that require legislation rather than governmental money. Fifth, however, some problems are outside the control of doctors or governments and are unlikely to be capable of full solution by government action or money.

One example of the more intractable problems is inequality in health. Many of the explanatory variables are within policy-makers' control only to a very limited extent. Le Grand (1982: 49–51) reviews three strategies. First, policies could be designed to change suppliers' behaviour, for example on training courses and different recruitment practices. Second, policies such as health education could attempt to increase working-class benefit. Third, policies such as geographical relocation or more means testing could raise middle-class costs. However, Le Grand (1982: 51) is pessimistic about the likely impact of such policies: 'it is difficult to resist the conclusion that there is little the Health Service can do to reduce inequality in its use or in the private cost of that use. The principal determinants are beyond its control. . . . Inequality in health care reflects inequality in society.' The domain of inequality can be limited, but it cannot be eradicated. A similar conclusion appears to have been reached by the Black Committee (Townsend and Davidson 1982). Most of their recommendations, like their discussion, focused on health rather than health care; on interventions outside rather than inside the NHS. In other words, there appear to be few global strategies across the whole NHS, and such mechanisms as are available for addressing class inequalities through the NHS are largely via the indirect route of geography (but see DoH (1996b) for a more optimistic interpretation of the role of the NHS).

This is hardly surprising. Increasing geographical accessibility for under-utilizing populations may be a slow and difficult process, but policy-makers have more control over it than they have over economic and cultural accessibility. It would be very difficult for governments to legislate on matters such as making doctors more equal in the sense of quality or in directing them how to treat their patients, making them live in the communities they serve, to be better communicators with working-class patients and to hold compulsory evening surgeries. Thus, not only are many of the NHS's ascribed objectives unclear, but some are effectively beyond the control of doctors and government.

CONCLUSION

The Royal Commission on the NHS (1979: 356) concluded that 'we need not feel ashamed of our health services and that there are many aspects of it of which we can be justly proud'. This judgement stills appears to be valid nearly 20 years later.

Whether in comparison with 1948, with other countries or with its stated objectives, our NHS has performed well. However, this must not blind us to its defects or to the fact that it might be able to perform better. The deficiencies of the service can sometimes be cruelly exposed at the individual level, either through the media or at a personal level. At such a time, the knowledge that such a person might not have been able to benefit from treatment in the past or in other countries or that their apparent neglect is the result of a 'rational' process of allocating scarce resources seems of little consequence. Nevertheless, the NHS is at root a collective enterprise, attempting to deliver in health terms 'the greatest good for the greatest number'. This requires constant vigilance and constant evaluation.

There can be little doubt that the NHS could make good use of more money. What is less clear is the precise amount of money needed, while even less clear is the best way of spending that money. It is arguable that the prime need is for a rational debate, which acknowledges that the status quo may not be the best way of achieving goals. Instead of placing a preservation order on the initial principles and structure of the NHS, both should be open to adaptation if it can be argued that they have become outdated or unachievable. The objectives of the service and the mechanisms for achieving them must be reassessed to ensure that they remain realistic and explicit. In other words, policies should be driven more by 'facts' than by 'values', and policy-making, like medicine itself, should be evidence based (Ham *et al.* 1995). The NHS should be a rhetoric-free zone, but it should not be a criticism-free zone. Thus, the view of Cochrane (1972) that 'evaluation should be the first priority of the NHS' remains as true today as when it was written.

REFERENCES

Aaron, H. and Schwartz, W. (1984). *The Painful Prescription*. Washington, DC: Brookings Institute.

Abel-Smith, B. (1964). *The Hospitals 1800–1948*. London: Heinemann.

Abel-Smith, B. (1976). *Value For Money in Health Services*. London: Heinemann.

Abel-Smith, B. (1984). Social welfare, in B. Pimlott (ed.) *Fabian Essays in Socialist Thought*. London: Heinemann, 169–84.

Addison, P. (1975). *The Road to 1945: British Politics and the Second World War*. London: Jonathan Cape.

Ahmad, W. I. U. (1993). Making black people sick: 'race', ideology and health research, in W. I. U. Ahmad (ed.) *'Race' and Health in Contemporary Britain*. Buckingham: Open University Press, 11–33.

Allen, D., Harley, M. and Makinson, G. (1987). Performance indicators in the National Health Service. *Social Policy and Administration*, 21: 70–84.

Allsop, J. (1995). *Health Policy and the NHS*, 2nd edn. Harlow: Longman.

Anell, A. (1995). Implementing planned markets in health services: the Swedish case, in R. Saltman and C. Von Otter (eds) *Implementing Planned Markets in Health Care*. Buckingham: Open University Press, 209–26.

Appleby, J. (1992). *Financing Health Care in the 1990s*. Buckingham: Open University Press.

Appleby, J. (1994). The reformed National Health Service: a commentary. *Social Policy and Administration*, 28: 345–58.

Audit Commission (1986). *Making a Reality of Community Care*. London: HMSO.

Audit Commission (1990). *A Short Cut to Better Services. Day Surgery in England and Wales*. London: HMSO.

Audit Commission (1991). *The Virtue of Patients: Making Best Use of Ward Nursing Resources*. London: HMSO.

Audit Commission (1996). *What the Doctor Ordered*. London: HMSO.

Avery-Jones, Sir F. (1976). The London hospitals scene. *British Medical Journal*, 30 October: 1046–9.

Baggott, R. (1991). Looking forward to the past? The politics of public health. *Journal of Social Policy*, 20: 191–213.

Baggott, R. (1994a). *Health and Health Care in Britain*. Basingstoke: Macmillan.

Baggott, R. (1994b). Reforming the British health care system: a permanent revolution? *Policy Studies*, 15: 35–47.

Balarajan, R. and Soni Raleigh, V. (1993). *Ethnicity and Health*. London: Department of Health.

Baldock, J. and Ungerson, C. (1994). *Becoming Consumers of Community Care*. York: Joseph Rowntree Foundation.

Bayley, H. (1993). Bridge over troubled water. *Health Service Journal*, 24 June: 24.

Beckett, M. (1995). Margaret Beckett's third way: cooperation and partnership. *British Medical Journal*, 311: 13–14.

Beech, R., Bevan, G. and Mays, N. (1990). Spatial equity in the NHS: the death and rebirth of RAWP, in A. Harrison (ed.) *Health Care UK 1990*. Newbury: Policy Journals, 44–61.

Benzeval, M. and Judge, K. (1996). Access to health care in England: continuing inequalities in the distribution of GPs. *Journal of Public Health Medicine*, 18: 33–40.

Berliner, H. (1995). The end of public healthcare. *Health Service Journal*, 19 October: 19.

Berridge, V. (1990). Health and medicine, in F. M. L. Thompson (ed.) *The Cambridge Social History of Britain 1750–1950. Volume 3: Social Agencies and Institutions*. Cambridge: Cambridge University Press, 171–242.

Bevan, A. (1946a). House of Commons, Second Reading on NHS Bill. *Hansard*, 30 April–2 May.

Bevan, A. (1946b). House of Commons, Standing Committee C on NHS Bill. *Hansard*, 14 May–19 June.

Bevan, A. (1978). *In Place of Fear*, first published 1952. London: Quartet Books.

Birch, S. (1986). Increasing patient charges in the National Health Service: a method of privatizing primary care. *Journal of Social Policy*, 15: 163–84.

Birch, S. and Abelson, J. (1993). Is reasonable access what we want? *International Journal of Health Services*, 23: 629–53.

Blaxter, M. (1990). *Health and Lifestyles*. London: Routledge.

Blendon, R., Leitman, R., Morrison, I. and Donelan, K. (1990). Satisfaction with health systems in ten nations. *Health Affairs*, 9: 185–92.

BMA (British Medical Association) (1991). *Leading for Health*. London: BMA.

Boulton, M., Tuckett, D., Olson, C. and Williams, A. (1986). Social class and the general practice consultation. *Sociology of Health and Illness*, 8: 325–50.

Bradford-Hill, A. (1951). The doctor's pay and day. *Journal of the Royal Statistical Society*, 114: 1–34.

Braithwaite, C. (1938). *The Voluntary Citizen*. London: Methuen.

Brazier, M. (1993). Rights and health care, in R. Blackburn (ed.) *Rights of Citizenship*. London: Mansell, 56–74.

Brooke, S. (1992). *Labour's War*. Oxford: Oxford University Press.

Bruce, M. (1968) *The Coming of the Welfare State*. London: Batsford.

Bunker, J., Frazier, H. and Mosteller, F. (1994). Improving health: measuring effects of health policy. *Milbank Quarterly*, 72: 225–58.

Butler, J. (1992). *Patients, Policies and Politics*. Buckingham: Open University Press.

Campbell, J. (1987). *Nye Bevan and the Mirage of British Socialism*. London: Weidenfeld and Nicolson.

Carling, Sir E. C. and McIntosh, T. S. (1945). *Hospital Survey: The Hospital Services of the North-Western Area*. London: HMSO.

Carpenter, G. (1984). National health insurance. *Public Administration*, 62: 71–89.

Carr-Hill, R. (1994). Efficiency and equity implications of the health care reforms. *Social Science and Medicine*, 39: 1189–201.

Carter, N., Klein, R. and Day, P. (1992). *How Organisations Measure Success: The Use of Performance Indicators in Government*. London: Routledge.

Cartwright, A. and Anderson, R. (1981). *General Practice Revisited*. London: Tavistock.

Cartwright, A. and O'Brien, M. (1976). Social class variations in health care and in general practice consultations, in M. Stacey (ed.) *The Sociology of the NHS*. Keele: University of Keele, 77–98.

Castle, B. (1980). *The Castle Diaries 1974–76*. London: Weidenfeld and Nicolson.

Chadda, D. (1995). Down payment on later life. *Health Service Journal*, 26 October: 28–9.

Charlton, J. R. H., Hartley, R. M., Silver, R. and Holland, W. W. (1983). Geographical variation in mortality from conditions amenable to medical intervention in England and Wales. *Lancet*, 26 March: 691–6.

Chernichovsky, D. (1995). Health system reforms in industrialized democracies: an emerging paradigm. *Milbank Quarterly*, 73: 339–72.

Cherry, S. (1992). Beyond national health insurance. The voluntary hospitals and hospital contributory schemes: a regional study. *Social History of Medicine*, 5: 455–82.

Chester, D. N. (1951). *Central and Local Government*. London: Macmillan.

Cochrane, A. (1972). *Effectiveness and Efficiency*. London: Nuffield Provincial Hospitals Trust.

Collings, J. S. (1950). General practice in England today: a reconnaissance. *Lancet*, 25 March: 555–85.

Collins, E. and Klein, R. (1980). Equity and the NHS: self-reported morbidity, access and primary health care. *British Medical Journal*, 281: 1111–15.

Collins, E. and Klein, R. (1985). *Self-Reported Morbidity, Socio-Economic Factors and GP Consultations*. Bath: University of Bath.

Cook, R. (1988). *Life Begins at 40: in Defence of the NHS*. London: Fabian Society.

Cooper, L., Coote, A., Davies, A. and Jackson, C. (1995). *Voices Off. Tackling the Democratic Deficit in Health*. London: Institute for Public Policy Research.

Cooper, M. (1975). *Rationing Health Care*. London: Croom Helm.

Cooper, M. and Culyer, A. J. (1971). An economic survey of the nature and intent of the British National Health Service. *Social Science and Medicine*. 5: 1–13.

Coulter, A. (1995). Evaluating general practitioner fundholding in the United Kingdom. *European Journal of Public Health*, 5: 233–9.

Crombie, D. (1984). *Social Class and Health Status: Inequality or Difference?* London: Royal College of General Practitioners.

Crossman, R. H. S. (1972). *A Politician's View of Health Service Planning*, Thirteenth Maurice Bloch Lecture. Glasgow: University of Glasgow.

Crossman, R. H. S. (1977). *The Diaries of a Cabinet Minister. Volume Three. Secretary of State for Social Services 1968–70*. London: Hamilton Cape.

Crowther, M. A. (1983). *The Workhouse System 1834–1929*. London: Methuen.

Culyer, A. J. (1976). *Need and the National Health Service*. London: Martin Robertson.

Curtis, S. and Taket, A. (1996). *Health and Societies*. London: Arnold.

Davies, B. (1968). *Social Needs and Resources in Local Services*. London: Michael Joseph.

Davies, C. (1979). Hospital-centred health care: policies and politics in the NHS, in P. Atkinson, R. Dingwall and A. Murcott (eds) *Prospects for the National Health*. London: Croom Helm, 53–72.

Dean, M. (1991). End of a comprehensive NHS? *Lancet*, 337: 351–2.

DHSS (Department of Health and Social Security) (1976). *Sharing Resources for Health in England* (report of the Resource Allocation Working Party). London: HMSO.

DHSS (1981). *Primary Health Care in Inner London* (the Acheson report). London: HMSO.

DHSS (1983). *NHS Management Inquiry* (the Griffiths report). London: DHSS.

DHSS (1988). *Community Care: Agenda for Action* (Griffiths community care report). London: DHSS.

Digby, A. (1989). *British Welfare Policy*. London: Faber and Faber.

Digby, A. and Bosanquet, N. (1988). Doctors and patients in an era of national health insurance and private practice, 1913–1938. *Economic History Review*, 41: 74–94.

DoH (Department of Health) (1989). *Working for Patients*. London: HMSO.

DoH (1992) *The Health of the Nation*. London: HMSO.

DoH (1993a). *Making London Better*. London: HMSO.

DoH (1993b). *On the State of the Public Health 1992. The Annual Report of the Chief Medical Officer of the Department of Health.* London: HMSO.

DoH (1993c). *Health and Personal Social Service Statistics for England.* London: HMSO.

DoH (1994). *The Patient's Charter. Hospital and Ambulance Services Comparative Performance Guide 1993–1994.* London: HMSO.

DoH (1995). *The NHS Performance Guide 1994–95.* London: HMSO.

DoH (1996a). *The NHS Performance Guide 1995–96.* London: HMSO.

DoH (1996b) *Variations in Health. What Can the Department of Health and the NHS Do?* London: DoH.

Donabedian, A. (1980). *The Definition of Quality and Approaches to its Assessment.* Ann Arbor, Michigan: Health Administration Press.

Donaldson, C. and Gerard, K. (1993). *Economics of Health Care Financing. The Visible Hand.* Basingstoke: Macmillan.

Doyal, L. (1979). *The Political Economy of Health.* London: Pluto.

Doyal, L. (1995). *What Makes Women Sick.* Basingstoke: Macmillan.

Drucker, P. (1968). *The Practice of Management.* London: Heinemann.

Duncan, C., Jones, K. and Moon, G. (1993) Do places matter? *Social Science and Medicine*, 37: 725–33.

Earl-Slater, A. (1996). Privatizing medicines in the National Health Service. *Public Money and Management*, 16: 39–44.

Earwicker, R. (1982). 'The Labour movement and the creation of the National Health Service, 1911–1948', unpublished PhD thesis. University of Birmingham.

Eckstein, H. (1958). *The English Health Service.* Cambridge, MA: Harvard University Press.

Edwards, B. (1993). *The National Health Service. A Manager's Tale 1946–1992.* London: Nuffield Provincial Hospitals Trust.

Enthoven, A. (1990). What can Europeans learn from Americans? in OECD (ed.) *Health Care Systems in Transition.* Paris: OECD, 57–71.

Eyles, J. (1987). *The Geography of the National Health.* London: Croom Helm.

Eyles, J., Smith, D. and Woods, K. (1982). Spatial resource allocation and state practice: the case of health service planning in London. *Regional Studies*, 16: 239–53.

Eyles, J. and Woods, K. (1986). Who cares what care?: an inverse interest law. *Social Science and Medicine*, 23: 1087–92.

Falconer, P. (1996). To charge or not to charge: the politics of health charges in Britain, in I. Hampsher-Monk and J. Stanyer (eds) *Contemporary Political Studies 1996. Volume Two.* Belfast: PSA, 933–43.

Finlayson, G. (1994). *Citizen, State and Social Welfare in Britain 1830–1990.* Oxford: Clarendon Press.

Foot, M. (1975). *Aneurin Bevan 1945–1960.* St Albans: Paladin.

Foster, P. (1983). *Access to Welfare.* Basingstoke: Macmillan.

Fox, D. M. (1986). *Health Policies, Health Politics.* Princeton: Princeton University Press.

Frankel, S. (1989). The natural history of waiting lists – some wider explanations for an unnecessary problem. *Health Trends*, 21: 56–8.

Fraser, D. (1984). *The Evolution of the British Welfare State*. London: Macmillan.

George, V. and Wilding, P. (1984). *The Impact of Social Policy*. London: Routledge and Kegan Paul.

Gilbert, B. B. (1966). *The Evolution of National Insurance in Great Britain*. London: Michael Joseph.

Ginsberg, N. (1992). *Divisions of Welfare*. London: Sage.

Glennerster, H. (1995). *British Social Policy since 1945*. Oxford: Blackwell.

Glennerster, H. and Matsaganis, M. (1994). The English and Swedish health care reforms. *International Journal of Health Services*, 24: 231–51.

Glennerster, H., Matsaganis, M., Owens, P. and Hancock, S. (1994a). *Implementing GP Fundholding: Wild Card or Winning Hand?* Buckingham: Open University Press.

Glennerster, H., Matsaganis, M., Owens, P. and Hancock, S. (1994b). GP fundholding: wild card or winning hand? in R. Robinson and J. Le Grand (eds) *Evaluating the NHS Reforms*. London/Newbury: King's Fund Institute/Policy Journals, 74–107.

Godber, G. (1958). Health Service; past, present and future. *Lancet*, 5 July: 1–6.

Godber, Sir G. (1983). The Domesday Book of British Hospitals. *Bulletin of the Society of the Social History of Medicine*, 32: 4–13.

Godber, Sir G. (1988). Forty years of the National Health Service: origins and early developments. *British Medical Journal*, 297: 37–43.

Goodman, J. (1980). USA: health services are superior, in A. Seldon (ed.) *The Litmus Papers*. London: Centre for Policy Studies, 126–32.

Gray, A. M. (1991). A mixed economy of health care: Britain's health service sector in the inter-war period, in A. McGuire, P. Fenn and K. Mayhew (eds) *Providing Health Care: The Economics of Alternative Systems of Finance and Delivery*. Oxford: Oxford University Press, 233–60.

Green, D. G. (1985). *Working Class Patients and the Medical Establishment*. Aldershot: Gower.

Green, D. G. (1986). *Challenge to the NHS. Hobart Paperback 23*. London: IEA.

Green, D. G. (1993). *Reinventing Civil Society: The Rediscovery of Welfare Without Politics*. London: IEA.

Griffith, B., Iliffe, S. and Rayner, G. (1987). *Banking on Sickness*. London: Lawrence and Wishart.

Griffiths, S. (1996). Men's health. *British Medical Journal*, 312: 69–70.

Grimsley, M. and Bhat, A. (1988). Health, in A. Bhat, R. Carr-Hill and S. Ohri (eds) *Britain's Black Population: A New Perspective*, 2nd edn. Aldershot: Gower, 177–207.

Guardian (1988). The national wealth. Editorial, 4 July.

Guha, S. (1994). The importance of social intervention in England's mortality decline: the evidence reviewed. *Social History of Medicine*, 7: 89–113.

Guillebaud, C. W. (1956). *Report of the Enquiry into the Cost of the National Health Service*. London: HMSO.

Ham, C. (1981). *Policy-Making in the National Health Service*. Basingstoke: Macmillan.

Ham, C. (ed.) (1988a). *Health Care Variations: Assessing the Evidence*. London: King's Fund Institute.

Ham, C. (1988b) A review of the literature, in C. Ham (ed.) *Health Care Variations*. London: King's Fund Institute.

Ham, C. (1992). *Health Policy in Britain*, 3rd edn. Basingstoke: Macmillan.

Ham, C. (1996). Contestability: a middle path for health care. *British Medical Journal*, 312: 70–1.

Ham, C., Robinson, R. and Benzeval, M. (1990). *Health Check. Health Care Reforms in an International Context*. London: King's Fund Institute.

Ham, C., Hunter, D. and Robinson, R. (1995). Evidence based policymaking, *British Medical Journal*, 310, 71–2.

Hansard (1946). House of Commons, Standing Committee C on NHS Bill. 14 May–19 June.

Hansard (1989). House of Commons, Written Answers. 22 March: cols 620–1.

Harris, J. (1992). War and social history: Britain and the Home Front during the Second World War. *Contemporary European History*, 1: 17–35.

Harrison, S., Hunter, D. J., Johnston, I., Wistow, G. (1989). *Competing for Health: A Commentary on the NHS Review*. Leeds: Nuffield Institute for Health Service Studies.

Harrison, S. and Hunter, D. J. (1994). *Rationing Health Care*. London: Institute for Public Policy Research.

Harrison, S., Hunter, D. J. and Pollitt, C. (1990). *The Dynamics of British Health Policy*. London: Unwin Hyman.

Hastings, S. (1941). *The Hospital Service*. Fabian Research Series 59. London: Fabian Society.

Haynes, R. (1987). *The Geography of Health Services in Britain*. London: Croom Helm.

Health Care 2000 (1995). *UK Health and Healthcare Services* (Chair: Sir Duncan Nichol). London: Health Care 2000.

Henwood, M. (1995). *Making a Difference? Implementation of Community Care Reforms Two Years On*. Leeds/London: Nuffield Institute for Health/King's Fund College.

Herbert, S. M. (1939). *Britain's Health*. Harmondsworth: Penguin.

Higgins, J. (1988). *The Business of Medicine*. Basingstoke: Macmillan.

Hindess, B. (1987). *Freedom, Equality and the Market*. London: Tavistock.

Holland, W. W. (1983). *The Evaluation of Health Care*. Oxford: Oxford University Press.

Holliday, I. (1992). *The NHS Transformed*. Manchester: Baseline.

Hollingsworth, J. R. (1988). *A Political Economy of Medicine*. Baltimore: Johns Hopkins University Press.

Hollingsworth, J. R., Hage, J. and Hanneman, R. A. (1990). *State Intervention in Medical Care*. Ithaca: Cornell University Press.

Honigsbaum, F. (1979). *The Division in British Medicine*. New York: St Martin's Press.

Honigsbaum, F. (1989). *Health, Happiness and Security: The Creation of the National Health Service*. London: Routledge.

Honigsbaum, F., Calltorp, J., Ham, C. and Holmstrom, S. (1995). *Priority Setting Processes for Healthcare*. Oxford: Radcliffe Medical Press.

Hopkins, A. and Bahl, V. (eds) (1993). *Access to Health Care for People From Black and Ethnic Minorities*. London: Royal College of Physicians.

Howell, J. B. L. (1992). Re-examining the fundamental principles of the NHS, in BMJ (ed.) *The Future of Health Care*. London: BMJ, 1–7.

IHSM (Institute of Health Service Management) (1988). *Alternative Delivery and Funding*, Final Report. London: IHSM.

IHSM (1993). *Future Health Care Options*, Final Report. London: IHSM.

Iliffe, S. (1988). *Strong Medicine. Health Politics for the Twenty-First Century*. London: Lawrence and Wishart.

Illich, I. (1975). *Medical Nemesis*. London: Marion Boyars.

Immergut, E. (1992). *Health Politics*. Cambridge: Cambridge University Press.

Jacobson, B., Smith, A. and Whitehead, M. (1991). *The Nation's Health: A Strategy for the 1990s*. London: King's Fund.

Jarman, B. (1993). Is London overbedded? *British Medical Journal*, 306: 979–82.

Jeffereys, K. (1987). British politics and social policy during the Second World War. *Historical Journal*, 30: 123–44.

Jeffereys, K. (1991). *The Churchill Coalition and Wartime Politics 1940–1945*. Manchester: Manchester University Press.

Jewkes, J. and Jewkes, S. (1962). *The Genesis of the British National Health Service*. Oxford: Basil Blackwell.

Johnson, N. (1990). *Reconstructing the Welfare State*. Hemel Hempstead: Harvester Wheatsheaf.

Jones, H. (1994). *Health and Society in Twentieth-Century Britain*. Harlow: Longman.

Jones, K. (1993). *Asylums and After*. London: Athlone.

Jones, K. and Moon, G. (1987). *Health, Disease and Society*. London: Routledge & Kegan Paul.

Jones, K. and Moon, G. (1993). Medical geography: taking space seriously. *Progress in Human Geography*, 17: 515–24.

Judge, K. and Solomon, M. (1993). Public opinion and the National Health Service: patterns and perspectives in consumer satisfaction. *Journal of Social Policy*, 22: 299–327.

Kemp, R. (1964). The golden bed. *Lancet*, 14 November: 1025–7.

King's Fund (1992). *London Health Care 2010*. London: King's Fund.

Klein, R. (1982). Performance, evaluation and the NHS. *Public Administration*, 60: 385–407.

Klein, R. (1988). Acceptable inequalities? in D. Green (ed.) *Acceptable Inequalities*. London: IEA, 3–20.

Klein, R. (1989). *The Politics of the NHS*, 2nd edn. Harlow: Longman.

Klein, R. (1995a). *The New Politics of the NHS*, 3rd edn. Harlow: Longman.

Klein, R. (1995b). Labour's health policy. *British Medical Journal*, 311: 75–6.

Labour Party (1943). *National Service for Health*. London: Labour Party.

Labour Party (1995). *Renewing the NHS*. London: Labour Party.

Laybourn, K. (1990). *Britain on the Breadline. A Social and Political History of Britain between the Wars*. Gloucester: Alan Sutton Publishing.

Le Grand, J. (1982). *The Strategy of Equality*. London: George Allen and Unwin.

Le Grand, J. (1991). The distribution of health care revisited. *Journal of Health Economics*, 10: 239–45.

Le Grand, J. (1994). Evaluating the NHS reforms, in R. Robinson and J. Le Grand (eds) *Evaluating the NHS Reforms*. London/Newbury: King's Fund Institute/Policy Journals, 243–60.

Le Grand, J., Winter, D. and Woolley, F. (1990). The NHS: safe in whose hands? in J. Hills (ed.) *The State Of Welfare*. Oxford: Clarendon, 88–134.

Leathard, A. (1990). *Health Care Provision*. London: Chapman and Hall.

Lee, R. (1988). Uneven zenith: towards a geography of the high period of municipal medicine in England and Wales. *Journal of Historical Geography*, 14: 260–80.

Leff, S. (1950). *The Health of the People*. London: Victor Gollancz.

Leichter, H. (1979). *A Comparative Approach to Policy Analysis. Health Care Policy in Four Nations*. Cambridge: Cambridge University Press.

Levenson, R. (1992). Patients and the market in health care. *Critical Public Health*, 3: 26–34.

Lock, S. (1989). Steaming through the NHS, in BMJ (ed.) *The NHS Review – What it Means*. London: BMJ, 1–2.

London Advisory Group (1981). *Acute Hospital Services in London*. London: HMSO.

Long, A. (1992). Evaluating health services: from value for money to the valuing of health services, in C. Pollitt and S. Harrison (eds) *Handbook of Public Management*. Oxford: Blackwell, 59–71.

Long, A. and Harrison, S. (1985). *Health Services Performance: Effectiveness and Efficiency*. London: Croom Helm.

Lowe, R. (1993). *The Welfare State in Britain Since 1945*. Basingstoke: Macmillan.

Macfarlane, A. (1990). Official statistics and women's health and illness, in H. Roberts (ed.) *Women's Health Counts*. London: Routledge, 18–62.

Macintyre, S. (1986). The patterning of health by social position in contemporary Britain: directions for sociological research. *Social Science and Medicine*, 23: 393–415.

Macintyre, S., McIver, S. and Sooman, A. (1993). Area, class and health: should we be focussing on places or people? *Journal of Social Policy*, 22: 213–34.

Macintyre, S., Hunt, K. and Sweeting, H. (1996). Gender differences in health: are things really as simple as they seem? *Social Science and Medicine*, 42: 617–24.

Mackintosh, J. M. (1953). *Trends of Opinion about the Public Health 1901–1951*. London: Oxford University Press.

Martin, J. P. (1984). *Hospitals in Trouble*. Oxford: Blackwell.

Marwick, A. (1967). The Labour Party and the welfare state in Britain, 1900–1948. *American Historical Review*, 73: 380–403.

Maxwell, R. J. (1981). *Health and Wealth*. Lexington: Lexington Books.

Maynard, A. and Ludbrook, A. (1982). Inequality, the NHS and health policy. *Journal of Public Policy*, 2: 97–116.

Mays, N. and Bevan, G. (1987). *Resource Allocation in the Health Service*. London: Bedford Square Press.

McKeown, T. (1976). *The Role of Medicine: Dream, Mirage or Nemesis?* London: Nuffield Provincial Hospitals Trust.

McLoone, P. and Boddy, F. (1994). Deprivation and mortality in Scotland, 1981 and 1991. *British Medical Journal*, 309: 1465–70.

McNaught, K. (1988). *Race and Health Policy*. London: Croom Helm.

McPherson, K. (1988). Variations in hospitalisation rates: why and how to study them, in C. Ham (ed). *Health Care Variations*. London: King's Fund Institute, 15–20.

McPherson, K. (1990). International differences in medical care practices, in OECD (ed.) *Health Care Systems in Transition*. Paris: OECD, 17–28.

McPherson, K., Strong, P., Epstein, A. and Jones, L. (1981). Regional variations in the use of common surgical procedures: within and between England and Wales, Canada and the United States of America. *Social Science and Medicine*, 15A: 273–88.

Means, R. and Smith, R. (1994). *Community Care. Policy and Practice*. Basingstoke: Macmillan.

Mechanic, D. (1995). The Americanization of the British National Health Service. *Health Affairs*, 14: 51–67.

Miles, A. (1991). *Women, Health and Medicine*. Buckingham: Open University Press.

MoH (Ministry of Health) (1944). *A National Health Service*, Cmnd 6502. London: HMSO.

Mohan, J. (1986). Private medical care and the British Conservative government: what price independence? *Journal of Social Policy*, 15: 337–60.

Mohan, J. (1991). Privatization in the British health service: a challenge to the NHS, in J. Gabe *et al.* (eds) *The Sociology of the Health Service*. London: Routledge, 36–57.

Mohan, J. (1995). *A National Health Service? The Restructuring of Health Care in Britain since 1979*. Basingstoke: Macmillan.

Mohan, J. and Powell, M. (1996). In what sense a national health service? Paper presented to the 7th International Symposium in Medical Geography, Portsmouth.

Mooney, G. (1986). *Economics, Medicine and Health Care.* Brighton: Wheatsheaf.

Mooney, G. (1994). *Key Issues in Health Economics.* Hemel Hempstead: Harvester Wheatsheaf.

Moran, M. (1992). The health care state in Europe. *Government and Policy,* 10: 77–90.

Moran, M. (1995). Health care policy, in J. Clasen and R. Freeman (eds) *Social Policy in Germany.* Hemel Hempstead: Harvester Wheatsheaf, 83–101.

Morgan, K. O. (1984). *Labour in Power 1945–51.* Oxford: Clarendon Press.

Morgan, M., Calnan, M. and Manning, N. (1985). *Sociological Approaches to Health and Medicine.* London: Routledge.

Mullen, K. (1990). Area and health in cities: a review of the literature. *International Journal of Sociology and Social Policy,* 10: 1–24.

Murphy, E. (1991). *After the Asylums.* Harmondsworth: Penguin.

Navarro, V. (1978). *Class Struggle, the State and Medicine.* Oxford: Martin Robertson.

Nettleton, S. (1995). *The Sociology of Health and Illness.* Cambridge: Polity.

New, B. (1996). The rationing debate in the NHS. *British Medical Journal,* 312: 1593–601.

NHS Executive (1995). *Priorities and Planning Guidance for the NHS 1996/97.* Leeds: NHSME.

NHS Executive (1996). *Primary Care: The Future.* London: HMSO.

North, N. (1993). Empowerment in welfare markets. *Health and Social Care in the Community,* 1: 129–37.

NPHT (Nuffield Provincial Hospitals Trust) (1946). *The Hospital Surveys. The Domesday Book of the Hospital Services.* Oxford: Oxford University Press.

NPHT/MoH (Nuffield Provincial Hospitals Trust/Ministry of Health) (1945–6). *The Hospital Surveys* (10 volumes). London: HMSO.

Nzegwu, F. (1993). *Black People and Health Care in Contemporary Britain.* Reading: International Institute for Black Research.

O'Donnell, O. and Propper, C. (1991). Equity and the distribution of NHS resources. *Journal of Health Economics,* 10: 1–19.

O'Higgins, M. (1987). Egalitarians, equalities and welfare evaluation. *Journal of Social Policy,* 16: 1–18.

OECD (Organization for Economic Cooperation and Development) (1987). *Financing and Delivering Health Care.* Paris: OECD.

OECD (1992a). *The Reform of Health Care.* Paris: OECD.

OECD (1992b). *US Health Care at the Crossroads.* Paris: OECD.

OECD (1993). OECD *Health Systems Facts and Trends 1960–1991. Volume 1.* Paris: OECD.

OECD (1994). *The Reform of Health Care Systems.* Paris: OECD.

OECD (1995). *Internal Markets in the Making.* Paris: OECD.

Office of Health Economics (1995). *Compendium of Health Statistics, 9th edn.* London: OHE.

Owen, D. (1988). *Our NHS.* London: Pan.

Oxley, H. and MacFarlan, M. (1994). *Health Care Reform: Controlling Spending and Increasing Efficiency.* Paris: OECD.

Packwood, T., Kerrison, S. and Buxton, M. (1994). The implementation of medical audit. *Social Policy and Administration,* 28: 299–316.

Parkin, D. (1991). Comparing health service efficiency across countries, in A. McGuire, P. Fenn and K. Mayhew (eds) *Providing Health Care. The Economics of Alternative Systems of Finance and Delivery.* Oxford: Oxford University Press, 172–91.

Parsons, L. G., Fryers, S. Clayton and Godber, G. (1945). *Hospital Survey: the Hospital Service of the Sheffield and East Midlands Area.* London: HMSO.

Pater, J. (1981). *The Making of the National Health Service.* London: King's Fund.

Paton, C. (1995). Change is as good as a rest. *Health Service Journal.* 6 July: 24–5.

Payer, L. (1990). *Medicine and Culture.* London: Gollancz.

Pearson, M. (1992). Health policy under Thatcher, in P. Cloke (ed.) *Policy and Change in Thatcher's Britain.* Oxford: Pergamon, 215–46.

PEP (Political and Economic Planning) (1937). *Report on the British Health Services.* London: PEP.

PEP (1944). *Medical Care for Citizens. Broadsheet 222.* London: PEP.

Phillimore, P., Beattie, A. and Townsend, P. (1994). Widening inequality of health in northern England, 1981–1991. *British Medical Journal,* 308: 1125–8.

Phillips, C., Palfrey, C. and Thomas, P. (1994). *Evaluating Health and Social Care.* Basingstoke: Macmillan.

Pinker, R. (1966). *English Hospital Statistics 1861–1938.* London: Heinemann.

Player, D. and Barbour-Might, D. (1988). *Health for All: The Practical Socialism of the National Health Service.* London: Tribune.

Pollitt, C. and Harrison, S. (1992). Introduction, in C. Pollitt and S. Harrison (eds) *Handbook of Public Management.* Oxford: Blackwell, 1–22.

Popay, J. (1992). 'My health is all right, but I'm just tired all the time': women's experiences of ill health, in H. Roberts (ed.) *Women's Health Matters.* London: Routledge, 99–120.

Powell, M. A. (1987). 'Access to primary health care in London', unpublished PhD thesis. University of London.

Powell, M. A. (1990). Need and provision in the NHS: an inverse care law? *Policy and Politics,* 18: 31–7.

Powell, M. A. (1992a). A tale of two cities: a critical evaluation of the geographical provision of health care before the NHS. *Public Administration,* 70: 67–80.

Powell, M. A. (1992b). Hospital provision before the NHS: a geographical study of the 1945 hospital surveys. *Social History of Medicine*, 5: 483–504.

Powell, M. A. (1992c). How adequate was hospital provision before the NHS? An examination of the 1945 South Wales hospital survey. *Local Population Studies*, 48: 22–32.

Powell, M. A. (1992d). Hospital provision before the NHS: territorial justice or inverse care law? *Journal of Social Policy*, 21: 145–63.

Powell, M. A. (1994a). The road to 1944: Labour, Tories and the NHS. Paper presented to the Socialist Historians' Group, University of London.

Powell, M. A. (1994b). The changing blueprints of the British NHS: the white papers of 1944 and 1989. *Health Care Analysis*, 2: 111–17.

Powell, M. A. (1994c). The forgotten anniversary? An examination of the 1944 white paper, 'A National Health Service'. *Social Policy and Administration*, 28: 333–44.

Powell, M. A. (1995a). The strategy of equality revisited. *Journal of Social Policy*, 24: 163–85.

Powell, M. A. (1995b). Did politics matter? Municipal public health expenditure in the 1930s. *Urban History*, 22: 360–79.

Powell, M. A. (1995c). A geographical analysis of the distribution of doctors in 1938. Paper presented to the Quantitative Economic and Social History Conference, St Catharine's College, University of Cambridge.

Powell, M. A. (1995d). A third way of pluralism without competition? The historical roots of quasi-markets in health care. Paper presented to the ESRC Quasi-Markets Seminar, London School of Economics.

Powell, M. A. (1996). The ghost of health services past. *International Journal of Health Services*, 26: 253–68.

Powell, M. A. (1997). An expanding service: municipal acute medicine in the 1930s. *Twentieth Century British History*, 8(3).

Power, C. (1994). Health and social inequality in Europe. *British Medical Journal*, 308: 1153–6.

Prochaska, F. (1992). *Philanthropy and the Hospitals of London. The King's Fund 1897–1990*. Oxford: Clarendon Press.

Propper, C. and Upward, R (1992). Need, equity and the NHS: the distribution of health care expenditure 1974–1987. *Fiscal Studies*, 13: 1–21.

Puffer, F. (1986). Access to primary health care: a comparison of the US and the UK. *Journal of Social Policy*, 15: 293–313.

Rae, D. (1981). *Equalities*. Cambridge, MA: Harvard University Press.

Raffel, M. W. and Raffel, N. K. (1994). *The US Health System*, 4th edn. Albany: Delmar.

Ranade, W. (1994). *A Future for the NHS?* Harlow: Longman.

Regan, M. (1992). *Curing the Crisis. Options for America's Health Care*. Boulder: Westview.

Reisman, D. (1993). *The Political Economy of Health Care*. Basingstoke: Macmillan.

Revill, J. (1994). NHS patients made to pay £10 to watch television. *Evening Standard*, 1 November.

Revill, J. (1995). Fury at teaching hospitals slur. *Evening Standard*, 5 July: 18–19.

Rivett, G. (1986). *The Development of the London Hospital System 1823–1982*. London: King's Fund.

Robb, B. (ed.) (1967). *Sans Everything: A Case to Answer?* London: Nelson.

Roberts, H. (1990). *Outcome and Performance in Health Care*. Discussion Paper 33. London: Public Finance Foundation.

Robinson, R. (1990). *Competition and Health Care. A Comparative Analysis of UK Plans and US Experience*. London: King's Fund Institute.

Robson, W. A. (1931). *The Development of Local Government*. London: George Allen and Unwin.

Robson, W. A. (1953). Labour and local government. *Political Quarterly*, 24: 39–53.

Royal Commission on the NHS (1979). *Report*. London: HMSO.

RSHG (Radical Statistics Health Group) (1987). *Facing the Figures*. London: Radical Statistics.

RSHG (1994). Statistics about the NHS – setting the record straight. *Radical Statistics*, 59: 6–40.

Sabo, D. and Gordon, D. F. (eds) (1995). *Men's Health and Illness*. Thousand Oaks: Sage.

Saltman, R. and Von Otter, C. (1992). *Planned Markets and Public Competition: Strategic Reform in Northern European Health Systems*. Buckingham: Open University Press.

Saltman, R. and Von Otter, C. (eds) (1995). *Implementing Planned Markets in Health Care*. Buckingham: Open University Press.

Sandier, S. (1990). Health services utilization and physician income trends, in OECD (ed.) *Health Care Systems in Transition*. Paris: OECD, 41–56.

Saper, R. and Laing, W. (1995). Age of uncertainty. *Health Service Journal*, 25 October: 22–5.

Schieber, G. and Poullier, J.-P. (1990). Overview of international comparisons of health care expenditures, in OECD (ed.) *Health Care Systems in Transition*. Paris: OECD, 9–15.

Schieber, G., Poullier, J.-P. and Greenwald, L. (1994). Health system performance in OECD countries. *Health Affairs*, 13: 100–12.

Seedhouse, D. (1994). *Fortress NHS*. Chichester: John Wiley and Sons.

Shackley, P. and Ryan, M. (1994). What is the role of the consumer in health care? *Journal of Social Policy*, 23: 517–41.

Shaw, G. B. (1946). *The Doctor's Dilemma* (first published 1911). Harmondsworth: Penguin.

Smaje, C. (1995). *Health, 'Race' and Ethnicity*. London: King's Fund Institute.

Social Services Committee (1985). *Community Care with Special Reference to Adult Mentally Ill and Mentally Handicapped People*. London: HMSO.

Social Services Committee (1988). *The Future of the National Health Service*. London: HMSO.

St Leger, A. S., Schneiden, H. and Walsworth-Bell, J. P. (1992). *Evaluating Health Services' Effectiveness*. Buckingham: Open University Press.

Stacey, M. (1977). People who are affected by the inverse law of care. *Health Service Journal*, 3 June: 898–902.

Stevens, R. (1966). *Medical Practice in Modern England*. New Haven: Yale University Press.

Stevenson, J. (1984). *British Society 1914–1945*. Harmondsworth: Penguin.

Szreter, S. (1988). The importance of social intervention in Britain's mortality decline c1850–1914: a re-interpretation. *Social History of Medicine*, 1: 1–37.

Szreter, S. (1994). Mortality in England in the eighteenth and nineteenth centuries: a reply to Sumit Guha. *Social History of Medicine*, 7: 269–82.

Taylor, D. (1990). Improved vision? British optical services for the 1990s, in A. Harrison (ed.) *Health Care UK 1990*. Newbury: Policy Journals, 62–76.

Taylor, S. (1946). House of Commons. Standing Committee C on the NHS Bill. *Hansard*, 6 June, col. 509.

Thunhurst, C. (1982). *It Makes You Sick: The Politics of the NHS*. London: Pluto.

Timmins, N. (1988). *Cash, Crisis and Cure. The Independent Guide to the NHS Debate*. London: Newspaper Publishing.

Timmins, N. (1996). *The Five Giants*. London: Fontana Press..

Titmuss, R. M. (1950). *Problems of Social Policy*. London: HMSO.

Titmuss, R. M. (1968). *Commitment to Welfare*. London: George Allen and Unwin.

Titmuss, R. M. (1970). *The Gift Relationship*. London: George Allen and Unwin.

Titmuss, R. M. (1974). *Social Policy*. London: George Allen and Unwin.

Tomlinson, B. (1992). *Report of the Inquiry into London's Health Service, Medical Education and Research*. London: HMSO.

Townsend, P. (1964). *The Last Refuge*. London: Routledge and Kegan Paul.

Townsend, P. (1981). Towards equality in health through social policy. *International Journal of Health Services*, 11: 63–75.

Townsend, P. and Davidson, N. (1982). *Inequalities in Health*. Harmondsworth: Penguin.

Townsend, P., Phillimore, P. and Beattie, A. (1988). *Health and Deprivation*. London: Croom Helm.

Townsend, P., Davidson, N. and Whitehead, M. (1992). *Inequalities in Health: The Black Report and the Health Divide*. Harmondsworth: Penguin.

Trevor-Jones, A., Nixon, J. and Picken, R. M. F. (1945). *Hospital Survey: The Hospital Services of South Wales and Monmouthshire*. London: HMSO.

Tuckett, D., Boulton, M., Olson, C. and Williams, C. (1985). *Meetings Between Experts*. London: Tavistock.

Tudor-Hart, J (1971). The inverse care law. *Lancet* 27 February: 405–12.

Tudor-Hart, J. (1988). *A New Kind of Doctor*. London: Merlin.

Tudor-Hart, J. (1994). *Feasible Socialism*. London: SHA.

Van Doorslaer, E. and Wagstaff, A. (1993). Equity in the finance of health care: methods and findings, in E. Van Doorslaer, A. Wagstaff and F. Rutten (eds) *Equity in the Finance and Delivery of Health Care. An International Perspective*. Oxford: Oxford University Press.

Vayda, E. (1973). A comparison of surgical rates in Canada and in England and Wales. *New England Journal of Medicine*, 289: 1224–9.

Vickridge, R. (1995). NHS reforms and community care – means tested-health care masquerading as consumer choice? *Critical Social Policy*, 15: 76–80.

Wagstaff, A. and Van Doorslaer, E. (1993a). Equity in the finance and delivery of health care: concepts and definitions, in E. Van Doorslaer, A. Wagstaff and F. Rutten (eds) *Equity in the Finance and Delivery of Health Care. An International Perspective*. Oxford: Oxford University Press, 7–19.

Wagstaff, A. and Van Doorslaer, E. (1993b). Equity in the delivery of health care: methods and findings, in E. Van Doorslaer, A. Wagstaff and F. Rutten (eds) *Equity in the Finance and Delivery of Health Care. An International Perspective*. Oxford: Oxford University Press, 50–87.

Wagstaff, A., Van Doorslaer, E. and Paci, P. (1991). On the measurement of horizontal inequity in the delivery of health care. *Journal of Health Economics*, 10: 169–205.

Wagstaff, A., Van Doorslaer, E. and Rutten, F. (1993). Introduction, in E. Van Doorslaer, A. Wagstaff and F. Rutten (eds) *Equity in the Finance and Delivery of Health Care. An International Perspective*. Oxford: Oxford University Press, 1–4.

Walsh, K. (1995). *Public Services and Market Mechanisms*. Basingstoke: Macmillan.

Walters, V. (1980). *Class Inequality and Health Care*. London: Croom Helm.

Watkin, B. (1978). *The National Health Service: The First Phase 1948–1974 and After*. London: George Allen and Unwin.

Webbe, Sir H. (1946). House of Commons. Standing Committee C on the NHS Bill. *Hansard*, 30 May: col. 367.

Webster, C. (1982). Healthy or hungry thirties? *History Workshop*, 13: 110–29.

Webster, C. (1984). Back to the thirties? *Radical Community Medicine*, 19: 23–31.

Webster, C. (1985). Health, wealth and welfare during the Depression. *Past and Present*, 109: 204–30.

Webster, C. (1988a). *Problems of Health Care. The Health Services since the War*. Volume 1. London: HMSO.

Webster, C. (1988b). Origins of the NHS. Lessons from history. *Contemporary Record*, 2(3): 33–6.

Webster, C. (1988c). Labour and the origins of the National Health Service, in N. A. Rupke (ed.) *Science, Politics and the Public Good*. Basingstoke: Macmillan, 184–202.

Webster, C. (1990). Conflict and consensus; explaining the British Health Service. *Twentieth Century British History*, 1: 115–151.

Webster, C. (ed.) (1991a). *Aneurin Bevan on the National Health Service*. Oxford: Wellcome Unit for the History of Medicine.

Webster, C. (1991b). The elderly and the early National Health Service, in M. Pelling and R. M. Smith (eds) *Life, Death and the Elderly*. London: Routledge, 165–93.

Webster, C. (1993). *Caring For Health: History and Diversity*. Buckingham: Open University Press.

Webster, C. (1994). Conservatives and consensus: the politics of the National Health Service 1951–64, in A. Oakley and A. Susan Williams (eds) *The Politics of the Welfare State*. London: UCL Press, 54–74.

Whitehead, M. (1988). *National Health Success*. London: S Birmingham HA and Association of CHCs for England and Wales.

Whitehead, M. (1992). The concepts and principles of equity and health. *International Journal of Health Services*, 22: 429–45.

Whitehead, M. (1994a). Is it fair? Evaluating the equity implications of the NHS reforms, in R. Robinson and J. Le Grand (eds) *Evaluating the NHS Reforms*. London/Newbury: King's Fund Institute/Policy Journals, 208–41.

Whitehead, M. (1994b). Who cares about equity in the NHS? *British Medical Journal*, 308: 1284–7.

Whitney, R. (1988). *National Health Crisis . . . a Modern Solution*. London: Shepheard-Walwyn.

Wilding, P. (1982). *Professional Power and Social Welfare*. London: Routledge and Kegan Paul.

Wilkin, D., Halam, L., Leavey, R. and Metcalfe, D. (1987). *Anatomy of Urban General Practice*. London: Tavistock.

Williams, I. (1989). *The Alms Trade*. London: Unwin Hyman.

Wilson, N. (1938). *Public Health Services*. London: William Hodge.

Wilson, N. (1946). *Municipal Health Services*. London: George Allen and Unwin.

Wistow, G. (1995). Continuing care: who is responsible? in A. Harrison (ed.) *Health Care UK 1994/95*. London: King's Fund Institute, 80–7.

Wistow, G., Knapp, M., Hardy, B. and Allen, C. (1994). *Social Care in a Mixed Economy*. Buckingham: Open University Press.

Wood, B. (1995). Federalism, implementation and equity: the importance of place in American health care reform. *Health and Place*, 1: 61–4.

Woodman, R. (1993). The painful dilemma of who not to treat. *Independent*, 2 March.

Woolhandler, S., Himmelstein, D. and Young, Q. (1993). High noon for US health care reform. *International Journal of Health Services*, 23: 193–211.

Yates, J. (1987). *Why Are We Waiting?* Oxford: Oxford University Press.

INDEX

HEALTH CARE REFORM
LEARNING FROM INTERNATIONAL EXPERIENCE

Chris Ham (ed.)

If you want a broad introduction to international health care reform, written by some of the best health policy analysts alive today, then this is it.

Chris Heginbotham

- What policies have been adopted to reform health care in Europe and North America?
- Which policies have worked and which have failed?
- What new initiatives are emerging onto the health policy agenda?

This book provides an up-to-date review and analysis of health care reform in five countries: Germany, Sweden, the Netherlands, the United Kingdom and the United States. It reviews experience of introducing competition into the health service as well as policies to strengthen management and change methods of paying hospitals and doctors. The experience of each country is described by experts from the countries concerned. In his lucid introduction, Chris Ham sets out the context of reform, and in the conclusion identifies the emerging lessons.

The book provides an authoritative introduction to health care reform in Europe and North America at a time of increasing political and public interest in this field. It has been designed for students of social policy and the full range of health service practitioners on courses of professional training.

Contents
Series editor's introduction – The background – The United States – The United Kingdom – Sweden – The Netherlands – Germany – Lessons and conclusions – Index.

160pp   0 335 19889 9 (Paperback)   0 335 19890 2 (Hardback)

MANAGING SCARCITY
PRIORITY SETTING AND RATIONING IN THE NATIONAL
HEALTH SERVICE

Rudolf Klein, Patricia Day and Sharon Redmayne

The 'rationing' of health care has become one of the most emotive issues
of the 1990s in the UK, causing much public confusion and political con-
troversy. This book provides a comprehensive and critical introduction to
this debate. It does so by examining the processes which determine who
gets what in the way of treatment, the decision makers involved at different levels in the NHS and the criteria used in making such decisions. In particular it analyses the relationship between decisions about spending
priorities (taken by politicians and managers) and decisions about
rationing care for individual patients (taken by doctors), between explicit
and implicit rationing. As well as drawing on research-based evidence
about what is happening in Britain today, *Managing Scarcity* also looks at
the experience of the NHS since 1948 and puts the case of health care in
the wider context of publicly funded services and programmes which have
to allocate limited resources according to non-market criteria.

Managing Scarcity is recommended reading for students and researchers
of health policy, as well as health professionals and policy makers at all
levels in the NHS.

Contents
Part 1: The context – Unpicking the notion – Politics and strategies – Prin-
ciples of resource allocation – Part 2: The NHS experience – The NHS: a
history of institutionalized scarcity – Priority setting in the new era – Lifting
the veils from rationing? – Into the secret garden – Part 3: The way ahead –
Money or science to the rescue? – What can we learn from the others? –
Policy options for the future – Appendix – References – Index.

176pp   0 335 19446 X (Paperback)   0 335 19447 8 (Hardback)

IMPLEMENTING PLANNED MARKETS IN HEALTH CARE
BALANCING SOCIAL AND ECONOMIC RESPONSIBILITY

Richard B. Saltman and Casten von Otter (eds)

- What lessons can be learned from the health reform process to date?
- What direction will future health reforms take in the industrialized world?

Implementing Planned Markets in Health Care brings together an international team of experts to address these important questions. Drawing on experiences in Northern Europe and the United States, it examines the key concepts behind the present push toward health reform in the industrialized world:

- contracting and solidarity
- contestable v. competitive markets
- the role of vouchers
- physicians' clinical autonomy.

Also included are case studies of planned market approaches based on contracts, patient choice, and on quality of care. The book concludes with a broad comparative assessment of the main themes and points towards the most likely developments in future *planned market* models of health care.

Contents
Introduction – Part 1: The politics of contracting – Contracting and the purchaser–provider split – Contracting and solidarity – Regulation of planned markets in health care – Contracting and political boards in planned markets – Part 2: Balancing incentives and accountability – Costs, productivity and financial outcomes of managed care – Vouchers in planned markets – Clinical autonomy and planned markets – Part 3: Constructing entrepreneurial providers – Self-governing trusts and GP fundholders – Implementing planned markets in health services – Competititve hospital markets based on quality – Part 4: Conclusion – Index.

Contributors
Anders Anell, Göran Arvidsson, Mats Brommels, Aad A. de Roo, Stephen Harrison, Nancy M. Kane, Christian M. Koeck, Julian Le Grand, Britta Neugaard, Ray Robinson, Richard B. Saltman, Clive H. Smee, Casten von Otter.

272pp   0 335 19425 7 (Paperback)   0 335 19426 5 (Hardback)